A FULL CONFESSION

*The Woman Who Took Down
the Dillinger Gang*

Thomas S. Hinds
Myrna Hinds Otte

Copyright © 2020 T. Hinds/M. Otte

All rights reserved. No part of this book may be reproduced in any form or by any electronic or mechanical means, including information storage and retrieval systems, without written permission from the authors, except in the case of a reviewer, who may quote brief passages embodied in critical articles or in a review. Trademarked names appear throughout this book. Rather than use a trademark symbol with every occurrence of a trademarked name, names are used in an editorial fashion, with no intention of infringement of the respective owner's trademark. The information in this book is distributed on an "as is" basis, without warranty. Although every precaution has been taken in the preparation of this work, neither the author nor the publisher shall have any liability to any person or entity with respect to any loss or damage caused or alleged to be caused directly or indirectly by the information contained in this book.

Cover design: Lisa Forde
Printed in the United States of America

Thomas Hinds wishes to dedicate this to his wife Karen Murgolo, a tolerant and giving publishing professional.

Myrna Hinds Otte dedicates this to the memory of Arland Otte, and with sincere gratitude to Michael, Sheldon, Rachel, Elena and Alison, her children; their help, encouragement, and pride in being a Hinds helped her complete this.

We wrote this book in memory of Raymond Hinds and Cleo Hinds Litz. Thanks for the stories.

A NOTE ON THE CONTENTS

The book is divided into four parts. Each part is preceded by a brief "illusion" or literary picture that purports to encapsulate the events in that part. Each part is divided into several chapters.

PART I: Dakotas and Saskatchewan 1898-1918

Bessie Hester and her early life on the last frontier, the middle border, in the Dakotas and Saskatchewan, and her first marriage; The family background in Ireland and Canada.

PART II: St. Paul 1918-1934

St. Paul's criminal history and Bessie Skinner/Beth Green's initial criminal background in St. Paul; The Green family; the real story in contrast to Beth's confessions.

PART III: HERE WE HAVE THE WILD BETH GREEN

Beth Green's association with John Dillinger, the Barker-Karpis gang, the FBI, and her initial confession connected to the first clean-up of corrupt St. Paul; Beth is tried and goes to Alderson prison.

PART IV: AUNT BESS--HER LIFE AFTER

THE END OF BETH GREEN

Bess Garrett's public life after prison, which until the early 1950s included illegal activity. (This part will also include her life as a mother and family member.)

CONTENTS

Title Page
Copyright
Dedication
A Note on the Contents
The Grand Illusion: In the Burn Barrel	1
Part I	5
Illusion: Of a New Life on the Prairie	6
Chapter 1	7
Chapter 2	22
Chapter 3	31
Chapter 4	39
Chapter 5	46
Part II	53
An Illusion: Shining in Pigseye	54
Chapter 6	56
Chapter 7	76
Chapter 8	90
Chapter 9	98
Part III	115
Illusion: On Rondo Street	116

Chapter 10	119
Chapter 11	124
Chapter 12	137
Chapter 13	150
Chapter 14	174
Chapter 15	196
Chapter 16	221
Part IV	231
Illusion: The Lumberman's Show	232
Chapter 17	234
Chapter 18	249
Chapter 19	267
Chapter 20	272
Coda	277
Acknowledgments	281
Bibliography and Research	285
Appendix	291
About the Authors	293

THE GRAND ILLUSION: IN THE BURN BARREL

On some mornings, in 1973, Cleo Litz felt that she was as old as her favorite aunt. She was, after all, 58 and she and her husband Curley were looking at taking a little less active role in running their resort in northern Minnesota. Cleo was thinking about this as she approached the mobile home where her aunt lived.

Aunt Bess was moving and to that end she was cleaning out the small home. Cleo was there to help but she was also determined to get any remembrances that Bess might have retained of Winnie, Cleo's mom, and of Cleo's early life.

Cleo's father, Almon, had sold the *Seguchie Lodge* to Cleo and Curley in 1947 and they had operated the resort on Lake Milles Lacs for more than 25 years. Cleo's Aunt Bess had worked for Almon, Bessie's brother, when he ran the resort in the forties. She had later worked for Cleo and Curley off and on. Cleo thought that Bess was a good employee, although she was too tough on other employees when she was allowed to manage the place. Bess was willing to do practically anything at the lodge; she had been a cook, a waitress and a hostess.

Bess had told Cleo many times how much that Cleo was like her mother Winnie. Winnie had died in the late 1940s, but Bess often spoke of her as if she would walk in at any time. Neither

Cleo nor Bess were overly fond of the woman that Almon had married after Winnie had died. She was much too sober, and Bess never missed a chance to remind Cleo of how much fun Winnie was, and the nights Winnie and she had spent at the *Streamline Bar*.

Bess was aware that her niece and her husband had achieved something Bess had only dreamed about with her husbands and lovers. Cleo and Curley had *The Seguchie Lodge*, a nice place with restaurant, tavern, and cabins, on a big lake called Mille Lacs in Minnesota. They had a launch, small boats, canoes, and a dock. In the dining room, displayed prominently, was a Gatling gun that Curley told the guests came from Pancho Villa's army. Other than that gun, there was nothing in the lodge that spoke of past violence.

Curley was a well-known fishing guide, with a nice mop of hair and a ready smile, and the place drew faithful fishermen and families who made the lodge their vacation spot in summer. Cleo and Curley had a good reputation in the community; they also had two daughters now grown but who were good students and good children.

When Bess had called Cleo and told her that she was going to move back to Minneapolis, Cleo had agreed to go over to Garrison, the town where Bess lived a few miles away, on the North-West corner of Lac Mille Lacs. Bess's winter job had collapsed, two of her friends from the old days had recently died, and there was little that kept Bess there.

Bess was a much older woman than Cleo, and Bess was now in much less happy circumstances, although she knew, as Cleo knew, that at least some of her family in Minneapolis, Northfield, and elsewhere regarded her as their favorite or, at least the most amusing, relative.

Bess always kept her mobile home as neat as a pin. She would joke that her penchant for cleaning was the only thing that she had learned from her mother. She would then add that this was not because her mother was a good housekeeper, but because her mother made Bessie keep house for all the men in the family starting when Bessie was very young.

When Cleo arrived that Friday morning, she found that Bess had packed up and was sorting through about ten cardboard boxes of pictures, newspapers, cards, menus, and imprinted cocktail napkins, address books, letters, obituaries, and mass cards. She was separating out a life on paper. She told Cleo, quite frankly, that there was material in the boxes that Bess did not want anyone to see.

When she was finished, Bess had reduced her memorabilia to one box to save. Cleo was given the opportunity to take pictures, letters from her mother, and other things as she wished, and she heard stories during the process that she had never heard before. When the sorting was done, Cleo helped her aunt carry the discarded papers out to a burn barrel close to the house, where without ceremony the biographical material was set on fire and burned. The history of Bessie Hester Hinds, of Bessie Skinner, of Beth from Aunt Grace's, of Beth Walsh, of Beth Green, and of Bess Garrett went up in smoke. Only Aunt Bess was left.

PART I

The Dakotas and Saskatchewan, 1898-1918, Bessie Hester Hinds

ILLUSION: OF A NEW LIFE ON THE PRAIRIE

"Men beheld in feverish dreams the endless plains, teeming with fruitfulness, glowing, out there where day sank into night- a Beulah Land of corn and wine!......'Now we're bound west!' said the young.... 'Wait a minute- we're going along with you!'" cried the old, and followed after. Human beings gathered together, in small companies and large- took whatever was moveable along, and left the old homestead without so much as a sigh."

(PG.227 *GIANTS IN THE EARTH*, HARPER AND BROTHERS, 1927, NEW YORK.)

"But more to be dreaded...was the strange spell of sadness which the unbroken solitude cast upon the minds of some. Many took their own lives; asylum after asylum was filled with disordered beings who had once been human."

(IBID. PG. 424)

CHAPTER 1

A New Life in the Wild West

In 1934, when Bessie Skinner was arrested as "Beth Green," she first told the FBI that she had been born in Montana. This was certainly not true. It was part of her attempt to protect herself and her family from the shame that her arrest might bring. At the time she was married as a girl in 1914, she told the Church of England rector who officiated at the ceremony that she was eighteen years old. This was also a lie- she was not yet sixteen.

Bessie married at age fifteen with reason and from example. The reason that she married was to get away from her mother and to escape the hard life that she was living in a small shack on the prairie in Canada. Much later, she said to her cousin, Robert Loutzenhiser, "I couldn't get out of that house fast enough." One way to get out was exemplified by her two older brothers. Pharos, and her brother Almon had escaped by route of marriage and she also saw marriage as a way to escape from her harsh mother, the shack and the equally harsh prairie.

Bessie had not been born in the shack in Saskatchewan nor into the hard circumstances that in 1914 she wanted to escape. From her birth in 1898 until she was almost thirteen years old in 1911, her life was not uncomfortable. Indeed for some of those years her family was locally prominent and better off than many in the communities in which she lived. Her family circumstances then promised a future.

At the time of Bessie's birth, her parents were part owners of a general store and a meeting hall and her father was also working his own acreage, growing wheat. Compared to many settlers around them, the family was well educated. Both Bessie's parents had been through the eighth grade. Both were readers.

Bessie at birth had an immediate family and an extended family, grandparents, uncles and aunts, who lived in some proximity to her immediate family. This whole group of relatives had moved and settled together several times before Bessie was born. Her mother and father, and grandparents, moved twice between the time Bessie was born and the time she was thirteen. While the reason for these moves before 1898 seems to be problems the families had in making a living, from that point they moved up. Her family became substantial citizens, in one case they founded a successful town. They were well thought of in each of the three communities in which they lived from 1898 to 1911.

In 1911, pushed by economic necessity, Bessie moved with her mother and father and two younger brothers to Canada. They moved from a small comfortable frame house in a North Dakota town of three hundred people with a school, to a 14' x 16' shack on the prairie, to a pioneer existence. Bessie's desire to escape from Saskatchewan was both a desire to go back to the places where her family had substance, and to go ahead, to a place where she could get ahead without family.

History, especially the history of an obscure individual, is difficult because of the lack of records. Formal records are births, deeds, and deaths. Informal records are letters, diaries and remembrances. It is hard, even when these exist, to travel back 100 or more years in time and understand what events and emotions caused what consequences to that individual. The formal and informal records show that:

Bessie Hester Hinds was born on June 28, 1898, at home, in Dale, North Dakota. Dale was a small town, and getting smaller, preparing to disappear. The county seat where her birth could be registered was in Linton, about 30 miles away from Dale, and in a different world. Bessie's certificate of birth is not in the County records due to distance, a courthouse fire there, or poor record keeping.

Except for a few deeds showing of her family's land holdings, there is no other record of her family, and indeed no local remembrances of these people. Bessie's only birth registry in Emmons County is a re-registration that she obtained in 1942 in Linton. She swore to her birth in Emmons County in this document presumably because such register information was needed in 1942 to obtain Social Security benefits for her in the future.

At the time that Bessie was born, the State of North Dakota was 9 years old. Her eldest brother, Pharos, was eleven. She was the third of five children who survived infancy (a brother died when he was two months old in 1891). She had one other older brother, Almon. A younger brother, Adelbert, was born in 1900 and another brother, Marvin David, was born in 1907.

But much of history is also written down and accessible. The surroundings of an individual and how those surroundings affected his or her life, form the person from before birth and inform them afterward can be found in history books, court records, newspapers and journals and other recordings. History tells us that although the great Dakota boom times had occurred almost twenty years before the year Bessie was born, in 1898 many people still expected to become wealthy, or at least comfortable, in the Dakotas. By 1898 this was an expectation based on the knowledge that a family would have to work hard to gain comfort. The Dakotas had already weeded out those who were awaiting wealth without much work, and most settlers coming in at that point, and there were not very many, were aware that their endeavors would only pay off over time.

There was mineral wealth in the state: the gold mines in the Black Hills were the most productive in the country, but they were controlled by Eastern interests. The farmland that was already developed, east of the Missouri river, was producing huge crops of wheat and many wheat growers were well established. These wheat growers in turn were enriching, and also dependent on, the railroads, the grain brokers and the mills in Minneapolis, all of which were also well established.

When Bessie was born, her mother and father owned farmland around Dale, North Dakota, and had part ownership of a general store in town. Her maternal grandparents, Rebecca and Pharos Pierce, also lived in Dale and owned a small hotel in the same community.

Dale, North Dakota, was founded in the boom of the late 1870s as a stagecoach stop on the way to the army posts and mining communities in the western Dakotas. But it never grew much, and by 1898 Dale was almost outside the orbit of civilization. The stagecoach line was closed and despite hopes of the inhabitants of Dale, no railway spur came to the town.

The farmers in that vicinity, toward the banks of the Missouri, had not benefited from the gold mining money. They worked all the time raising crops and families. Most of the acreage was much less productive than the wheat farming land further to the east. The Peterson family, neighbors of Bessie's family, described the land as "grit and gumbo." In 1902, several families living in or close to Dale became tired of the difficulty of raising wheat on the land, and transporting it about forty miles to a railhead. They moved to towns where railways existed and bought acreage closer to these towns when they could afford it.

The serious wheat growers, those who took over large holdings, buying out their neighbors, and raising the grain aided by modern equipment, stayed on. Among those who stayed on were members of the considerably extended Peterson family, who were later to become in-laws of Bessie. But most families moved toward the nearby towns, towns that had at least a railhead.

In 1902, Bessie's mother and father and grandparents had sold out their land holdings in Dale for cash. They disassembled the buildings that were valuable and moved the lumber and hardware to a town started that year, and rebuilt.

They reinvested the little cash from their transaction in this town. Bessie's family was proud to be among the founders of the brand-new town of Pollock, S.D.

The railroad went through Pollock, and with it came opportunities that did not come to Dale. The town was on a bend in the Missouri River. The cropland immediately around Pollock appeared to be excellent. One of the first civic efforts in town was the establishment of both a grade and a high school. Bessie's parents were active in this endeavor. Bessie's two older brothers immediately started school in Pollock and Bessie was enrolled in the first grade there in 1904.

But before this there was family history; there were records of where Bessie's family came from, what they were like and what formed them to eventually form her. There are also two different sides to the story about how Bessie's family ended up in North Dakota. One side is about the family, the other is about the land. The extended family in the early 1900s included relatives named Pierce, Peterson and Loutzenhiser. These people hold some interest as individuals, and as types. They are, indeed, typical in origin.

The other side is a story of location and frontier; whatever it was in the Dakotas that lured the latest batch of pioneers to settle in a desert, whatever it was that made them believe that just ahead, or maybe right here, was better and more fertile land. To understand the milieu and background to Bessie then it is necessary to understand something of the history behind her.

The great push west was almost over by 1880, but the myth of the land of opportunity was as alive for farmers and city folk seeking to harvest success, as it was for immigrants who were coming into Boston and New York from Europe.

Three of "Bessie's families" were on this continent for at least three generations before Bessie was born. These were the Hinds, Loutzenhiser and Pierce families. All had settled in America several generations before and then kept moving. All had moved, a generation at a time or even faster, further west until they fetched up in the "Golden Dakotas" next to each other. The fourth family, one that plays a more minor role in Bessie's story, the Petersons, were more recent arrivals. Bessie's contemporaries in that family were the first generation born on American soil.

Bessie's father, David Hinds, was born in 1857 in Allenford, Ontario to a family that had settled two generations earlier in Canada from Ireland. When David was born, Allenford was relatively civilized, but he did not stay there. David finished eighth grade and shortly thereafter did what his father and grandfather had done: move on westward.

Bessie and her siblings were told by their father that they were Irish and Orangemen. The family identified with William and Mary, William of Orange, who insured a Protestant Kingdom of England and Ireland at the Battle of the Boyne on July 1, 1690. This battle and the distinctions that it made still resonate in Northern Ireland and the Irish Republic. But the battle meant far less in the Americas in the mid-19th century and its distinctions meant still less as time went on. Nonetheless, as time went on the Hinds family continued to mark the difference between their Protestant background and that of the "others." They remained anti-Catholic, and against non-English speaking immigrants.

Bessie's great-grandfather from County Cavan in Ireland, Walter, first settled in a small town that would become Guelph City, Ontario. There the Protestant Irish and Anglican Scots formed an early majority According to family genealogical records, Bessie's great-grandfather was a "founder" of the town. He, and his wife, certainly contributed to its population.

Walter, Bessie's great-grandfather, had married Elizabeth Anne Beatty in Ireland in 1823. He was 20 years old; she was sixteen. They had their first of nine children in 1824. After arriving in Canada, Walter worked close to Guelph following his two older brothers to take up land and work on the main *Waterloo* highway (now N.24) for the contractor and entrepreneur, Absolom Schade. Walter Hinds owned a farm just outside Guelph and, according to family records, traded to some success in the town. Other family members came to the area and roads and corners there were named after the family; descendants still live in the town.

Walter, however, went mad sometime in 1841 and was confined to an asylum for 38 years. His disposition and indisposition were treated very gently by members of his family researching genealogy.
One familial researcher stated," He was a victim of the rugged existence immigrants found in Guelph in the 1820s(sic). His lack of good mental health (partly inherited and partly due to poor nutrition) and a tendency toward violence when drinking Brandy was a major factor in his confinement."

His wife, Elizabeth Ann, could not legally divorce him and remarry and she was unable to find any help from her family in running the farm. According to local records, her oldest child was fifteen at the time that Walter was sent to the asylum, and her youngest an infant. Bessie's grandfather, Beatty Hinds, was six years old in 1841, and the seventh child of nine.

In Ontario, the Hinds family first encountered the railroad and the gifts of the railroad. Elizabeth sold land to the railroad to pay for Walter's confinement and sent her children out to work early, some on the railroad. Beatty may have gone out to work on the Grand Trunk first when he was in his early teens.

When Walter finally died in 1879 without leaving a will, a court case ensued among members of the family over who was to get the little that remained of the farm. By 1879, Walter's son, Beatty, was himself a patriarch, sane, and was long gone from Guelph. He was following the railroad.

Beatty married Elizabeth Goodrow in 1855 when he was 19 years old and also reproduced early, like his Irish father and grandfather. Beatty was twenty-two years of age in 1857, when his first son David, Bessie's father, was born. He had been making a living for himself for seven years at this point. He had very early on established a small farm, took railroad work when he could, and engaged in civic affairs. Among other accomplishments, he produced seven children with his first wife.

Beatty and Elizabeth had enough success to buy a larger farm in Allenford, Ontario, and to ensure that the six children of this marriage who survived infancy, got a primary education. David went to school through the eighth grade there.

Beatty in his obituary in 1913, was called "honored and esteemed" in his community. David named his firstborn son, Pharos Beatty, after his father, and his wife's father. David was obviously impressed with what his father had accomplished.

According to what family told his grandson, David Hinds went to Chicago from Guelph, at age seventeen, in 1874, where he became a "commission man" for the stockyards, searching for herds of cattle of a quality required at the packing plants. Even if this story is true, however, David seems to have gone back to Allenford and next went into the United States following the railroads through Canada, Wisconsin and Minnesota.

At the point when David left home at age 19 in 1876, the Canadian Pacific Railroad was well established and that road was looking to make incursions into the United States. It was thought that shipping wheat along the St. Lawrence River by a railroad that avoided Chicago would allow cheaper access to the sea. David's long-lasting excursion into the United States followed the establishment of the predecessor lines to the Minneapolis, St. Paul and Sault Ste. Marie railroad (the "Soo" line).

With a decent education and the ability to write a nice hand. David probably started as a laborer when he first signed on to work for the railroad, but he seems to have been a clerk at least part of the time.

* * *

At the same time that David was working his way into the United States, the great Dakotas boom was starting. In 1875, gold was discovered by soldiers associated with Custer at Lead in the Black Hills of south-western Dakota Territory. Many ambitious young men went there to find wealth. Their movements further spurred the development of the railroads. (David Hinds was in the United States and had access to transport. There are some indications that David made a brief excursion into the Dakotas with a brother when he was 20, in 1877, the year after the battle of Little Big Horn.)

Many thought the land in the Dakotas was better than gold

and the railroads were promoting it as such. They were poised to reach down from the north. The newly incorporated *Chicago, Milwaukee and St. Paul* railroad company, which in the late 70s had its termination in St. Paul, made plans to drive west to what was considered to be the best wheat farming land in the Dakotas.

The *Milwaukee* railroad under the enterprising direction of its founder and President, Alexander Mitchell, was not only driving the line east to west through Wisconsin, Minnesota and the Dakotas, it was doing so using all the latest equipment, and it was not only connecting towns but creating new ones as it went along such as Aberdeen and Mitchell, South Dakota.

Because the road was profitable carrying grain from its beginning, and because the speed of rail building was high, the Milwaukee Road was able to pay twice the going daily wage to its laborers, it could pay them a princely $2.50 per day.

David worked his way to Aberdeen with the Milwaukee line starting when he was 24; the records give no indication whether he was laborer or among lower management although his past education could have placed him as a "clerk" easily enough. When he fetched up, in Alexander Mitchell's Aberdeen, whatever he did getting there, he had money in his pocket.

Although David stopped following the rails in 1882, he was to remain their pawn. In 1882, in Aberdeen, however, he was unmarried, he had money from his work, and he had a desire to invest it. With more than $600 in his pocket he was able buy both farmland and city plots. This was a wise investment. At the time this town at the end of the Milwaukee line, Aberdeen, was a boomtown and David appeared to have it made.

Close to the place where he lived in town was a livery stable managed by a gentleman named Pharos Pierce. David was 28 years old when he and Minnie Pierce, Pharos's daughter, were married in 1885. She was 18. He was very handsome, with dark curly hair and a handlebar mustache, and she too was handsome, with a determined set to her jaw, pride and ambition.

Minnie Pierce's family's dreams and background at that point could not approach David Hinds's real position; he was ambitious, young, mostly unencumbered, and buying property. Minnie, on the other hand, may have been impressive to look at in 1885, but her family's financial situation was more tenuous.

In Aberdeen, and later elsewhere in the Dakotas in Dale, in Pollock and in Burnstad, David, seems to have had more money than the Pierces. Minnie's father and mother followed their son-in-law when he made decisions to move.

At the time that David married Minnie in 1885, he helped to establish, with his father-in-law, the *Pierce Construction* company. In late 1885, this company contracted with the Milwaukee railroad to build a railroad grade along the present route of the *Sunshine Trail* in South Dakota. David and Pharos Pierce hired people to do the work, and bought equipment, but a national depression intervened. The railroad did not pay independent contractors for two years. David said that it was for this reason that *Pierce Construction* went broke.

If you look at a map of the railroads of the United States in 1890 (As illustrated by Webb in his book "The Great Plains") you find that the rail lines look like veins and capillaries from the east coast up to a point in western Minnesota and the eastern Dakotas. Then nothing or almost nothing. The blood of commerce moves along a few big lines through the great American desert as fast as possible, in order to get across and over the mountains to other rich veins on the west coast.

Disappointed by the railway, left with little cash and few prospects in Aberdeen, David and Minnie Hinds, their newborn son Pharos Beatty and Minnie's family, Rebecca and Pharos Pierce sold their properties and went west in the Dakotas to homestead and grow wheat.

The major initial push of agricultural immigration into the "golden Dakotas," in the 1870s and early 1880s, came from the Indiana, Illinois, Minnesota, and Iowa wheat and corn farmers and their sons. These families had busted the sod on the more eastern prairies, and then moved to wilder locations as the farms in those states diversified in crops and livestock and became more fenced in.

Wheat was the upscale crop, celebrated as "amber waves of grain" (first penned in 1893), and its golden and alive kernels promised to allow the Great Plains to feed the world. There seems to have been a species of settlers who wanted to plant wheat on the moving "middle border" of the United States. They felt something like contempt for people who practiced "mixed farming" raising vegetable crops, cattle, dairy cows and feed for livestock.

David's wife, Bessie's mother, Minnie Pierce, and her immediate family, had followed this pattern of wheat farmers, a pattern that is described in Hamlin Garland's *Son of the Middle Border*. That is, they followed the western trail, increasingly toward the Dakotas, planting the golden grain.

Bessie's mother, Minnie, was born in Iowa in 1867. Pharos and Rebecca Pierce had, in addition to Minnie, a son Berton, a son named Wilbert and another daughter, Blanche. The family had put the children through several grades in schools along their route.

The Pierces had seen hardships equal to, if not greater than David's family. In October of 1880, the Pierces were living in Redwood County, Minnesota and Berton Pierce was 15 years old. A great early snowstorm struck, and Berton, Minnie and Wilbert were engaged in fall plowing about four miles from their cabin. They struggled home and took the plow horses inside the cabin with them. Soon, all the family was inside the cabin. They all lived with the horses for three days, unable to get out of the house even to find the way to the barn. After three days they had to dig up from under the snow to get out the door.

The girl Berton Pierce was to marry, Harriet Lucinda Loutzenhiser (called Hattie, and a sister of Frank Loutzenhiser), was already living in the southern Dakotas in Union County, that October, age 13, with her family. The same storm that hit Redwood County had also come to Union County. In that area, however, the snow did not seem to stop falling for any time from October 1880 until April 1881.

The Loutzenhiser family lived seven miles from the nearest grist mill, and they were only occasionally able to get out of the homestead that winter to grind their grain. In fact, the snow often covered the house, which was of sod and built into the side of a hill. Each time Hattie's father went out to clean the chimney, he would have to shovel snow inside the house to be able to start to get out. They would carry food to the animals in the barn and lower it through a hole in the roof.

The family's chief diet that winter was boiled wheat and "snow birds" (prairie chickens?). The trap they used to kill the birds was an old tabletop propped up with a string attached to the prop and pulled through an open window of the hut; they used wheat for bait. None of the settlers in that area had meat that winter except as they could improvise.

Perhaps the snow drove Pharos to move from Redwood County. But he probably didn't need that excuse. Later generations of Pierces described Pharos as having "itchy feet" and "always looking for the promised land." Pharos Pierce kept moving west. Every landscape that he inhabited after leaving the rich farming area of Redwood County, Minnesota in 1880, was bleaker and less productive than the previous one. Pharos abandoned 80 acres in Jackson, Minnesota, in 1884 to move with his wife and three children to Aberdeen, Dakota Territory. He was there long enough to see his daughter married and to see *Pierce*

Construction established and fail. He next moved on to Emmons County (La Grace) in 1885. In 1887, he was joined by his son-in-law, and they moved to Dale. After that, Pharos moved to Pollock, South Dakota. Berton Pierce, his son, at age 37, having had his fill of the prairie moved back eastward to the lake and woods country of Minnesota in 1902.

Several other groups of immigrants came for the free land that was offered by the government as the Indian tribes were suppressed in the eastern part of the Dakota territories in 1870-1871. Among the first emigrants from overseas to Minnesota and later the Dakotas were Norwegian fishermen and farmers, sailing in boats crammed full from Stavanger to Boston or Halifax.

These settlers, who some in the Dakotas called, with deprecation, "Norwegans" (pronounced "Nor Vague Ans") planted and they worked and they built their houses out of sod. The earliest settlers saw their beautiful Dakota wheat crops eaten by hordes of grasshoppers each year from 1871 to 1878. These folks thought about what happened to them in terms of biblical plagues and wondered where they had sinned. (These early settlers are the people described by O.E. Rolvaag in his wonderful book *Giants in the Earth*).

Fresh off the boat that arrived from Stavanger, Norway, in 1881 in Boston were the Petersons. Even if grasshoppers had wreaked havoc earlier on the first Dakota settlers like a biblical plague, the middle border had something that many poor emigrants wanted, free land. Settlers were lured by the "low, dry grass and the gorgeous colors of dawn." Rolvaag describes how they were lured from Norway by advertisement and cheap, if crowded, means of travel.

Many Norwegians had come into Minnesota quickly in the early 1870s. By the early '70s, the area around Rushford, Minnesota was filled with Norwegians, those who owned land nearby and those stopping with relatives on the "way west" to find land. St. Olaf College was being set up in Northfield Minnesota, and Lutheran churches and schools were springing up all over.

So, the more recently arrived Norwegians looked for free land to the west, in the Dakotas. This was what the Petersons, the Norwegian players in Bessie's family story did. They came from Stavanger, Norway to Rushford, Minnesota. Then they started moving west. By 1876, they were farming near Lamberton, Minnesota, but did not own the land. With three children, they moved again in 1879 to the Mitchell, Dakota area to take advantage of free land. In the Dakotas, six more children were to be born to this hearty couple, George and Tena.

George and Tena Peterson did not really go as lonely pioneers to the Dakotas. Rather like Per Hansa and Hans Olsa, and the rest in *Giants in the Earth,* they moved as a group, thus gaining considerable acreage.

CHAPTER 2

Stories and their Surroundings

In 1889, North and South Dakota, became states. The progenitors and in-laws of Bessie were in the "golden Dakotas" by then. The Dakotas were made states both because of the gold rush and the sudden influx of miners, and because wheat and corn farmers continued to move in, looking for cheap arable land. David Hinds, the Pierces, the Petersons and the Loutzenhisers had added to the swelling population.

The means of getting to the good land in the Dakotas and getting the wheat and corn out to be milled was the railroad. There has never been a question that the railroads transformed the life on the Great Plains, providing connection and communication where nothing else did until Eisenhower put in his highways. But like Ike's highways that allowed communication at high speed over long distance, the railroads did not rely on much "in-between." The railroad companies had urged people to move to the new prairie land, and many towns grew up and died out based on where railroads <u>said</u> that they would build lines and where they <u>actually</u> built lines.

Among the towns that were born based on being a stagecoach stop and soon died when the railroads did not come through was Dale, North Dakota. Dale was at a crossroad in a valley (hence the name) It was at Dale that the four families (Hinds, Peterson, Loutzenhiser and Pierce) were to mingle.

The post office in Dale was established in 1891 and was a log house with a dirt roof when David Hinds had his farm very close to the town. Also, there was a Presbyterian church, which the Hinds and Pierce families attended, a store, the Pierce hostelry, the Loutzenhiser saloon, a grade school and a Grange Hall.

Farming not too far away and to the west were George and Tena Peterson, their sons and daughters and grandchildren by this time, a large family of Norwegians who shopped at the Dale store. The various Petersons owned about 900 acres in the vicinity making them substantial community members. Emmons County, where Dale was located was also where, a few miles to the west, the wild town Winona provided entertainment for the soldiers at Fort Yates.

During the time that Bessie's extended family and parents were homesteading and then running businesses in the Dakotas (1881-1911) and when Bessie's parents homesteaded in Canada in 1911-1915, the cities of the east and west were getting public sanitation, public transport, telephone exchanges, electric lights and power, and public hospitals. It was a normal thing for a child in New York State to go to school until he was sixteen. This was not true in the Dakotas. Dale was typical of the hardscrabble towns that sprang up and collapsed. Pollock, where Bessie's family moved in 1902, was an exception.

Much of the Dakotas appeared to be outside the normal U.S. boundaries where progress was measured by technology. It was 1911, when Sioux Falls saw its first airplane when a barnstorming team visited. In 1917, Hamlin Garland in his biography, pictured Sioux Falls as the place where civilization ended. Granted that Garland was writing about an earlier Sioux Falls, the frontier that was depicted by Garland still existed for Bessie's family, at least until they moved to Pollock in South Dakota.

They found the frontier again in Saskatchewan when they left for Canada in 1911. (This late frontier lasted into the early 1920s and has been eloquently described by Wallace Stegner in his autobiographical book, *Wolf Willow*.) While Frederick Jackson Turner was completing his thesis on the significance of the frontier on the emerging urban America, Bessie and her family were still living the frontier.

Berton Pierce, Minnie's brother and Bessie's uncle, born in 1865, told stories of the Dakota frontier to his son, Wilbert. Wilbert and his daughter later incorporated these stories in a small book. Berton's stories seem to have been as much a tale of everything that was said to be happening in the area as the truth about his experiences. Along these lines, he said that his father and mother, Pharos and Rebecca, were in Northfield, Minnesota during the Jesse James raid in 1876. Berton said that his mother, Rebecca reacted to this story, when he asked her, by saying that it was more or less true. She said, "Yes, Pharos went with the posse [chasing after the James gang], but the posse went one way and Pharos went the other."

There is little evidence to support the story that Pharos Pierce was in Northfield the day that the James gang rode in. It is faintly possible, and would be a great addition to Bessie's later story if true. Pharos and Rebecca did move to Minnesota from Iowa in time for them to have been where Berton said they were, and they worked their way west in Minnesota, as wheat farmers. Northfield, in 1876, was a milling town for wheat.

To add to the hardness of farming in the Dale area, there remained the real fear of the "savage" Native American neighbors when Bessie's parents moved there. As a good example, the land on which the Hinds family settled was expropriated from the Ogallala Sioux after gold was discovered much further west in the Black Hills in 1875. Furthermore, in the late 1880s, such theft of Indian lands did not stop; as they continued West, more land was taken by the railroads and their commercial agents.

The Sioux had struck back from 1862 on, making war on the US government troops and the squatters, miners and homesteaders that the troops were guarding. This was only a sporadic war. But its battles ranged from the Minnesota massacres in the mid-1860s to the Little Big Horn in 1876 to Wounded Knee in 1890. At Wounded Knee, the Sioux were massacred (it was called "defeated") and enclosed.

By 1890, few war parties could be raised among the starved Sioux. Sitting Bull was assassinated that year, only a few miles away from where Bessie's family lived, but this did not end the mutual killing. Small bands of Sioux "renegades" continued to roam the area. Even farther east in Minnesota, where the settlements were thicker, it happened that local families were slaughtered in a most gruesome fashion. But hatred of the Indian, tales spread by settlers, and constant worry probably lent the tales of murder more credence than they deserved. And if a family was slaughtered it was hard to prove the identity of the real perpetrators.

As late as 1910, there were bloody episodes of Indian resistance and reprisal. In the small new towns, the dangers were less than they were for the small farmers, although everyone was acquainted with, or had heard of someone, usually of the preceding generation, who had been attacked or killed.

On February 17, 1897, all the members of the Spicer family from two miles outside old Winona, North Dakota were killed. The Spicer farm was less than ten miles away from the Hinds and Pierce homes in Dale, and about equidistant from the Peterson and Loutzenhiser farms. A visitor to the Spicer farm described the scene of carnage at the place and blamed the "savages." From the stories given in the local newspaper, and by Wilbert Pierce, it appears that the assailants had killed the farmer in the barn by beating him to death. Then they called his wife from the house and killed her. Next they killed Mrs. Spicer's mother, Mrs. Waldron, and then attacked Spicer's married daughter Mrs. William House, and her twin babies. It was apparent from the scene that Mrs. House had put up a fight with a hoe, and it remained caught up on a wire where the stove pipe attached to the house.

Immediately, suspicion centered on six Sioux. One of them was part African-American and called "Blackhawk." The others were named Standing Bear, Alex Cadotte, Ireland, Holy Track, and Defender. It was said that a local saloon owner had precipitated the murders by telling some or all of these people that they could not drink any longer in his place but that they could find plenty to drink at the Spicers. (This was a dark jest, the Spicers were teetotalers, and had objected to all the drinking in Winona.)

In any event, a few days after the murders, a posse was raised and after several more days, five of the six suspects were arrested; Ireland could not be found. Two of the accused were to be defended by a lawyer down from the state Capitol and were held locally.

The story that goes on from here has been told in several versions, and Bessie's cousin tells the one related here: The two Sioux men who were captured and turned over to the local law for local incarceration were safe. The other three were taken 40 miles to Williamsport to jail. A "jury," informally gathered in Williamsport, found all three guilty of murder. The jury included Jacob Loutzenhiser, the brother of Bessie's uncle and aunt from Winona environs. Shortly after the "trial," a mob in which Jacob did not participate, followed the prisoners, broke into the jail and took out Cadotte, Standing Bear and Holy Track, "and hung them up from the neck on a rack used to hang game for drying." Jacob was not there at the end, having other business to attend to, but he lent his good saddle horse to the executioners

Wilbert Pierce, who tells this story in his small book, as he recalls his father Berton's experiences and remembrances, also tells of his father's best friend, named Robert Marsh, who had a terrifying reputation in the State. Marsh would stake out the Missouri river on the east bank where Sioux were not allowed to cross and shoot any that appeared in that area. On the steel plate on his rifle he had more than forty scratch marks, each purportedly marking the creation of a "good Indian."

※ ※ ※

Progress almost seemed to be the antidote to savagery. In the late 1870s and 1880s, on the side of progress, the settlers had both scientific and social scientific justifications for believing that they could make the middle desert bloom. They had "dry farming" and Henry George. Department of Agriculture tracts on "dry farming" and political tracts derived from Henry George's writings could be found in the Pierce's small library in the Dakotas.

"Dry farming" was a scientific certainty according to the US government. Farmers were told that enough water would come from the rains and the rivers, irrigation and water tables, and if they chose the correct varieties of wheat and corn, they could raise grain for the bread of growing America. Prairie grass and new varieties of hay could also be sold as fodder to the horses and oxen that provided most of the power for cultivation of the grain.

Those Washington soothsayers, and the almanacs that promised the rain that came in the late 1890s, that filled the rivers and raised the water tables, were preaching a new, and rational, gospel. And they were right those years. "Dry farming" works well in the Dakotas when it rains above the area's annual average.

Henry George, the New York sociologist and philosopher and his arguments in *Our Land and Land Policy* (1871) and later in *Progress and Poverty* (1879) may have been of more real relevance to the urban poor than to those who wanted some land or lots of land in the Dakotas. But his choice of villains: railroads, capitalists and old money certainly had its appeal, and every lyceum and grange on the middle border boasted his books, and many had Henry or his disciples as lecturers. His views became bedrock for later progressives, bi-metalists and farmer-laborites across the west Midwest.

Those farmers who believed that above average annual rain would continue into the early 1900s or that dry farming would work without it, were not lucky. However, if your land holdings were large enough, farmers could survive even with low production per acre. The Petersons survived. Local politics for the small holder might become increasingly populist but both winter and spring wheat could grow and make the big land holders rich by comparison with their small holding neighbors.

In the late 'Eighties and early 'Nineties, the dry shores of Frank Norris's "oceans of wheat" were thus pushed further west, beyond the small towns on the middle border, as the population of America increased substantially and wheat farming expanded. The wheat had already been harvested for ten years in vast quantities in Nebraska, Kansas and southeastern South Dakota. Now it was being grown out toward the Missouri River, and shipped by rail to Kansas City and to Minneapolis from new towns in North and South Dakota. These towns included Pollock, South Dakota, and Burnstad, North Dakota.

By the early 1900s, it was becoming quite clear: to survive even on this land a farmer had to farm more than just a quarter section. Twice this much might ensure that he made enough profit one year to tide him through bad crops and prices the next year. So, problems arose for those farmers whose holdings were smaller or who were in the dry cusp area east of the Missouri river. Many of these farms were a quarter section or less, and there was little wood, fewer hills and less water. The land itself was described by the Peterson family as thin soil on the top of the hills and clay and runoff at the bottom. Plows hit stones soon at the top and could not break through the bottom.

It was not bad land for grazing if you could afford to have enough livestock. But Bessie's family were now farmers. Sodbusters lived their lives as sod-hut homesteaders and what they went through has been described graphically by O.E. Rolvaag in *Giants in the Earth* and *Peder Victorius*.

Small farmers had to diversify, and some like Bessie's family took up work in town as well as farming. But finally, the actual instrument that determined whether the farms and small towns would live or die was the railroad.

Along with a belief in "dry farming," and Henry George, Bessie's relatives believed that the railroads, no matter how monopolistic, would fulfill the promise of connecting the small Dakota towns to the world. Here also they were wrong.

By 1901, Bessie's parents and the Pierces had moved a few miles south from Dale, North Dakota, and across the border to Pollock, South Dakota. The Pierces were founders of the town of Pollock, South Dakota, where they built, owned and operated the "Pierce Hotel." Pollock was a railroad town, a creation of the Milwaukee railroad. As noted earlier, the family had great pretensions, and it appears to be there that it claimed a Captain Pierce as "captain of the second Mayflower crossing" and as an ancestor.

FROM UPPER LEFT: DELBERT, ALMON, BESSIE (AGE 8), PHAROS (FRONT) IN POLLOCK, S.D., 1906 (PRIVATE COLLECTION, MHO).

In Pollock, Minnie Pierce Hinds worked for the local doctor, a young man named Shockey who was fairly recently out in the Dakotas and had young children. She became a nurse/midwife and she was to pursue this calling later in Canada.

CHAPTER 3

Bessie and Her Family Go to Burnstad

> "Come to Logan County. The price of land in Logan County is going up. There is no better time than now for securing a home [in Burnstad, North Dakota] where cheap lands can be bought for a fraction of the cost of no better land in Iowa or Illinois. It is your privilege to locate... where the <u>climate is ideal</u>, where the <u>summers are never hot</u>, and where, because of the dry air in winter, <u>it seldom seems cold</u>. You may have a home where <u>crop failures are never known</u> and where <u>everyone who works prospers</u>."

(ADVERTISING BROCHURE FOR LOGAN COUNTY, EARLY 1920S. EMPHASIS ADDED.)

In Pollock, South Dakota, Bessie's family had lived for the last time as a single unit, mother, father and five children together under one roof. In 1905, the family consisted of Pharos, the oldest son, 18, and teaching at the grammar school; Almon, the 16-year-old second son; Bessie who was seven; Adelbert, the third son, who was five years old, and the baby Marvin. By 1908, the family was smaller and living in Burnstad, North Dakota, in lovely Logan County.

Pollock still exists today as a town, albeit a small town. Find

Burnstad, North Dakota on even a decent sized map today. You cannot, although it still clings to a tenuous existence on the border of Beaver Lake State Park. You can find it as an "US" (unincorporated settlement) in the North Dakota Gazeteer. It is a mark on the county roads of the North Dakota highway map. In 1908, the town had 350 people in it, today it has three. There are more buildings in good repair in town than there are people today, thanks to the efforts of its few denizens.

Minnie Pierce Hinds had done midwife work in South Dakota, working for Dr. Schokey as he traveled around the countryside; she delivered children when he was around and when he wasn't around. Dr. Schokey himself delivered at least one, the last, of Minnie's children, Marvin, born in Pollock when she was 40 and David was 49. When David and Minnie moved to Burnstad, Minnie continued to practice her trade.

Even in her early days as mother and wife, Minnie was strong, and throughout her long life the baby in the family, Marvin, was tied to his mother's apron strings after David's death in 1925, until Minnie herself died in 1953. The other children all left home early.

Both from the fact that Minnie worked outside her home as a midwife, and from the fact that she later was to undertake farming operations by herself when David died, it is obvious that Minnie was a survivor and unafraid of labor. Her pride in the Pierce family name, and the stories that she told and probably believed about her origins, however, was another side to her character. According to her family, even when she was dirt poor, she acted as if she was better than anyone around her; she did have her standards. Those standards were stretched somewhat in the social sphere, just prior to the move to Burnstad, when her headstrong, and ambitious, oldest son had gotten married.

Pharos (named after Minnie's father) was a semi-professional (paid) catcher with the local baseball team and, after teaching for a year, had chosen to work for someone other than himself, as the manager of a branch lumberyard in Burnstad, N.D. Those steps certainly placed Pharos in the middle of better life. He helped his younger brother, Almon to get work with the lumber company as well. The young men were taking "ways to get ahead."

Minnie was proud of Pharos when he graduated high school in Pollock and then took up a teaching post in town. But she had some questions about his choice of wife.

Pharos had been seeing a maid at the Pierce family hotel in Pollock, S.D. The girl's family, and Pharos's parents were acquainted back in Dale, N.D. This girl, slightly older than Pharos, behaved as if her Norwegian, immigrant background was as good as anyone's in Pollock; yet she was a servant; she changed beds and sewed and cooked for money! She was born "Grace Peterson" but had adopted the spelling "Grayce" for her name. Her parents spoke more Norwegian than English, and yet she appeared arrogant.

Pharos had judged his chances when he married Grayce, and he was right; his wife was to outshine his mother socially in every respect. His wife's family, the Petersons were to go on to practically own the community of Pollock and prosper in the Dakotas long after Minnie and David were gone.

The marriage ceremony itself was understated:
"The marriage of Mr. Pharos B. Hinds and Miss Grace Peterson occurred at Linton, North Dakota, Wednesday, July 1, 1908. The Wedding was a quiet affair and only a few friends were present. The news came as a great surprise to their many friends in Pollock where both have lived for several years. Pharos is the eldest son of Mr. and Mrs. David Hinds formerly of this place. He was a graduate of the Pollock School and formerly a teacher in this place. He is one of the most enterprising [*AMEN*] and popular of the young men who have grown up here and left the town to enter business elsewhere and he will be long remembered in

Pollock. The bride is the daughter of Mr. and Mrs. Geo. Peterson of near Winona. She is a most excellent young lady in every way, and very popular among her acquaintances. The young couple will make their home at Burnsted (sic), North Dakota, where Pharos is the manager of the North Star Lumber Yards." (*Campbell County News*, Pollock, S.D., Friday, July 3, 1908). Pharos was 21, Grayce, 22.

Whatever she might have thought about her new daughter-in-law, Minnie knew that young P.B., as he was now calling himself, had what it took to get ahead. David and Minnie did not; they had only been marginally successful in Pollock. So, it is not surprising that these older people with "itchy feet" followed P.B. and Grayce to Burnstad, North Dakota in 1908. David was hired to manage a general store there, one of three general stores.

P.B., on the other hand, was the manager of the local lumberyard. Burnstad looked as if it might grow and there was considerable building going on. P.B. received a salary of around $600 per year. Based on this munificent sum and their expectations, the newlywed Pharos and Grayce set up housekeeping in a house they purchased.

Burnstad, indeed, looked like it might "go." The Soo line was expanding through town. There were two hotels in Burnstad, there was a butcher shop and a drug store. There was a creamery, a blacksmith shop, a machinery and hardware store, and a flour mill. There was a bank and, a newspaper, "the Burnstad Comet," run by the lawyer in town, and a grade school.

By 1910, however, it was clear to Bessie Hinds's parents that they had backed a losing proposition by going to Burnstad, indeed, by staying in the Dakotas. Burnstad was still in a "dry farming" region and here too they were small holders, placing them in a similar position that they were in before they left Dale.

This land was on the desert's edge, and was fated to remain largely unsettled and uncivilized whatever the century. In 2001, a New York Times correspondent, reporting from Fort Yates, in the neighborhood of Winona, Dale, Burnstad and so on, told how the land was finally going back to what it was; that 3.7 million acres were to be without roads, and the buffalo were back.

People were still coming into North and South Dakota to homestead and farm, but they looked more and more desperate, not the sturdy "scot-irish" or even the "norwegans," they were called "bohunks" (South Germans, Czechs and Slovenes), speaking god knows what, and worshipping Rome not home. Some Czechs farmers had migrated into Minnesota as early as 1857, and farmed successfully and set up New Prague, which was wealthy enough in the 1890s to invite composer Antonin Dvorak for a visit. But the new settlers to the Dakotas from Bohemia tended to be from cities and unskilled in farming and were moving to an area that bordered the great American desert.

In Burnstad, son P.B., and his new wife, Grayce, were in a better financial and social position than Minnie and David. It was P.B. who was buying and selling land and looking about for ways to get ahead. While business at the North Star Lumber Company was thriving and P.B. owned land next door to C. P. Burnstad, the community's founder, he was already angling to move to an even more substantial community.

Bessie was in school in Burnstad and very happy there. She had a teacher whom she adored and, since this was a country school, the teacher advanced the very bright Bessie quickly. Bessie completed the eighth grade when she was twelve. Just after she finished the grade, her parents took her, and themselves, away to what to her at least was comparative nothing.

David and Minnie, unable to make it in Burnstad, decided to move to Canada. David Hinds, born Canadian, had taken American citizenship by declaration. (Bessie later told the prison authorities that he was not an American citizen). But David had not been in Canada for twenty years.

David's motivations in going to Canada seem less clear than Minnie's. He expressed his disappointment with how little he had accomplished in the Dakotas and he was willing to go back to the developing Canadian west and take along any of the family he could talk into going.

Minnie, who saw her comfortable life ending in the Dakotas, wanted to go someplace where people spoke good English and knew the value of being of old stock. She thought that she could find this in Canada. Minnie and her parents, who had come out from Minnesota, Iowa and points further east, pretended to remember better times and places that they came from. They would certainly now face something different.

Already some from the Pierce family had struck out for Canada and they seemed to be doing well. Minnie's sister and brother-in-law, Blanche and Frank Loutzenhiser had emigrated from the Winona, North Dakota, area to Moose Jaw, Saskatchewan by 1910. They were urging David and Minnie to look at the land in that area, and were asking the older Pierces, who were still living in Pollock, to move.

Minnie's father Pharos (of the "itchy feet") and mother Rebecca were willing to try something else and follow youngest daughter Blanche to the Canadian prairie where, according to Blanche, life was good. And free land, the chance to start again, was a powerful draw.

In 1911, they cashed out for what they could get. Unfortunately for them, the next step Minnie and David took was a step that was to bring them even further down the social scale. The Burnstad times were the last relatively good times that Minnie was to have for 35 years.

Pharos and Grayce were left behind to grow in the essential glory of America.

This is not to say that P.B. really was pioneering and took chances or bet on much. He may have been strong-willed but he was also cautious. Although he became the "successful son," he was always a big frog in a little pond. (Much later, Bessie would say, "He only had two jobs in his life… ." This was intended both as sarcasm and as praise.)

After the elder Hinds couple went to Canada, Pharos and his mother seem not to have been much in communication. Much later, Minnie was to praise Pharos as her most successful son and Grayce as her neatest and cleverest in-law. By doing so, she may have been denigrating the other children and their choices. Still, by that time, it was obvious that Pharos was far and away the most successful of the lot.

While David was alive, the increasingly successful Pharos helped out and visited his parents. Not so, once David died. Then, Pharos did not visit his mother often and, he did not often help Minnie financially. After his father's death in 1923, he did not go to Canada except very occasionally. Rather than go to his mother's house, he and Grayce vacationed with friends from their social level and developed their own ambitions for their only son. Even when Pharos was relatively rich and well established in Northfield, a good Minnesota town, when he was chairman of the local school board and active in local politics, Boys Scouts, Rotary and an usher at the establishment Lutheran church, and Grayce was active in the Eastern Star and Rebekahs, and sought after for her household skills and organizing ability, P.B. did not see his mother frequently. He did not attend Minnie's funeral.

Bessie learned several early lessons from the familial relationships. Lesson one from Brother Pharos was that marriage, even at a young age, could take you away from Minnie's control.

Lesson two was that if you used your brain and were pleasant to people you could advance yourself more quickly. Finally, Bessie may have learned to keep her own counsel; this would be a result of her parents' contrary attitude. They did not feel that their failure was their own fault, and said so.

Bessie's immediate family was not slow in placing blame for their steadily declining fortunes, and, in the abstract it could be argued that a great deal of the fault of their failure did lay outside of the family with the railroad monopolists, the banks, and perhaps with immigrants who did not speak English and were willing to work cheap.

The Hinds family had "always" been Orangemen (Protestant Irish), and a Currier and Ives print of William of Orange at the Battle of the Boyne hung prominently in David and Minnie's houses, as it did in their son and grandson's houses. The Canadian Hinds immigrant family remained attached to Protestant and Orange secret societies, and David and his sons were Free Masons. They had a conservative and visceral distrust for government and foreigners. They defined foreigners as people who did not speak English, who had arrived on this continent a generation or more after the Hinds family had arrived and who were in all likelihood Roman Catholic. There were any number of institutions and people who could be blamed for the problems that spoiled their chances to be rich in the USA. When Beth Green lived in sin with a Roman Catholic, this was an act of insurrection. When she had African-Americans and Jews as good friends, these were acts of insurrection.

CHAPTER 4

Bessie and Her Family Go to Canada

> *"The geologist who surveyed southern Saskatchewan in the 1870s called it one of the most desolate and forbidding places on earth...Desolate? Forbidding? There was never a country that in its good moments was more beautiful."*

> PP. 6&8, *WOLF WILLOW*, WALLACE STEGNER, PENGUIN, 2000.

In March, 1911, as the financial situation had got worse in the Dakotas, son Almon headed north to scout out the situation in Canada. He got work there and encouraged his parents to come. David Hinds paid the $10 filing fee on a "blind" piece of land in Saskatchewan, and persuaded Minnie's parents to do the same.

In April 1911, David and Minnie packed up their belongings in Burnstad and went from the Dakotas to homestead in an even bleaker place. With them, and planning to bust sod, plant three years-worth of crops, to "prove up" on a separate homestead went Minnie's parents, Rebecca and Pharos Pierce, then in their early 70s.

David was fifty-three years old and Minnie forty-four when

they left for a new life. David had come up and scouted the territory shortly after his son Almon had gone and given an initial report. David thought he knew what the family needed and it was in Canada.

So, in April 1911, Minnie brought Bessie and Marvin up on the Canadian Pacific railroad and David set out with the eleven-year-old Adelbert in a Soo Line boxcar, via Portal, Saskatchewan, to bring the family effects to the unplowed prairie. Almon was waiting for them in Swift Current.

A short time after their arrival in Swift Current, David and Minnie hired a buggy and tried to locate their land. In his wonderful memoir, *Wolf Willow*, Wallace Stegner describes at first hand the country into which they drove. This was a place recently abandoned by cattle men whose ranges were being enclosed and cut up by the railroad. It had been abandoned before that, or not quite abandoned, by the Indian tribes who had established under Sitting Bull and other great leaders a redoubt in the hills of south western Saskatchewan. It appeared one of the best places where wheat crops might be raised, wheat, only wheat, and that those who wanted to plant only wheat could go.

Mid-April was early spring in southwestern Saskatchewan and the creeks and coulees were running full. After going twenty miles from Swift Current, south and slightly west, Minnie and David, in a rented buggy, were forced to turn back because of the high water of the spring thaw.

When May started, they set out again, this time taking along the four-year-old Marvin and eleven-year-old Adelbert. When they finally located "their" land, they found it was almost in Montana, and there were neither farms nor other homesteaders nearby. Even worse, it had the same problem as the farms in Dale, North Dakota: it was too far from a railhead. The closest town was still Swift Current, more than 60 miles away. En route, they stopped at one of the few homesteads in the area and a woman came out; when she saw Minnie she began to cry; she had not seen another woman in two years.

The family also stopped at a ranch where oxen were broken and sold to be used to pull the plows that "busted" the sod. The prairie out there needed deep plows and great power to break up; David was used to farming with horses. David had no doubts; to settle so far from a railroad, and with such land, would be a mistake. The Hinds and Pierce families chose to retreat to Swift Current and stay there until they could find land closer to the rail lines, and closer to being like the farm land that David knew from Ontario.

Because the land immediately around Swift Current was in an area that was already settled, the family would have to accept farming a smaller piece of land still some distance from town. David decided to farm a small piece, 320 acres with horses. David was, in effect, back in Dale, North Dakota. Unlike in Dale, the Hinds and Pierce families could not homestead on adjoining plots. They had planned to do this so that the older members of the family could provide care for the younger and vice versa.

David and Minnie, for another filing fee, got 160 acres about twenty-eight miles southwest of Swift Current and bought another 160 acres on the same site. Rebecca and Pharos Pierce acquired 320 acres about one-half mile away from the Hinds homestead. The Canadian Pacific Railway was running close by and the distance to a granary and elevator, which were being built in a new town, Webb, was about five miles.

Having decided to take up land closer to civilization, the next responsibility for the immigrants was to build on it and produce a crop. To that end, David, Minnie, Adelbert, Marvin and Bessie drove down on the first of June in a covered wagon. That night they pitched a tent made from the canvas on the wagon top. There was a rainstorm and the tent flooded and blew over.

The next day they re-pitched the tent on the acreage that they had just purchased, drove round and marked the boundaries and then went back to Swift Current to pick up their belongings and son Almon.

When they had arrived in Swift Current, David and Minnie purchased one horse by way of livestock. Almon brought down a mare, a cow and a calf. The cow died and the calf was fed watered gruel. But the mare foaled, and the family wealth expanded slightly. The family set back out for the homestead with two horses pulling a wagon/hayrick and more belongings, the calf in a box of straw on the rick, and the colt tied on behind.

This family of six people had to stay in the 7 by 9-foot tent for about two months. Because the land was almost devoid of trees, there was no wood at hand for building. So, for their first weeks in the wild of Saskatchewan, David and all the family cut the prairie grasses by hand as hay and loaded up the rick. (This was not the "short grass" prairie.) David and Almon drove the hay back to Swift Current to sell it. With the proceeds, they bought timber for house frame, rafters and rough siding. They then framed in the house, sided it rough, added to the walls sod from the prairie that they were already plowing, and roofed it over.

When they were finished, they had built a 14 by 16-foot hut. They were not so foolish as to put sod on the roof but used oak shakes with tar in the joints. Bessie lived in that hut for three years with her parents and brothers, at first with frequent visits to and from her Pierce grandparents. David started a small garden right away, and according to Marvin's remembrances, David and Delbert hunted for deer and upland game. The family had adequate food.

Although Almon came along at first to help his parents and grandparents move to the homesteads, and get settled, grubbing out a living there did not appeal to him, and shortly thereafter he went north to Pennant, Saskatchewan, to work for a lumberyard.

Almon did not abandon his parents entirely, however. For a few years he came south regularly to help out on the homestead. In Pennant in 1914, he married Winnie, a young woman who already had an infant daughter. He was 21 and now out from under Minnie's thumb.

The prairie family was busy those three years, cutting grass from the plains for hay, selling it, selling produce from their garden, buying and breaking more horses, breaking up the sod beneath the stubble and planting wheat and other crops. Minnie could earn cash as a midwife and she preferred to do this to being in the hut.

Minnie also preferred working the fields to being in the hut. According to her children and grandchildren, this was because Minnie did not like housekeeping. The chore of watching out for Adelbert and David, and watching the infant Marvin, fell to Bessie. David did not go out to the fields as much as time progressed; a strange lassitude seemed to have settled on him. His disability was later to be diagnosed as diabetes.

Not only was Bessie confined to the hut because of her mother's wish to be outside it, the family was away even from the small society and schools that the Dakota towns had provided. The trip to Swift Current and back took a minimum of two full days and if Minnie went along to midwife or make purchases, frequently it took more time. When this happened, the children were left alone with Bessie, then fourteen years old, in charge.

There was no doubt that Minnie was both tough and hard. She was certainly hard on Bessie and Bessie hated her for it. Bessie told a story again and again about how her parents and Almon left on a three-day trip for supplies to Swift Current from the homestead, leaving the fourteen-year-old Bessie in charge of Adelbert (twelve) and the baby Marvin, age five. There was no wood at hand for Bessie, except rejected railroad ties, which David and Almon had hauled in. These burned well but required tremendous effort to split and carry from several hundred yards away to the hut. Bessie, in her mother's absence, did what most people in the area did all the time. She collected and burned sun dried cow and buffalo chips and used them to heat the hut and cook the food.

David and Minnie decided not to put up in Swift Current to save the expense, so they arrived home early, after two days. From far away, Minnie could see, floating above the hut, the brown smoke of the chips, rather than the white smoke of railroad ties. When Minnie got home, Bessie was shamed, physically punished, and told that her family did not use such a fuel.

Minnie would later tell her granddaughters, Marvin's daughters, many tales of the hard life on the prairie. She told of how she delivered babies in snow and rainstorms and only lost a few patients. She told of taking sick herself after a few years in Canada and how "her" Doctor, with for whom she worked, removed a sixty (?) foot tapeworm from her gut. She told of David's illness, diabetes, which got progressively worse over a period of nine years until he died in 1923; how David could not work after 1918 and the boys, Marvin and Adelbert took over farming, good crops were coming in and more land was bought. She also told how the neighbors had erected a barn in 1912 that the farmers around used both for business and pleasure. The neighborly Potter family was musical and its members played violin and piano. "Robert McInnis was good on the Jews-harp and was a noted step dancer." Amusements and romance were either manufactured, or found.

In late 1913, or early 1914, when Bessie was about 15, son Pharos and daughter-in-law Grayce visited the homestead and Swift Current. A studio photograph of this group was taken at the time. It shows a remarkably handsome family. Grayce and Minnie are almost smiling, and Pharos and David look suitably solemn. It is Bessie to whom your eyes are drawn, however. Her expression is direct and challenging, and it belies her age. (See back cover.)

CHAPTER 5

Bessie Gets Tangled in Webb

There was a developing community called "Webb," which was five miles away from the family homestead. The family believed in the values of education. Because the farmland and shack were isolated, Minnie attempted immediately to get a rural school organized for Bessie, Adelbert, and especially Marvin to attend. (The effort failed; and no school was established close to the homestead until 1918.)

In 1911, the people in town, in Webb, were building a school. Bessie wanted to continue at school there; both her older brothers had graduated high school and taught for a time afterward. But times had changed from Pollock, South Dakota. The homestead farm required a strong young person to work it, especially since Bessie's father, David, was regularly debilitated by his diabetes. In addition, Webb was far enough away that, if Bessie went to school every day, she would have two plus hours each way to travel. The other option, should Bessie attend school in Webb, was boarding Bessie in town but the family was poor and decided to invest in little Marvin's schooling and later boarded him in Webb when they could lay their hands on the money.

So, Bessie was stuck out in the middle of nowhere without

even the minimal social life she had known in the Dakotas.

In 1910, the citizens of Swift Current, Saskatchewan, had started a weekly newspaper. This paper, called "*The Swift Current Sun*" was an immediate success. It carried news of Webb, as soon as that town began to boom. By January 1913, the *Sun* went semi-weekly and one edition each week featured a page with the masthead "*The Webb Moon.*" In fact, Bessie and her mother were featured but not named in one of the early stories from Webb. The story did not redound to anyone's credit, and almost ninety years later, because some families involved continue to live in the area, there is a hesitancy to talk about the details.

It may have been that Bessie had a wild streak, but all evidence points to her as a victim and the story seems to have gone something like this:

Bessie may not have gotten to Webb daily for school but she did get there off and on. And Bessie, who was clearly well developed, and had a strong opinion of herself and life at age fourteen, was well on her way to being "ruined' by a man from Webb, about 22 years old, who with his brother, ran one of the pool halls in town, and who had uncovered her charms when she visited there.

This man was known to be rather wild and several entries in the *Webb Moon* tell about his social life. He and a friend, Peter Dudley, mocked the proprieties of the time and when they rented an apartment, their pool hall doing well, they inserted an amusing and mocking announcement in the *Moon* advising, "that they were home and will receive visitors on Wednesday afternoon."

In 1912, the man was involved in a land deal where he was accused of falsifying land records. About the same time, when he came to call on Bessie at the homestead, he was met at the door by Minnie, with a pistol that she pulled from under her apron.

She told him to get off the farm and out of the county. This story was still remembered and told in that area of Saskatchewan many years after the event occurred.

Bessie felt that she needed a ticket out, and wanted to go farther than Webb. Shortly after she became either a victim or a "bad girl" as adjudged by neighbors, Bessie met Nelson Edward Skinner, age 21, probably at one of the Potter family's barn soirees. This Skinner, a bachelor farmer, was homesteading land with his married brother and they all needed help. Nelson Skinner was also from across the border, the United States. His parents, Fred and Martha Styles Skinner, moved to Saskatchewan from a farm outside of Portal, North Dakota, right on the Saskatchewan line where Nelson had grown up.

Minnie Hinds was not impressed with this young man either, although two facts indicate that Nelson's family may have been better off than many in Webb. They are frequently mentioned in the social pages of the Swift Current Sun, and they traveled to California regularly, coming back and talking of moving to Long Beach. Minnie may only have objected because of Bessie's age. Bessie was a bit of an embarrassment and the Skinners were established. Nelson should have been more suitable to Minnie than Bessie's previous suitor.

Bessie clearly saw Nelson Skinner as an opportunity. Bessie, as she said "Couldn't get out of that house fast enough." But Bessie did not wait until her mother could be persuaded: Nelson Edward Skinner and Bessie Hester Hinds eloped and were married in Swift Current, Saskatchewan, on June 13, 1914. They were married at St. Stephen's Church (Church of England) and the bride listed her religion as Methodist, the groom, Presbyterian. The witnesses to the marriage were Nelson's brother, Robert, and Nelson's sister-in-law. Bessie gave her age as 18. In actuality, she was two weeks shy of her 16th birthday.

Bessie and Nelson honeymooned in California at Nelson's

relatives' home. They came back in July and began to live with Nelson's brother. But events were to make any honeymoon short-lived. In August, the Dominion of Canada, part of the British Empire, went to war with Germany and with the Austro-Hungarian Empire. Young Canadians from the prairies were among the first to enlist and Canadians were soon fighting abroad as they had twenty years earlier in the Boer War.

There was a practical side to their enlistment. Soldiers going to fight the Hun had expectations of free land at the end of their service. Such were the rewards for veterans of the Boer War. And they, and everyone else, did not expect the war to last long.

Nelson had renounced his American citizenship when he had homesteaded in Canada with his brother in 1911. But citizenship was a looser concept in 1914 than it was later in the century, and Nelson could easily become an American citizen again by moving to the United States and reapplying for his "birthright." He would thus avoid "patriotic necessity" in his adopted land and any military draft should such be enacted. Nelson and Bessie went back to California.

Marvin Leonard Skinner was born to Bessie and Nelson Skinner on June 10, 1915 in Santa Rosa, California. Bessie was 16 years old and Nelson 22. When Leonard was 18 months old, Bessie and Nelson returned to Canada again to live with Nelson's parents. Bessie later admitted to her family that she was lonely in California and that Nelson's attitude toward her had changed with her pregnancy. She said that he blamed her for getting pregnant and for continuing the pregnancy until the birth of Leonard.

Their relationship did not improve after they went back to Webb. In fact, it worsened when Bessie discovered that Nelson was seeing other women. She decided to leave him. When she informed Nelson's parents that she and their son were separating, they offered to care for Leonard for her. With no job skills and the need to support herself, Bessie dared not refuse the offer made by the Skinners to take Leonard and raise him. Nelson wanted to go back to the West Coast.

* * *

Bessie's life divides into three acts. First, 1898 to 1918, she led a sometimes hard, sometimes not so hard existence as a frontier girl and young wife. In 1918, she ran away from that and she was taken up by Danny Hogan, a St. Paul criminal boss and mob fixer. At that time, she lived as married, with at least two gangsters.

In this middle act, Bessie's life became difficult after Danny Hogan was blown up by the mob in 1928. She had to adjust to a new, more violent, boss, who replaced Danny, Harry Sawyer. She had to manage legitimate and illegitimate businesses, a family, and her money in an increasingly dangerous and violent environment as the crimes of Prohibition became the post-Prohibition gang crimes of kidnapping and bank robbery. She was criminally involved with John Dillinger and went to Federal Prison. She had to deal, as did America, with the collapse of the economy.

The final act of her life was neither as attuned to the history of the Middle Border, nor as dramatic as her involvement with the Dillinger and Barker-Karpis gangs. After her full confession to the FBI, the courts and in prison she was empty. Her words brought down many mobsters and helped to clean up the Twin Cities, which desperately needed honest police and courts. But her words were a secret that she tried to keep from family and friends.

She was Bessie Skinner and then, in an act of even worse judgment, Bess Garrett. She was a sometime hostess, a sometime bar owner, and a sometime Madame. She probably failed as a mother and her life, except in the eyes of her family and nieces and nephews and their children was a downward trajectory. So, let us see, after her life on the Middle Border and age 18 how she lived.

PART II

St. Paul, 1918-1934

AN ILLUSION: SHINING IN PIGSEYE

December 4, 1928 looked more like March in the streets of St. Paul; snow was melting and it was gray. There was no particular need for Bessie Walsh to hurry that morning. She was to be picked up by her employee, Opal, at 10 a.m., but if Opal did not make it, she could always grab a ride with her neighbor, and sometime boss, Danny Hogan, who lived close by.

Rain had been falling that night but it had only been rain and not sleet and Bessie had looked out the kitchen window into the alley when she was up, not too early, fixing Bob's breakfast. When she had gotten up to pee earlier, at 6 a.m., she could look slantwise and see that Danny Hogan was not home yet. His garage door stood open and his car was not there. He kept late hours. He could not drive her that day.

She had gotten up again at 7:30, and fixed breakfast for Bob before he went out on his route and for Leonard before he was picked up for school. Bessie was "married to" Bob for almost four years and it appeared to her likely that he was getting tired of her and the wild life. She was 30, he was 28 and he was now looking at all the younger women in the speakeasies.

At 10 a.m. when she looked out, she could see that the alley was full of slop. There was a central steamy pile dropped by a horse pulling a milk wagon. Dirty snow was piled against the curb and nothing looked green except the Paige coupe now in

Danny Hogan's open garage across the way. Because his car was there, Bessie knew that Danny was back home. But she wouldn't get a ride from Danny, and anyway Opal was pulling up. Bessie still wasn't dressed. She would invite Opal in for a cup of coffee, and get ready to go to work.

Two people to get ready today: first, the ten a.m. Bessie who had to get to the *Holly Wood Inn,* check the books and deal with deliveries, the runners and the cook, Lucy. Later this afternoon she would have to get the six p.m. Bessie ready, Bessie the hostess, splash of water and cologne under the arms and between and under the breasts, silk dress.

She also had to check what and how her son Leonard was doing at school when she came back and get him settled for the evening, have Opal cook his dinner, before heading back to work. It helped that he was in a parochial school and could spend the whole day. The nuns would look after him and he would have "proper" playmates. The usual worries, but this December morning she could take her time.

THE ALLEYWAY BETWEEN BETH GREEN AND DANNY HOGAN'S HOUSES. (PRIVATE COLLECTION MHO)

CHAPTER 6

Wild Pig's Eye: An Introduction to the Twin Cities Criminal Life (St. Paul, 1918-1928)

The Twin Cities, Minneapolis and St. Paul, were conceived and born in deception and sin. Traces of their birthright were to be found more than a century after they first struggled out and up. St. Paul was the earlier twin, and when it saw daylight, it saw it with a squint. After all, the town had almost been called Pigseye after its founding father, "Pigseye" Parrant.

Parrant was an early trader and innkeeper along the Mississippi, at a location close to the place where Hiawatha's girlfriend's grandmother lived. He, that is, Pigseye, sold fire water to anyone who could pay and kept a small brothel as well. He set the tone for a part of St. Paul life that led through "Swede Hollow,",up Wabasha Ave. to St. Peter, and in a much classier fashion on to Summit Ave.

The banks of the Mississippi where the Minnesota River joins were first settled by a mixed bag of white folk moving west in the late 1830s. The territory, upon which the early settlements stood, were at least still partially under the legal control of Ojibway tribes who had taken it from the Sioux shortly before.

The early settlements were, therefore, in large part "illegal." The illegal settlers were, however, guarded by the U.S. Army at Fort Snelling, on the west bank of the Mississippi.

Pigseye's establishment was on the east bank of the Mississippi. The soldiers at Fort Snelling, did not have to cross the river to that side and Pigseye's cave/tavern to find their amusements. Any of the Fort's troops who wanted to, could get drunk regularly at "Brown's Groggery" without the crossing. Brown's was an establishment in a community of about 150 souls, however lost, who made their living in Indian Territory, from the soldiers and trading.

Official opinion at the Fort was negative about the settlements. Fort Snelling's commander, Major Plympton, wanted to enforce discipline, and the treaty with the Native-American neighbors. He wanted the soldiers to be drunk less frequently, and not to have easy access to liquor. He also wanted the neighboring Ojibway to be less easily riled up. To these ends, in 1840, he drove the 150 settler/squatters off the west bank of the Mississippi and across the river to the east. These rejects settled around the cave where Pigseye had held sway, and in his honor called their new town after him.

For one year, the town that was later to be the capital of Minnesota had a name that every child learning State Capitals could remember. Then Father Lucian Galtier came in to reform the settlers, and set up a chapel and dedicate it to St. Paul. Ah, well, progress.

Brown's Groggery was close to a small attractive creek that flowed over a charming waterfall, appropriately enough called Brown's Falls. A cave was tucked behind the waterfall. In the 1850s, Henry Wadsworth Longfellow was to see an engraving in Harper's Magazine of this waterfall, and take inspiration from it for an epic poem he wished to write on Native-Americans. (The local literati took back this inspiration and since the late 19th century the place, and a city park established there, has been called Minnehaha Falls.)

As St. Paul developed from 1860 to 1880, wheat was grown on the fertile plains stretching west of the Mississippi, and most grain mills were local. But mixed farming by Anglo-Saxons was more the rule, and the towns that were growing around the rivers and fields were reminiscent of New England towns. They were also named either in the style of the French explorers (e.g., Mille Lacs), in New England reminiscences (Northfield) or, with supposed Indian names (Mankato). The eclectic frontier also allowed Native-American sounding names that were actually from the Greek such as Minneapolis.

The great grain milling companies and the railroad tycoons who carried the grain in their almost endless grain cars on the tracks, (as described by Frank Norris in The Octopus and The Pit, as well as in his planned Oceans of Wheat), were the stuff, no, the integument of Minneapolis and St. Paul.

The large international grain companies which grew up in Minneapolis and St. Paul included Pillsbury, General Mills, Cargill, and Archer, Daniels. Then (and now) they processed the waves of amber grain harvested in western Minnesota and on the great acre farms that were increasingly reaching the Dakotas. By the early 1900s, crop diversification, transportation costs and declining fertility in the spring wheat areas of the upper Midwest meant that the value of flour milling products declined, in fact fell to less than one quarter of their previous value. This had an effect to the west, in Burnstad, North Dakota, as already seen.

Other industries remained solid. South St. Paul continued to be the meat packing center for the area with plants operated there by both Armour and Swift. Another major industry which boomed in the early 1900s in St. Paul was publishing with the big three firms being Brown and Bigelow (calendars), Webb Publishing (*The Farmer* magazine) and West Publishing.

The contrast with the frontier and the settlers' lives was stark. The frontier was Bessie's heritage. She came from a family always moving into the great beyond where railroads were built, timber was cut or grain was grown, and where the men and women who cut, built and hewed from the forests and dug up the prairies, continued to believe that they would be rewarded for their labor.

Her parents and grandparents were not rewarded. They moved from failure to failure; they depended on, but did not profit from railroads, nor did they profit from raising up those amber waves. Their stores and hotels mostly failed as the economy around them changed. When the family went broke in the first part of the century, there was nothing but more back breaking work in front of them, certainly nothing for Bessie. So, she tried to move on, and as she moved, Bessie tried very hard to catch up with whatever really made money.

❈ ❈ ❈

In the summer of 1918, Bessie Hester Hinds Skinner, age 20, left her in-laws' home on the Saskatchewan prairies, leaving behind her husband and her three-year old son. Her husband was pursuing other women and her son was loved and taken in by Nelson Skinner's folks. Bessie left hard scratch for a life in any city, and she was not, by any means, the first. Advertisements from the YWCA and other Christian groups during the decade warned girls like Bessie to take care, to not be taken advantage of: "Do not go into the large cities for work unless you are compelled to.... Do not ask questions of strangers nor take advice from them." Bessie knew that advice, like taking advantage, ran in two directions, unlike the Mississippi.

Her first stop was at the home of her brother, Almon, and sister in law, Winnie in the growing railroad and wheat burg, Fargo, N.D. In Fargo, she got work as a waitress for a few months. Her close relationship to Winnie developed here; her relationship with her brother was less warm. After six months in Fargo, she was still poor, still dependent on family and there was no chance of improvement in sight.

Bessie left Fargo to find an independent life but also because her brother and sister-in-law were at a difficult time in their marriage. According to his daughter, Cleo, Almon had lied to get himself a job. Almon had passed bad checks, and his wife, Winnie had to keep him out of jail. Winnie left Almon shortly thereafter taking her two daughters, Maxine and Cleo with her. She divorced Almon and soon married another man. Later she divorced again and remarried Almon. Watching her brother's minor crimes, and unconventional life, and judging her chances, may have helped Bessie set a pattern for her life.

One of Bessie's café customers in Fargo offered Bessie a job in Hibbing, Minnesota, an iron mining boomtown on the Mesabi Iron Range. She went to work in Hibbing at a little railroad café with a slight improvement in wages from her job in Fargo. In Hibbing, however, the unions, the bosses and the poor miners were locked in a dance that was post-boom. She soon found this rough and tumble poor mining and railroad town a place where she could not get ahead. Like Robert Zimmerman (Bob Dylan), forty years later, she had an urgent desire to get out of that place.

Hibbing had one lesson for her. It was the first place that Bessie was free of family and restraints; it was where she learned that she could make it on her own. But Hibbing was too confining. After three months, once again she hit the road, this time for the bright lights of the Twin Cities.

✻ ✻ ✻

Bessie seems to have inherited some of her mother's pride. She always considered herself to be as good as anyone else and better than many. Bessie kept, from age twelve to the end of her life, the beautiful valentine that her Eighth Grade teacher grade teacher in Burnstad had given to her, and remembered what her teacher had said about her.

She could have headed into dire poverty in the Twin Cities. The St. Paul equivalent of Seattle's "skid row" also existed, located in a miasmic lowland at the foot of the hill upon which the big brewers and railroad men had their mansions. It was flooded with the very poor, cheap bars and brothels and many times by the Mississippi. From the 1890s to the late 1920s, Swede Hollow was the part of St. Paul where its down and out days were very open to public scrutiny, and Pigseye could look around and recognize his progeny.

When Bessie arrived in the Twin Cities in the spring of 1919 from Hibbing and the disagreeable railroad café, she initially settled in Minneapolis. There she worked as a waitress for two years, and perhaps as a little more, at a cheap restaurant at 414 ½ Hennepin Avenue, in the heart of downtown. Shortly after taking this job, she went to work at a second job at the Minneapolis Elks Club at Second Avenue South and Seventh Street. The Elk's Club was a place where men with some money gathered. She seems to have worked in both places, on different shifts, for about eighteen months. Then she moved to St. Paul.

St. Paul was not finished with being part Pigseye in the year that Bessie arrived in the Twin Cities, and that fact was to help her find her true calling. She was good with customers, especially men. She knew how to get them to relax, and understood how she had to behave toward them to get ahead. Armed with a quick mind, a ready smile and a risqué (some later said raucous) sense of humor, she quickly got acquainted with those people who patronized cheap cafes and the Elk's Clubs in Minneapolis and St. Paul. Her contacts turned out to be good for finding better jobs, and her forwardness and strong work ethic also provided extra cash if she chose to work extra hours.

Bessie Skinner would never have to worry about inhabiting a place like Swede Hollow. Pleasures of the most mundane sort were available there, in Swede Hollow, at discount prices. Bessie had energy and looks and had learned early what it takes to scratch your way up as well: buy cheap, and especially, sell dear. She grew to know about Minneapolis and St. Paul, from the cheap crooks in Swede Hollow, to the Hamm and Bremer families on the hill, to the Archbishop in the St. Paul Cathedral.

St. Paul continued its rakish history; it was given a new energy as the inheritor of Pigseye's saloon by Prohibition, or rather by defying Prohibition. Bessie seems to have joined in with this defiance. By 1922, she was living at 460 St. Peter Street in St. Paul and listed her occupation as "clerk," but she already knew some of the major players on the St. Paul bootlegging scene.

Prohibition, only three years old, was still an abstract concept to St. Paul and Minneapolis drinkers. Minnesota as a whole was torn between wanting to be a "Prohibition State" and knowing that it never could succeed completely.

Minnesota had had this dichotomy since its founding days. Towns were established in the Minnesota territory on "dry" or prohibitionist principles before the State existed. For example,

Northfield, Minnesota's founder wrote into its charter in 1855 that it was to remain "dry." This was to frustrate several generations of students at Northfield's two colleges.

Some Minnesotans were not content with prohibition at home. The State sent its anti-alcohol reformers out into the wider world. It was, after all, a Minnesotan, the immensely upright, and popular in his own district, sixty-year-old "Judge" Volstead, Republican of Granite Falls, Minnesota, who had written the law that provided criminal penalties for violating the Eighteenth Amendment. Although President Wilson was still compo mentis enough in 1919 to veto Congressman Volstead's attempt to enforce prohibition, Wilson's veto was overridden. Volstead's constituency supported him. Still, one can judge from their behavior that most people in Minnesota thought Volstead was a fool.

Two simple facts made Minnesota a good spot for folks who disagreed with Volstead to defy foolish Prohibition and its laws. First, drinking was something that everyone, or almost everyone, (discounting the denizens of Swede Hollow) did there privately; the image is of stern Norwegian farmers downing aquavit straight in the family kitchen, and being slightly ashamed of what they were doing. The scene is described with Per Hansa and Hans Olsa playing the lead roles in O.E. Rolvaag's *Giants in the Earth*.

Second, the amber waves of grain were easily brewed into amber beverages or stilled into hard liquor. Lumbermen, slaughterhouse workers, millers, miners, all wanted a beer after work. The need for a steady liquor supply in the upper Midwest, and the grain, had ensured that considerable industry in St. Paul was founded on spirits and the current big brewers had substantial interest in politics and life in the state. Money was to be made from booze.

Along with no shortage of locally produced product at hand for local consumption, there was also lots of unpatrolled and unpopulated border with Canada to make smuggling easy, and the Twin Cities also served as a transport hub. The water of life could be shared with neighboring states. Importing and exporting along the rail lines that ran from New York through Detroit was also an easy option. Boats carried booze up and down the Great Lakes. There was a grain alcohol axis between St. Paul and Cleveland.

Outsiders pictured Minneapolitans as dour, Scandinavian and Lutheran (all synonymous). St. Paul seems to have been viewed as a beer-drinking town of Irishmen (or Germans). Neither the self-images, nor the outsider's images were particularly accurate. Both towns had some ethnic diversity, both had cultural claims and both had a rich but limited criminal life.

The Twin Cities had an adequate share of criminal problems throughout Prohibition and into the gangster era of the Depression. Here is where Bessie fit in by 1924. The towns that were born wild continued that way. Bessie found her truly wild side there. At that time the sinfulness, especially of St. Paul, was pointed out in the national press and by officials of the Federal government. The newspapers and the revenue and postal inspectors thought that the Cities were pretty evil places. Although she was wild, no one was to think Bessie was "evil," not even J. Edgar Hoover, then getting his start too.

From the mid-twenties to the end of the thirties, the major papers in the two towns, especially the *St. Paul Daily News*, ran crusading stories and editorials aimed at cleaning up the town. The stories were prominent, the places were prominent.

In the twenties and thirties, Minneapolis and St. Paul formed the largest urban area in the Northwest, i.e. that area north and west of Chicago and as far as the Pacific Coast, north of San Francisco. The twin towns had already fallen into their two distinct patterns of self-imaging: Minneapolis residents thought of their town as richer, better educated, more intellectual and more self-controlled. St. Paulites thought of their town as better established and more historical, more influential because it was the capital city, more ethnically diverse, and more "blue collar."

Bessie lived between the towns, at times in St. Paul, at times in Minneapolis. She too had two separate images, but one she kept well hidden from the authorities, the press and her family.

The criminals with whom Bessie consorted were likely to have ethnic identities very different from that of the majority of people in the area. Very early on, Bessie seems to have chosen many of her friends and colleagues from a very small ethnic population in the area's melting pot. Harry Sawyer (born Sandlovich), Jack Peifer, Leon Gleckman, the Gleeman brothers and many others with whom she dealt were of Eastern-European-Jewish background. By the 1930s, the number of Jewish citizens in the Twin Cities had increased to about 40,000 in total, but this number represented less than 5% of the total population.

An even smaller group of citizens was African-American. The 1940 census showed that there were about 4,500 African-Americans living in the area. Most of these people were employed as cooks, waiters, sleeping car porters, domestics, and stockyard and meat processing workers. Bessie counted several African-American women among her friends and colleagues.

Those acquaintances that she did not choose, her relatives, were much less tolerant than she was. But most, not knowing her real story in full, remained tolerant of her, indeed loved her, despite "some faults."

Neither her letters, nor her family's memories indicated that she paid much attention to the religion or race of her friends.

She was much less prejudiced than her relatives. Who knows why? But being a single divorced, self-supporting mother and having had, at first, to work with all sorts in cheap railroad spots and cafes, and as a "clerk," she may have admired other self-made types. Her friends were not those that would have been approved by her parents; but that part of her family, the Pierces, with their prejudices, were struggling up on the Canadian prairie. It was in the Twin Cities' nightclubs, restaurants and speakeasies that she learned to work with her peers.

* * *

There was a distinct layering in the criminal society in St. Paul when Bessie Skinner arrived there in 1922. At the top, tolerated and perhaps even encouraged by the Mayor, was the Chief of Police, Frank Sommers. Sommers was heir to the "O'Connor layover system," invented and perfected by St. Paul Police Chief John J. "the Big Fellow" O' Connor in the early 20th Century, whereby any criminal of any proportions arriving in St. Paul, paid obeisance and tribute to the designated representatives of the police force and pledged not to do anything criminal within the St. Paul borders.

Next came the big bosses, the "capos di tutti capi," in Mafia terms. These men, and they were all men, were at a parallel level to the Chiefs of Police in St. Paul, On the "crooks" side, gaining hegemony in 1922, was the up and coming mob boss Leon Gleckman, who was just moving into control of the liquor syndicate. In 1922, when Prohibition agents raided Gleckman's "St. Paul Blueing Company" they found a brewing company instead, with thirteen stills that generated an estimated <u>profit</u> of over $1,000,000 a year. Bessie was the paramour of a Teamster Organizer and regular mobster who was part of this criminal syndicate.

The top levels of the St. Paul and Minneapolis mobs, those bosses whose names will reoccur in criminal activities long after Bessie "went straight," were her acquaintances at this time. Chances are very good that she had at least met Leon Gleckman by 1922. She was well acquainted with his underlings and worked in the places he frequented. (In 1927, after serving eighteen months in Leavenworth for bootlegging and related crimes, Gleckman returned to St. Paul, resolved to ensure that he did not go back to prison. He began by buying his way into politics and became de facto co-Mayor of St. Paul by 1930. At one point in the early thirties, he even considered running for the real office, at the urging of local wealthy citizens. Gleckman did go back to prison, however, sent up by the U.S. Treasury for tax evasion in 1934.)

Gleckman's biggest rival for capo di tutti capi in St. Paul was Jack Peifer. Jack Peifer was a man who Bessie knew and feared more than Gleckman. From some accounts, it seems that Peifer gave the appearance of being more legitimate than Gleckman. He owned many of the restaurants and nightclubs where Gleckman's liquor was sold and had substantial "straight" business interests. But as his influence began to grow in the late twenties, Peifer was more and more notoriously engaged in the dirtier rackets. And if you look closely you can find his name listed in a court case as a thug--a liquor hijacker--employing violent underlings back in the early twenties.

Peifer, by the early 1930s, was a man who planned crimes bigger than hijacking and got others to carry them out. For example, there is evidence that Jack Peifer actually ordered the hit on Margaret "Indian Rose" Perry and her friend Sadie Carmacher in early 1932 as a favor for for another boss, Harry Sawyer. This crime had a great influence on Bessie during the time she was Beth Green, 1932-1934. While these murders benefited

Sawyer more, Peifer was said to have been better connected to the "Murder Incorporated" boys in New York. There was fairly positive proof that a New York hit man actually shot and burned Margaret and Sadie. Peifer, according to Alvin Karpis, was also the man who planned William Hamm's kidnapping in 1933 and engaged the Barker-Karpis gang to carry it out. There is another Beth Green connection with this kidnapping, for a later Chapter.

As far as there was territory, it appeared that Peifer operated out of locations around St. Paul, while Gleckman controlled the town itself. Peifer did, however, own the most elegant restaurant and casino within St. Paul, the Hollyhocks Club, above the Mississippi River and close to the current International Airport. (It is now a private residence.)

At the next level down in 1922, from Peifer and Gleckman were the fixers and bootleggers. The King of the Fixers was "Dapper Danny" Hogan. He was ex-Chief Frank Sommers' partner, from 1922 to 1928, operating out of his restaurant/night club, the "Green Lantern" saloon, earlier named "Dapper Danny's," Bessie was Danny Hogan's protegee from sometime before 1924 on, and a lifelong friend of Danny's wife Leila.

Bessie's associates in St. Paul then, from 1924 to 1934, even before she was arrested by the FBI, were bosses, crooks, whores, and fixers. They were people well got up in a mob which had a national reputation. When Danny was murdered in 1928, it marked an inflection point in Bessie's life. She had been involved with whores, gamblers and bootleggers before that time. After, she was to become involved with bank robbers, sociopathic killers, and kidnappers. This came not from choice of occupation on her part, but from choice of lovers.

In early 1932 she took up with Eugene "Eddie" Green. He had first met Beth in early 1932 when she ran the Alamo. The Alamo was a joint of considerable disrepute located between St. Paul and White Bear, Minnesota out on Highway One just past the Keller Golf Club. It was a place where the demimonde and more solid citizens had dinner, gambled and partied. It was co-owned by Jack Peifer.

Beth's history with men was rich before she met Eugene "Eddie" Green. Immediately before Beth took up with Eddie, she lived with a man named Ray Moore for about two years, after Bob Walsh. Ray was a minor hoodlum, and gambler, and who was a card dealer there when she took over the Alamo. Ray was abusive; Beth had other options and she left him. Fearing Ray, she hid out with a good friend from earlier days, "Aunt Grace" Rosenthal, who still ran one of St. Paul's most up market brothels.

Between 1929 and 1931, before Ray and at the beginning of the time Bessie ran the Alamo, she was working out a business relationship with Harry Sawyer who was trying hard to be head of the St. Paul mob. Harry had "inherited" Beth from Harry's sponsor, Danny Hogan, when Danny was murdered.

❋ ❋ ❋

As noted, when Bessie Skinner first came to St. Paul in 1922, she lived on St. Peter Street in the downtown area and her occupation was listed in the city directory as "clerk." Bessie was an attractive and intelligent young woman and she could read, had a nice hand, and could do arithmetic, despite the fact that when she came to the Cities, she had only an eighth-grade education and no clerical experience.

In 1922, the second rung brothels were on St. Peter's Street, and one of the common designations in the directories then for the ladies of the demi-monde was "clerk." Frank Marzitelli told Paul Maccabee, "During the O'Connor days, St. Peter [Street from West to College streets] had a string of whore houses on the second stories, protected by police. Rumor had it that the county coroner would give the prostitutes medical examinations." This was where Bessie roomed. If Bessie did start out as a prostitute, it would help to account for many of her later associations and occupations.

A short distance away from Bessie's first capital city residence was the most famous brothel in the city run by the most famous Madame in St. Paul history, Nina (pronounce Nye-nah) Clifford. Nina was born in 1851, and by 1888 she had completed her magnum opus, a three-story brick brothel across the street from the St Paul central police station and county morgue on Washington Street.

Nina's role in the history of commercial St. Paul is both a matter of local documentation and legend. Her renown reaches to the present day. But Nina herself kept it up for a long time: she did not die until 1929, and up until that time she both reigned and ruled. When she did die, after a duchess's funeral laid her well-traveled remains to rest, her place in St. Paul was taken over, (or so they say in Minneapolis), by the most recent girl friend of Isadore "Kid Cann" Blumenfeld, the boss of the Minneapolis mob.

Whatever vague connections, Bessie Skinner may have had to Nina Clifford and Nina's era, she had a connective link to "Dapper Danny." This man, Danny Hogan, had arrived in the Twin Cities in 1909, ten years before Bessie. If one looks at his image in photograph, Danny looks like someone drawn for a "Dirty Dick of Deadeye" magazine. He looks like the bad banker in the 1930s Western who lies and hires the fellows who are going to destroy the town.

Danny Hogan, her great protector in her first association with the mob was the living definition of a "fixer" in the mob hierarchy. He moved and negotiated among the different mob bosses and the police and politicians, as well as the lower level gangsters and the police. He delivered warnings, news of impending raids, and weapons to the crooks. He laundered money and bonds gained from fraud, robbery and embezzlement. He planned crimes although he was usually not directly involved in them. He carried payoffs to police and politicians, and he took his cut of everything. He was, in mafia terms, a "capo." He was Bessie Skinner's mentor, friend and boss.

While Danny was still alive, between 1924 and 1928, Beth lived with Bob Walsh. Bob drove a beer truck and was an organizer for the Teamsters. Also, at that time, Bob associated with the Gleeman-Gleckman bootlegging Syndicate, and was very much involved in one of the most famous crimes during the bootlegging era. Bob was involved with "logistics"; moving the stuff.

At the time Beth lived with Bob Walsh in 1924, however, she was better got up with the mob than he was. Beth had risen through good contacts and her own efforts. Those were her best years, 1924 to 1928, when she was first a protégée then a colleague of "Dapper Danny" Hogan. During this period, she had a house next door to where Danny and his wife, Leila, lived, in a good section of St. Paul. She also worked, off and on, at Danny's main place of business, the Green Lantern saloon. She worked there, but this was not where she earned most of her money. She had other business interests, and many of them resulted from her contacts with Danny.

When Beth Green was arrested in 1934 her legal name was Bessie Skinner. Danny Hogan knew her by this name when he took Bessie under his wing in 1924. Twelve years later, this was the name that J. Edgar Hoover used when he wrote about her.

How Bessie and Danny first became acquainted is a matter of speculation. "Aunt Grace" probably introduced them. But what is sure is that Bessie became very close to Danny's wife, Leila. This seems to have been a real friendship, almost a family relationship. It was to last until Leila died in 1973.

The stories about Hogan, the Gleeman brothers, Gleckman, Harry Sawyer and Beth's domestic partners have passed into footnotes in the history of a criminal era. J. Edgar Hoover's name survives and sells books, but more because of outrage with his effrontery than his reputation as a gang buster.

During that time and in that place, the people whom Beth Green knew made national headlines, were discussed by Cabinet members and on the floor of Congress, and inspired newspaper stories, magazine articles, movies, "true crime" books and novels.

Danny Hogan came in for his share of publicity, and when he was killed, 3,000 people attended his funeral, including the Mayor, Police Chief, and Archbishop of St. Paul. There was little doubt then why he was famous. Danny was a master of ensuring that crime, civic corruption, and "law and order" could mutually exist and be profitable for a large number of St. Paul citizens while the "little guy" was not harmed and could easily find amusements.

The criminal was then guaranteed a modicum of protection from being arrested while in St. Paul for crimes committed elsewhere than St. Paul. Chief Sommers would get regular delivery of crisp green bills. (Perhaps these rake-offs did not provide enough income because Chief Sommers switched sides officially in 1924, joining the bad guys as an active partner of another big fixer in the area and helping to plan crimes.)

Police Chiefs rotated through the job in the Twenties, after Sommers left, sometimes retiring much enriched, sometimes forced out for being too obviously corrupt. When the position of Chief was occupied by Tom Brown in 1930, Brown was paid the same courtesy as his predecessors, and the "O'Connor Layover system" looked secure. Greed and the Depression were, however, already in the process of destroying the system.

St. Paul had already established its reputation as one of the safest places in the country for a crook to go before Danny set up shop in 1922. The O'Connor Layover system was in place for seven years by 1922, and it worked. From 1922 to 1928, Danny was the person with whom crooks, newly arrived in town, would check in. He was also the person who kept the Division Chiefs and detectives on the St. Paul police force happy. Danny Hogan was an exemplar of an era, worth his own book.

At the next level down from Hogan were the more specialized fixers, such as Danny's deputy, Harry Sawyer, who got rid of hot jewels, bonds and securities and provided the protection rackets for Gleckman. Myron J. Quimby, writing about Bessie in 1969, gives her a prominence that she may or may not have really had before 1932, when he says, "Bessie Skinner was an early accomplice of Harry Sawyer's."

At this level too were the madams of brothels, and the bookies and set up men for all kinds of gambling, and the labor organizers and union leaders at the breweries and trucking depots. In lower middle management, there were specialists in hot or clean cars. These included Thomas Filben and his Federal Acceptance Corp. Tom Filben had another specialty, he was undisputed "King of the Slot Machines" and he ran all the slots for the tri-county area through his Patrick Novelty Company. He also handled hot diamonds for the mob.

(Tom Filben is a good example of the long careers that criminals could have in the Twin Cities and Minnesota. Tom Filben will be encountered again during the "penny ante" prohibition days of the late 1940s and early fifties.)

Beneath this level were the actual crooks that carried out the jobs.

Bessie status was ambiguous, perhaps because she was a woman and the mob was a man's game. She was acquainted early on with members of the several syndicates in St. Paul, especially those who worked with Leon Gleckman, and who hung out with Danny Hogan. Among the successful specialists, and operators of their own syndicate, were the Gleeman brothers, Abe and Ben, whose much younger brother, Irving, was to help Bessie during the time she was associated with Dillinger.

The Gleeman bootleg booze storage and transport syndicate, with the cooperation of Harvey Gellman from Minneapolis, was made up almost exclusively of Jewish hoodlums, and they distributed liquor and kept accounts for the various bootleggers. They would purchase their booze from Gleckman, and hire drivers, often from the breweries. In 1924, the Gleeman brothers employed a Teamster organizer, Bob Walsh, for loading and unloading trucks. Along with Walsh, they also employed George Hurley. We know for sure that Bessie was living with Walsh at this time, early 1924 when she was 26 years old. George Hurley was to come into her life again several years later when she worked directly for the man at the Green Lantern, which he managed, and where he tended bar.

There were other rumors around that hinted at Bessie's involvement with the mob that early, for example, the rumor of a tunnel from the Schmidt Brewing company to Bob Walsh's basement (the house where Bessie and Bob lived.) This is probably not true; the tunnel actually seems to have gone to another house, nearby. But Bob Walsh was named in papers. There is also no evidence about how Bob and Bessie met. But a supposition exists that Bessie became sexually acquainted with Bob early. Certainly, she knew him in 1923.

Besides being employed by Danny Hogan or his cohorts in several of their different "business enterprises," Bob and Bessie Walsh, as they called themselves, became neighbors of Danny and Leila Hogan on West Seventh Street in St. Paul in late 1924. Bessie remained a close friend of Leila Hogan, long after Danny's untimely demise and Leila's remarriage.

CHAPTER 7

"Dapper Danny" Hogan Goes to His Reward

> *"[Danny Hogan] is, no doubt, one of the most resourceful and keenest criminals in the United States and has always been able to cover his tracks so as to avoid detection."*
>
> SPECIAL ASSISTANT JOHN S. PRATT WRITING TO THE U.S. ATTORNEY GENERAL, MAY 24, 1927, QUOTED BY PAUL MACCABEE.

Danny Hogan, in St. Paul, was an ex-convict from the wild west. He had spent time in San Quentin, as well as in jails in Wisconsin and South Dakota, for theft and general malfeasance. But he only seems to have found his true genius after he moved to St. Paul, and his true genius was organizational. It took a few years to show up, but when it did, in about 1920, Danny began to make a solid name and position for himself. He showed himself the master at planning crimes and cleaning the gains that resulted, i.e., laundering the money, securities, bonds, jewelry or postage stamps.

When Danny took his cut, it was not onerous, he gave good value and he paid a percentage of his cut up the line. Danny did

A FULL CONFESSION

not have to point pistols in peoples' faces to get them to go along with him. He could smile and serve drinks. And he could always hire mopes to carry out the dirty work.

One can assume that Danny had started on the path which would lead him to be the chief fixer in St. Paul, soon after he arrived. Although he came into town earlier, according to Paul Maccabee, he cannot be found figuring in St. Paul records until 1918, however, when he was mentioned in police reports, and in the papers, as a "prominent figure" in the St. Paul underworld.

Before Danny Hogan came into the ascendancy, in the late teens according to these reports, the citizenry of Minneapolis and St. Paul were of different temperaments and neither town cooperated in controlling or advancing illegal activities. The twin towns were each controlled by different gangs.

Despite local differentiations however, the Cities were not really contested between crooks. There were only different jurisdictions in a big metropolitan area. It was eminently practical for the controllers of gangs to come to arrangements both at the big boss level and among the fixers so that business in the two towns could be conducted without too much competition among the potential rivals; such competition often could result in more deaths, police involvement and diminished profits.

Thus, according to the FBI records, in the early twenties, Danny Hogan came to an agreement with Edward Morgan, the chief fixer in Minneapolis. This agreement stated simply that the two bosses would not interfere with each other's territory. This agreement held until Danny's successor, Harry Sawyer, suffered from a surfeit of greed in the early 1930s.

In the history of Beth Green/Bessie Skinner, this agreement

would mean that, as a rising protégée of Danny Hogan, she could work in both the twin towns and be protected. Her work history at the time has her both in Minneapolis and St. Paul, sometimes as a "clerk," sometimes as a waitress, sometimes as a cashier.

❋ ❋ ❋

In a move that Dashiell Hammett was writing fiction about at the time, the mob in St. Paul in 1924 decided that it would be better to do business with the U.S. Attorney and his chief prosecutor, than to face him in court. The mob, Danny Hogan in front, bought the federal prosecutor William Anderson, and the U.S. Attorney, Lafayette French. French actually came cheaper than Anderson for he was a fool. This purchase was to stand Danny in good stead, when he was later accused of having planned the April 1924 robbery of a South St. Paul mail messenger.

This robbery was a federal crime and was investigated over several years. During the robbery itself, some $35,000 was stolen from the Chicago Great Western station, and as various crooks who were involved in the robbery were caught over the ensuing years, it became clear that Danny Hogan and Frank Sommer, the ex-police chief, had planned the robbery sitting in the *Green Lantern* . They later received their 10% cut there. One crook, John Moran, was arrested for and had taken a fall for the robbery in 1924. Following his conviction, it was reported that Prosecuting Attorney Anderson, a man owned by Danny, <u>apologized</u> to Moran, for having had to convict him!

Knowing that Hogan and Sommer's were involved in the robbery, even on the part of the Justice Department <u>and</u> Postal inspectors, and being able to prove it were two separate things. Danny and Frank began to feel the heat when in 1926, when

Moran and others began to talk. Moran talked because he felt betrayed; he was set up to take the fall for the whole robbery and he had not been sprung in the ensuing time.

But when Moran snitched, his information was not adequate to prosecute the gang in Minnesota. St. Paul was Hogan's town and it would be difficult to bring him to trial there. He was well known and well liked and he had the police in his pocket. In addition, the Feds suspected with justification that the U.S. Attorney's office in St. Paul was incompetent at best and at worst on the take from the syndicate.

Indictments were therefore brought in the Cleveland Federal court against Danny Hogan, Frank Sommer, Leon Gleckman, Abe Ginsberg, S.J. Grohman and Detective Sergeant Thomas Brown (yes, that Tom Brown). Almost immediately the case against Hogan, et. al., began to suffer from forgetful witnesses, changing stories and disappearing informants. Max F. Burger, Special Agent of the FBI was assigned by the U.S. Attorney General to investigate not only Hogan, but the United States Attorney's office in St. Paul. He reported his investigation on June 26, 1926 in a comprehensive report.

In this document, several years before the Dillinger days, a detailed view of the crooked goings on in *Pigseye* were supplied with absolute clarity. The charge was laid that in addition to William Anderson (Assistant U.S. Attorney), the Clerk of the U.S. Court at St. Paul and the Chief Deputy U.S. Marshal at St. Paul, were all also "apparently working against the interests of the Government," and in the interests of Danny Hogan. The Burger report and subsequent reports of other investigators contained great quantities of supporting evidence and testimony to these charges.

This was the milieu that Bessie Skinner became part of. She was an intelligent woman, who read and listened to the news her whole life. Her history at this time, whenever recorded by her, or Leila, or Aunt Grace or in the newspapers, certainly went up in that burn barrel in 1973. What is left is a real history of those times recorded in many places without Bessie's help. Also left the memories of her relatives, mostly of people from the Danny Hogan era that Bessie associated with.

* * *

Bessie and Leila Hogan became neighbors as well as close friends. Leila was ten years older than Bessie. She enjoyed the company of the younger woman, and the Hogans had a house north of the Twin Cities on Big Bass Lake. They loved to get away to their cabin in the Minnesota lake district and go fishing. Bessie and Bob Walsh were invited to this lake to stay over.

BESSIE IN HER STUDIO PORTRAIT FROM 1927 (PRIVATE COLLECTION-MHO)

After Danny died, Leila Hogan bought a house on Twin Lakes by Brainerd, Minnesota. Bessie stayed with Leila at that house also and remained friends with Leila Hogan until Leila died in 1973.

By mid-1924, thanks to her association with Hogan, Bessie was living in a good section of town and spending considerable time with the man she called her husband, Bob Walsh. Bob Walsh was a confederate of Danny's and of Leon Gleckman. Bob's day job was at the *Schmidt Brewery* where he was a truck driver and an organizer for the Teamster's Union. During this time *Schmidt* was providing beer to the *Green Lantern*, and numerous other establishments as directed by Danny Hogan. In his spare time, Bob was a driver for the Gleeman's liquor distribution syndicate.

Bessie lived as if she was married to Bob Walsh and her relatives thought that she was. During their four-year relationship, Bessie herself believed that their life together was both stable and legitimate. Her family treated Bob like family. Her family also knew that she was acquainted with Danny Hogan, but Danny's reputation among most people who read the newspapers in Minnesota was as a colorful restaurant entrepreneur.

Bessie's older brother, P.B. had moved to Minnesota in 1926, and he and his wife Grayce accepted that Bessie and Bob were married. They let their only son, eleven-year old Raymond, visit at the home Bessie shared with Bob. In later years, Raymond used to love telling of being entertained by Danny Hogan when visiting his cousin, Leonard, at Beth's home.

Despite the appearance of legitimacy, from the first days of her association with the Hogans, Bessie knew what was going on with Danny Hogan and his gangs. In her confession to the FBI, Bessie told the agents that in the mid-twenties, Danny Hogan had installed a lady informant within the Prohibition Bureau in St. Paul. She also described the mob's workings, going back as far as 1926.

Bob Walsh, however, in 1926, was not in either a stable or

legitimate position at work. He was up to his eyeballs in the biggest court case brought during the Prohibition era, a case that involved millions of dollars of profits, betrayal within the mob, wrongful prosecution and conviction, murder, and of course, Leon Gleckman.

The case revolved around liquor distribution, it was described in brief earlier. Central to this distribution under the general authority of Gleckman, was the *"Gleeman/Gellman Syndicate,"* as it was called in the press. This syndicate was made up of Morris Roisner, Nate Bader, Harry Gellman, Sammy Harris, Abe Ginsberg, Morrie Miller, Tommie Webber, and Bennie Weisman in addition to Abe and Ben Gleeman. The *syndicate* had its offices in the Builders Exchange building in St. Paul and in the 622 Plymouth Building in Minneapolis.

The syndicate's operations involved storage and distribution facilities, trucks identified by (faked) names as belonging to moving companies, and autos used in the transport of booze.

As part of its work, the *Syndicate* would purchase grain alcohol in bulk from Cleveland, Ohio, where it was manufactured and sometimes "denatured"; they would distribute the booze for Leon Gleckman once the alcohol (whatever its source) became liquor. If European liquor was imported from the East Coast, from Ben Weisman in New York City, the *syndicate* would handle its distribution once it was moved in cases to St. Paul by train.

Morrie Miller and Tommie Webber were gunmen and guards for the *syndicate*. Morrie Miller in particular was known to be a killer. The *syndicate* employed George Hurley and Bob Walsh for loading and unloading liquor. According to newspaper accounts, Hurley and Walsh were also employed to transfer liquor from large containers to bottles, and to place the bottles of booze into cartons. The cartons were then stacked and ready for Hurley, Walsh and others to deliver to another storage facility.

They would perform this task at night at a *syndicate* warehouse, where they would be locked in, both for their own protection and to ensure that some of the goods did not go missing through pilferage.

One morning in February 1925, Abe and Ben Gleeman picked up Bob Walsh and Bob Hurley at the Royal Hotel in St. Paul. The four men went to breakfast together and the Gleeman brothers explained to the two other men that they needed considerable quantities of liquor moved, in two "Moore Transfer Company" trucks from the freight yards of the Milwaukee line to a mob-controlled warehouse. At breakfast, they also discussed the fact that a hijacking gang was operating, and preparing to hit the Gleeman facilities. This gang (according to Abe Gleeman) consisted of Burton Stevens, Eddie LaSalle, Roy Rogers, Frank Riley, Jimmie O'Keefe, Charlie Adams, Jack Peifer, and Gasoline John Miller, also known as John Gallagher.

Hurley, Walsh, Abe and Ben Gleeman took trucks down to the yard and began to transfer booze from the freight cars. They found that they were being shadowed by the young hoodlum, Burt Stevens, who warned the Gleemans that federal agents were ready to arrest them. The Gleeman brothers did not believe this, and they suspected that they were being set up for a hijacking. They had access, through Danny Hogan, to information on where the federal raids were to be conducted. So, they warned Stevens off.

Several mornings later, on February 16, Ben Gleeman had another confrontation with Stevens, and that afternoon, as Gleeman and Morrie Miller were in downtown St Paul, they saw Stevens. During an ensuing argument, Morrie Miller shot Burt Stevens dead. (Ben Gleeman claimed in court that he was not aware of the shooting, just of Morrie Miller jumping into his car and telling him to take off.)

An investigation into this murder could, in the view of the St. Paul bosses, reveal the whole mob and bootlegging structure in St. Paul. They hid the Gleeman brothers and their partners for a few days, but Abe Gleeman, and then Ben, surrendered to authorities. They were eventually tried twice and at the second trial found guilty of Burton Steven's murder. They were sentenced to life in prison at Stillwater, Minnesota.

In 1926, the Gleeman brothers decided that they did not want to spend their lives in prison for a crime that they had not committed. They turned states witnesses and provided evidence about the structure of the *syndicate,* and the information that they gave, before a Federal grand jury in Cleveland, Ohio (the same grand jury which was looking into Danny Hogan's involvement in mail robbery) turned out to have as powerful an effect as the St. Paul mob had feared.

According to Paul Maccabee (p.33), the grand jury indicted more than 60 Minnesota residents, (41 of these from St. Paul), and some 60 others from around the country. The indictments showed more than 100 illegal acts in twelve cities. The money taken in, in the Twin Cities area alone, amounted to $200,000 per week or about $10 million a year. Thirteen of the defendants in the trial pleaded guilty, and these and others went to prison. Leon Gleckman went to Leavenworth penitentiary in 1927 for 18 months. However, a St. Paul police detective, Tom Brown, who was also indicted (yes, that Tom Brown), had the charges in the case against him dropped and he went free. Bob Walsh, a player in the *Syndicate,* also escaped incarceration.

In 1926, Bob's "wife," Bessie Skinner, became a hostess at the *Holly Wood Inn* in Mendota, a short distance from St. Paul, and on a bluff overlooking the river. This was a dining and dancing establishment with a large casino in the rear. It was owned jointly by Danny Hogan, Harry Sawyer and two other partners. Beth

Green/Bessie Walsh conveniently forgot about this place in talking to the authorities at the Alderson reformatory in 1934.

The *Holly Wood* was not a dive. In fact, it was respectable enough that Bessie's niece and nephew, and her son Leonard, when he re-arrived in her life, at age twelve, could visit occasionally during daylight hours, and other family members would come to dinner. Leonia Goodman who lived on Rondo Street in St. Paul was the cook here and it was here that the two women became acquainted. Opal White, was another African-American employee at the *Holly Wood*. She frequently drove Bessie to and from work there. Opal also continued to work for Bessie until the Dillinger days, and remained a lifelong friend.

Many years later Bessie stated that it was also in 1926 she had appendicitis and at the same time had her "tubes" tied. At this time, she had realized that she would have to take full responsibility for raising her son, Leonard, and perhaps she wanted to insure there would be no more children to be responsible for. Ultimately, she may have regretted this decision. Certainly, in later years she became something of a surrogate mother to her nieces, nephews and then later to her great nieces and nephews.

1926 was a breakout year for Bessie. She was 28 years old and a trusted member of Danny Hogan's inner circle Her immediate family was moving closer; P.B., the most stable brother, was 35 miles away in Northfield managing a lumber yard there, and her brother Almon had moved to Minneapolis in 1922 and remarried his ex-wife, Bessie's favorite, Winnie. In 1926, Bessie was making lots of money, projected a quasi-respectability, and had loyal friends. She had found her place.

* * *

Her son also found a place about then, and it was with her. When Bessie and her husband, Nelson Skinner had separated in

1918, their son Leonard initially lived with his paternal grandparents, Frederick and Martha Skinner, on their farm near Webb, Saskatchewan. His father had returned to the West Coast (Washington State) where he managed a chain store.

According to Leonard and Raymond's cousin, Cleo, Leonard was living with his father prior to his move to St. Paul. Leonard was first sent from Saskatchewan to his father in Washington state. Bessie and Nelson were not in touch but Bessie was communicating with Nelson's parents, her son's grandparents, through her family that lived in Webb. She had not seen Nelson Skinner since 1919. She was divorced from him in the late spring of 1923. The divorce was granted on the grounds of Skinner's desertion of her. Nelson remarried not too long after they finally divorced but Nelson's new wife was unable and unwilling to take on a preadolescent "son." So, Leonard continued to live with his grandparents in Saskatchewan.

Nelson Skinner's parents suffered both illnesses and financial reversals. These were hard times for little Leonard, who was shuttled around. Although, since 1918, Bessie had sent money to help with Leonard's support, she was notable by her absence; Leonard did not know her well. Now, Leonard was sent to St. Paul to live with his mother. He was twelve years old and described by his cousin, Cleo as a "sad kid when he arrived, with the clothes on his back which were like him, small and ragged."

Leonard, like Bessie, had a good mind, a strong back and an engaging personality. By 1927, Leonard was better off than he ever had been. His mother was living a fairly stable life with bootlegger and union organizer Bob Walsh and working for her neighbor and good friend, Danny Hogan. On Danny's suggestion, the Protestant Bessie enrolled Leonard in an excellent Catholic private school, where he would get more individual attention and, from the nuns, learn some of the manners and polish that he lacked. (Again, for the record, Bessie's Orange Irish brothers were not pleased about this.) Bob Walsh was a good father stand

A FULL CONFESSION

in, liked by Leonard and all Leonard's cousins for his playfulness and warmth. Life was good for him and his mom for a change... for a while. Danny Hogan's spectacular death in December 1928 was to change this.

❋ ❋ ❋

One sloppy morning, in early December, 1928, Danny Hogan who had come home very late, had risen too early. He left his house, went out and stepped on the starter of his green Paige coupe. The resulting explosion, a nitroglycerin charge wired to the starter, blew off Danny's right leg and sent him on a short circuit to answering his greater judges. But Danny did not die immediately, there was time for the entire St. Paul mob to pay their final respects at the hospital where he was taken still alive, and to offer their blood for his in the transfusions that were badly needed. But he did die and was buried with all pomp and ceremony. Three thousand of his intimate friends attended his funeral.

The "good" times were real for Bessie up to this point, but not always very happy. She was destined to live an even wilder life in even less happy times. Shortly after Danny went beyond, Bob Walsh left Bessie, and indeed left the mob life. Perhaps he had brushed too near to real problems too many times and Danny's death was the final straw. He married in 1930, and spent the rest of his life on the correct side of the law, still working for Schmidt's Brewery. Bessie went on to become an associate of Harry Sawyer. Bob Walsh and Bessie remained friends.

❋ ❋ ❋

Danny Hogan was a man who made a large impression on

the people in Minnesota from 1918 to his death ten years later. While assuming that real life and literary parallels can be easily identified is a mug's game, there are still a few coincidental matters between the greatest of all American "making it" stories and Beth Green and her friends' milieu. The ways in which Minnesota influenced Fitzgerald's *The Great Gatsby* (1924) have been widely researched.

There is little doubt that Gatsby's "colleague' Meyer Wolfsheim is based on Arnold Rothstein. There is little doubt that when Fitzgerald talks of Gatsby's "vast pipeline" to the south he is talking about importing booze from Canada. And *St. Olaf* is a very real college in Northfield, Minnesota, whether or not James Gatz attended it. The same golf courses where Fitzgerald caddied, were later favored by the thugs Holden and Keating, visiting St. Paul, under Danny Hogan's protection, and out for an afternoon.

But one connection that has not been made, and might be, is a connection between Dan Cody, Gatsby's Minnesota mentor, and "Dapper Danny" Hogan. What little is told us of Dan Cody's background by Fitzgerald bears a similarity to Hogan's western experiences. Hogan's love for the water, fishing and boating, can run parallel to James Gatz meeting with Cody, a sailing enthusiast. And finally, Hogan was a man who, at least in the case of Bessie Skinner, tried to develop a promising young person.

❋ ❋ ❋

There was considerable speculation among family, friends and newspaper writers, that Danny's fatal push on the starter was planned from far away. While the thread of evidence was not thick, it did lead to New York and favors for friends. Arnold Rothstein, Fitzgerald's Meyer Wolfsheim, was shot down on the streets of New York on November 4, 1928. According to later reports in the St. Paul press, the pistol that killed Rothstein came from Danny Hogan in St. Paul and perhaps the shooter did too. The killer was never identified.

The belief that Danny was done in by the mob in revenge for Rothstein's killing is romantic, and perhaps even literary, but unlikely. The most reasonable theory about who killed Danny Hogan is that it was his protégé Harry Sawyer; *Cui bono*? There is little doubt that Harry Sawyer had the most to gain from Danny's death. Still, there is a streak of romance, and Gatsby-like invention, that makes the Rothstein story a better one.

CHAPTER 8

Harry Sawyer Comes into His Glory: Bessie Skinner/Walsh/Moore/Green and Harry Sawyer, 1928-1933

As already stated, the center for planning crime and taking payoffs in St. Paul was Danny Hogan's Green Lantern saloon. From the time it was first "Dapper Danny's" until the police closed it down in 1933, it was the gathering spot for crooks from all over. There are only limited descriptions of the joint during the time that Danny Hogan owned it. There is no reason to think, however, that its nature changed much between 1924 and 1932.

So, we can take it that the most fabulous, but proto-typical, moment for the place occurred New Year's Eve, 1932. Public Enemy Number One and autobiographer, Alvin Karpis, describes, in great detail, what he saw as the moment of most glory for the *Green Lantern* and for Harry Sawyer, the man who took over Danny's "business interests" in 1928.

On New Year's Eve, 1932, Harry Sawyer gave a party: "The greatest blow out Sawyer ever gave in the place.... There was probably never before as complete a gathering of criminals in one room in the United States as there was in the *Green Lantern* that night. There were escapees from every major U.S. penitentiary."

What Alvin Karpis says is true and among those present at the *Green Lantern* were Tommy Holden and Francis Keating, best known as the "Evergreen" bandits because of their robbery of a train in Evergreen Park, Illinois; they were also famous for their 1930 escape from Leavenworth Federal Penitentiary. Also present was Murder Incorporated hit man Gus Winkler, hired killer Shotgun George Ziegler, Crane-Neck Nugent, Fred Burke, and Johnny Moore. Johnny may have been the brother of Bessie's boy-friend who she was dumping at that time, Ray Moore.

Two of the most successful bank robbers in American history were also there. These were Harvey Bailey who had robbed the National Bank and Trust of Lincoln Nebraska of $2.6 million dollars in 1930 and who also robbed the Denver Mint, and Big Homer Wilson, another successful bank robber who had never been arrested; Tommy Gannon, who like Homer "had never been made" for his many robberies was there. Frank Nash, who was to die in the Kansas City Massacre, helped to round out the group.

Representing the upper levels of the St. Paul and Minneapolis mobs were Tom Filben, Tommy Banks, and Isadore "Kid Cann" Blumenfeld, the boss of bosses in the Mill City. Bessie Skinner/Beth Green knew them all. Young ladies from Aunt Grace's establishment and several other pleasure palaces were also there. Beth Walsh? She well may have worked the party. She was a great hostess.

Bessie, in the first year after Danny's death, was either an employee of Harry Sawyer, or a business associate of his. She was working at the Holly Wood Inn gambling casino in Mendota across the Mississippi from St. Paul. Both Danny and Harry had owned part of the place and Bessie later told the FBI that she acted for Danny's widow, Leila, in continuing to manage the nightclub.

Although the record on her exact status apropos Harry is rather fuzzy, there is little doubt that Bessie continued to do well financially when Harry took over. In 1929 she lived at 565 Portland Avenue South in St. Paul and in 1930 she lived on Grand Avenue, both respectable addresses and Leonard lived with her. Her mother, Minnie, came to visit Bessie and Leonard that year from Webb, Saskatchewan. Minnie and her last son at home, Marvin, were struggling to make ends meet on the farm. Beth financed the trip, and this appears to be the only time that Minnie came to St. Paul. (Bessie did visit Canada infrequently and also saw her mother in northern Minnesota in the 1940s).

Harry Sawyer, although he was Danny Hogan's protégé, as was Bessie, had quite a different personality from Danny's. He seemed to lack all of Danny's "loveable colorful rogue" characteristics. Instead, Harry "Dutch" Sawyer was a thoroughly bad man.

Harry Sawyer climbed a crooked path to get to be chief fixer in St. Paul. As already pointed out, he was born in Lithuania in 1890 to an Orthodox Jewish family named "Sandlovich." His family had settled in Lincoln, Nebraska, which is where Harry grew up. Harry's criminal career was first noted by authorities there in 1915 when he was arrested for robbery. Six years later, after he was again arrested for theft in Lincoln, he jumped bond and sought the protection of Danny Hogan in St. Paul. Hogan put him to work, first as a "tough guy" and then as a fence.

Those who knew him from the early days, when he served as a gofer for Danny Hogan, did not trust him. The betrayals surrounding the murder of Burton Stevens, the postal robberies, the Gleckman liquor affairs all had Sawyer's involvement. Those who knew him later did not trust him either. When he arranged to have his enemies, or his supposed enemies, murdered, his "friends" trusted him even less.

Harry was greedy and Danny's empire was hard to manage. It was not inevitable that Sawyer would take Danny's place after Danny's death, but it did seem likely that Sawyer would profit from Hogan's demise as he profited from Danny's tutelage while Hogan was alive.

It was not until mid-1930 that Harry Sawyer's ambitions began to expand beyond the limits that Danny Hogan had observed. This was when Harry not only provided sanctuary for criminals but let criminals engage in activities within the Twin Cities. The time from December 4, 1928, when God "Paiged" Hogan, until Holden and Keating, the "Evergreen" bandits, went to hide out in St. Paul in February, 1930, was a period of consolidation on Sawyer's part. He tested to see who was loyal and who was not and God help you if you were not. But this was all local stuff. Danny was dead and the Depression was starting and the Feds were turning their attention elsewhere.

Sawyer, like many Twin Cities mobsters had ties along the Great Lakes to the "Purple Gang" in Detroit. When a crook got too hot in Detroit, Harry would help him hide out in St. Paul. A reciprocal arrangement existed. There were certain parallels between the St. Paul and Detroit gangs: Harry Sawyer's crowd in St. Paul and the bosses of the "Purple Gang" were middle European and of Jewish background. Both gangs were well known for sudden violence and harsh enforcement of loyalty. Rumor had it that the "Purple Gang" supplied most of the hit men for the mobs around the country. It has been said that they were known as the "Purple Gang" after a Detroit newspaper stated that they were full of colorful characters, and another journalist commented that the color that should be associated with the gang was "purple, like rotten meat."

In the years immediately after Danny's murder, Sawyer

sought to rival Jack Peifer, the other up and coming St. Paul fixer, and set himself up as a club owner, buying both classy as well as very downscale joints around the Twin Cities. Bessie did not want trouble with Harry Sawyer, nobody did, and she could make money with him. She later told the FBI that the St. Paul gangs had "naturally migrated" to Sawyer, after Hogan's death. She certainly did.

Her concerns at this point were broader than just whether Harry was a good person to attach herself to. She needed to continue providing for Leonard.

Bessie began operating the *Alamo* nightclub in 1929, and worked there during the summer, continuing to be a hostess at the *Holly Wood* in the winter. Although Bessie said that she owned the *Alamo*, it is possible that she only fronted for the "real" owners, Harry Sawyer and Jack Peifer, and Ray Moore may have been her fellow manager while she was there.

The FBI files say that she <u>sold</u> the Alamo to Harry Sawyer <u>and</u> Jack Peifer in 1930. But Bessie said to the Alderson prison authorities that she sold it in 1933. She lived and worked there until 1933. Bessie was busy and continued to hold down several jobs at one time. Among establishments for which Bessie worked during this period were *McCormick's Sandwich Shop*, another front for the *Green Lantern* and owned by Frank McCormick, another hood. In 1931, Bessie worked directly for Harry and was hostess at the *Green Lantern* for a short time. Her status there was unambiguous, she was under Sawyer's direction.

In any event Bessie was at the *Alamo* until 1933. While she was there and at the *Holly Wood* in winter, Leonia Goodman went back and forth with her. Bessie worked with Opal Whyte at the *Holly Wood* as well, and Opal was the person to whom she entrusted the *Alamo* for several months in 1931 when she was "laying low," i.e. living with "Aunt Grace," after her breakup with Ray Moore, the man who succeeded Bob Walsh in her life.

If Bessie Skinner was working for Sawyer after Danny's death, she was also making her own way, having become associated with the hoodlum and card shark Ray Moore, during her time from 1929 to 1930 at the *Alamo* nightclub and casino. She was probably Ray's boss there, but she was also searching for a serious relationship post-Bob Walsh. Ray Moore was a good-looking dealer at the casino who liked to gamble himself, and he offered Bessie some excitement to counter the boredom of her life of domesticity as a single mother.

When Bessie was with Bob Walsh, her son, Leonard, was living with them at home, and she was sending him to a private school. By 1930, Leonard was in public school, enrolled in Johnson High School in St. Paul from which he went on to graduate in 1933. Earlier in 1931, about the time Bessie took up with Ray Moore, she arranged for Leonard to board full time with a series of respectable families.

Leonard had boarded and lived away from Bessie off and on before she took up with Ray, he was staying with her on weekends and living with her for the period in 1931 when Bessie's mother was visiting; and he had "helped her" and lived with her summer months when she was running the *Alamo* club out on White Bear Road.

She was setting aside money, from 1926 onward, in the hope her son would go to college. Leonard, while not outstanding was a competent student and she tried to impress on him that her lack of even a high school education had meant a great difference to her life. But she was also saving for herself. She wanted to have enough money to buy her own place and wanted to own a fancy joint, a resort, on one of Minnesota's many lakes.

In fact, she regretted bitterly the fact that she could not continue her schooling. She blamed her mother. She said that when she was Leonard's age, there were no schools for her to attend on the prairies of Saskatchewan. She attributed the different direction her life had taken from that of her older brother, Pharos, to not finishing school. (Pharos had graduated from high school in North Dakota before Bessie's family left for Canada. He had gone on to be successful, honest, and comfortably ensconced.) But Bessie was not living in a small college town with a good reputation and a steady job like P.B., her brother was. She was working for and with Harry Sawyer.

※ ※ ※

For his first years after Hogan's death, Sawyer consolidated his power. Sawyer got a break in 1930, when he got his own "Frank Sommer." This was Tom Brown who was named Chief in the St. Paul police department in June. (Yes, that Tom Brown.) From this point on, and in parallel to Bessie's increasingly dangerous life, Sawyer, who up until then had offered protection, sanctuary and money laundering to bootleggers and gamblers, and local gangsters, expanded his criminal portfolio. His new investments were the much more nationally famous bank robbers, murderers and kidnappers.

Almost immediately when Brown became Chief, Sawyer began to get inside information from the police. This paid off handsomely, for example when the Barker-Karpis gang, not a local gang, who had paid Sawyer for protection, was informed well in advance that their hideout in West St. Paul was going to be raided. (In fact, according to Paul Maccabee, the police informed the gang about the possibility of a raid while the chief witness to the gang's presence, an occupant of the same house, was still sitting in the station waiting for the police to take some action on his complaint. JDSH p.109)

To look at the St. Paul police department in 1931 is to see that the crooks were in charge of the cops. The corruption ranged from the mayor's office through federal and state courts and prosecutors and down to the cops on the beat. Such corruption was not only known to the people who read books like Dashiell Hammett's *Red Harvest.* Newspapers, magazines, and the movies all pointed out the mob control of certain cities, both in fiction and in life.

Dashiell Hammett would have agreed with Alvin Karpis, one could choose the town that was friendliest to criminals from a lot of contending communities. Karpis named the towns in the center of the country; Kansas City (of course); Miami, Ohio; Fort Scott, Kansas; Cleveland, Ohio. ("The fix was really in in Cleveland" p.99 TAKS [The Alvin Karpis Story]); Hot Springs, Arkansas; ("many crooks chose it for their vacations... like Lucky Luciano" ... ibid); "But," Karpis went on to say, "of all the Midwest cities, the one I knew best was St. Paul, and it was a crooks' haven."(p.100 ibid)

Karpis had considerable information to provide about the two main fixers he dealt with in St. Paul. The two main people ("the most important guys" p. 100 ibid) were Harry Sawyer and Jack Peifer, "and they swung a lot of weight." Karpis knew for sure. And Bessie Walsh/Moore was there. Through Harry Sawyer, Bessie was very closely linked with Alvin Karpis and his associates, Fred Barker, "Doc" Barker, Larry "the Chopper" Devol, Verne Weaver, William Miller, Jess Doyle, Earl Christman.

In 1931, Bessie left Ray Moore because Ray was getting abusive. He also was disturbed by Bessie's success, and she felt that he was stupid. She was also getting rich. In order to hide out from him, she searched out her friend, a well-known Madam in St. Paul, "Aunt Grace." Bessie went to live with "Aunt Grace" Rosenthal for a while; then she brought Leonard home to live with her after Ray disappeared.

CHAPTER 9

Eddie, Bessie, Ma, Doc, and Freddy (and Alvin): Remember the Alamo

The changes that Harry Sawyer was making in the way that criminal activities were carried out in St. Paul were based on two factors: the approaching end of prohibition, and Harry's willingness to work with gangs who cared not at all if they carried out their crimes in the Twin Cities.

As the end of Prohibition became inevitable with Roosevelt's election, the active brewing industry in the Twin Cities continued to operate much as it had earlier. The breweries produced on some shifts legal "near beer" (.2% alcohol content) and the "medicinal" alcohol that had just been extracted from and later could be surreptitiously added to it; and on other shifts, illegally, the real thing.

When it became legal to make "3.2 beer" in 1933--beer that was 3.2% alcohol by volume--these breweries were particularly well positioned to follow the law. They were manufacturing the "near beer" to which the other 3% alcohol could be added legally from their stocks of "medicinal" and "industrial" alcohol. Beer joints sprang up all over the place. The Bremer (*Schmidt's Beer*) and the Hamm (*Hamm's Beer*) families became even richer.

Alvin Karpis said, in this regard in his biography, "Well, Jesus, this was the beginning of the end of the dry era. Prohibition was now staggering on its last legs. Millions of Americans went wild in the rush to buy and drink this new, powerful beer."

There was a down side to this, and not just for William Hamm, Jr. who was rolling in lots of immediate cash when 3.2 beer was allowed on the market in 1933, and who was a target for kidnappers. As Prohibition lay dying, the gunsels, gangsters and mob were turning toward other ways to make profits, Harry Sawyer allowed robbery to move into the St. Paul area, and the local plutocrat, Hamm, was kidnapped by Karpis and his gang.

It was at this point that Bessie's life took a turn that would provide her with increasing wealth and lead her to prison. It may have been difficult for Bessie to avoid the exciting life, and continue to make good money. Be that as it may, from 1931 to 1934 she was situated at the local hub for bank robbery and kidnapping, working with Harry Sawyer and Jack Peifer. Then, in the summer of 1932, she met Eddie Green.

At that point Eugene "Eddie" Greem had risen well above where he had started when he robbed the Crane Ordway Company in Minneapolis of its payroll on May 16, 1922. Eddie was fingered for this job but not arrested until later in that year and he had an opportunity to make headlines in the St. Paul Dispatch before his arrest. Eddie was a common, or garden variety, robber then. He worked for Leon Gleckman and drove taxi, taking fares and delivering booze. On September 15, 1922, he was arrested for conspiring to violate prohibition for making deliveries for Gleckman. He pleaded "not guilty" to that crime but while under arrest was "ratted out" on the *Crane Ordway* robbery, tried and convicted. Very mundane.

Eddie's brothers, as well, lived outside the law. The parole officer who handled Eddie's case in 1922 said about him "whether it will ever be safe to parole him is to my mind very doubtful." The physician who examined upon admittance to the state reformatory said, "This is the type with criminal tendencies, selfish, impulsive, and hard to manage." It is also obvious that Eddie was as unlucky in his early career as he was in his later. In 1922 he was turned over by the gang for the *Crane Ordway* robbery and received a very tough sentence, although he did not have an extensive past record, or too many juvenile problems. But, eight years was a long time to spend in jail, especially when his "family doctor," Dr. Clayton May, had provided an alibi for him.

Whatever, Eddie's faults as a member of society, he was feisty, he did not lack a sense of humor and he was faithful to his family, as they were to him. He spent several different times in solitary confinement when he was first imprisoned, and the infractions for which he was confined indicate a high-spirited young man: He was confined for "fighting in the dining room," and "striking a fellow inmate." More tellingly he was cited for making an "immoral," and probably impossible, invitation to a guard in front of his prison mates. Best of all, he was confined for a "disturbance in the cell house after he came from chapel, imitating the ladies' singing [which] started the whole house [singing]."

In Eddie Green's letters to his family he expressed concern for his mother and brothers and told Margaret Green that he was OK. He could also joke about being in prison. In one letter from Stillwater to his mother, on June 22, 1923, he said: "We only got beans [to eat] three times today, there must be a shortage on the outside, the way they give them to us lately."

When he finally got out of jail in 1930, he had to begin, again, to work his way up. This time he chose a specialization that would give him a niche and also make him useful to Harry Sawyer. It also provided him with plenty of cash. He became a "jug marker," and bank robber.

Bessie Skinner did not know Eddie Green in 1919, when she first arrived nor did she know him more than eight years later when he got out of prison. Around the same time in 1932, that the Barker-Karpis gang was introduced by Harry Sawyer to Eddie Green and another Minnesota freelancer, Tommy Carroll, she also began to manage the *Alamo* club. Bessie soon made the acquaintance of Tommy and several of his girlfriends, most notably Jean Delaney most likely at the *Alamo,* which was co-owned by Harry Sawyer. Starting in late 1932 and lasting through that bloody April in 1934, Bessie Skinner/Walsh/Moore became Beth Green.

There are two different stories that Beth gave to two different sets of authorities about her life as Beth Green. One was the story that she told the Alderson prison authorities. The other is the story that can be pieced together from the FBI files, stories in the Twin Cities press, and some personal remembrances.

To the Alderson authorities she said that during this time "she never had to call the police about the club." (the *Alamo*.) She said that she never had questionable characters patronize the place, and it was not raided for liquor. She did not sell liquor either. (N.b., Bessie's partners in this place were bootleggers and crooks, including Harry Sawyer, so we may suspect that Beth Green is being a bit disingenuous in her story about her abstemious nature and her "dry" place of business.)

Beth stated that the "best people" patronized the *Alamo* and that she did employ her son, Leonard, to help clean after school. Bessie said that she did most of the cooking herself, although she gave some employment to Leonia Goodman and her sister and to Opal Whyte.

Beth claimed, truthfully enough, that the *Alamo* was very successful. She also told why she worked elsewhere after late October: The club itself was not heated, and it was too far from town for a winter crowd. So, every year, in early November, Bessie would close it down and go back to work in St. Paul as the hostess at the *Holly Wood Inn*, where she was paid $25 per week, she said to the prison interviewers. This was the majority of her income, she implied. But she was also willing to work at other jobs to turn a dollar and she talked about the savings account that she started in her son Leonard's name.

Her story about meeting Eddie Green is the only one extant and how true it is, is questionable, if only because she kept a lot of information about her relationship with Eddie to herself.

She said that in August 1932, Eddie Green began to eat regularly at the *Alamo*. Jimmy Green sold beer to the *Alamo* and Eddie's brothers, Jimmy and Frank, would also come there to eat. Eddie first came with them. A short time later he began to come in for dinner by himself and hang around after all the guests had left. He would help Bessie clean up. He was kind to Bessie, and after Ray Moore, she may have felt that she deserved some kindness. He was also kind to Leonard and he soon introduced Bessie to his mother, Margaret. Bessie fell in love with him.

In November 1932, when Bessie closed the *Alamo* for the winter, Eddie asked her to live with him. He gave her some of his back ground and told her that he had been in prison. He told her that he was born in Colorado, but that his mother came from Northfield, Minnesota and that his father had died of pneumonia when Eddie was quite young. He told her that he had stopped school, like Beth, as he called her, in the Eighth Grade to go to work.

He told her that he was divorced as Beth was. The only evidence that exists that Eddie was previously married is in his prison records from the Minnesota State Reformatory in St. Cloud where Eddie had first served a part of his term for robbery in 1922 and 1923. These records state that he was arrested for "wife abandonment" in 1922. He may have been married at 21, and still have been married when he met Beth. If this were the case, it would help to explain some of Eddie's statements on his death bed about a wife who does not seem to be Beth Green. In any event, Bessie was not a Catholic, and she was divorced, so they could not be married in the Church.

Whatever their actual status under canon and State law, Eddie and Beth considered that they were married in the eyes of God. Eddie's family treated her as his wife. She was happy again. Bessie became Beth Green.

Beth told the prison authorities that when she met Eddie "she had not had much dealing with men since her divorce [from Leonard Skinner in 1924]." She may have also told Eddie this lie.

Although the club and casino were closed, there was a heated apartment at the *Alamo*. Eddie and Beth lived there together from November 1932 to June 1933. During that time, Beth made arrangements for her son Leonard who was attending high school in St. Paul, to board with a respectable family, the Harkness family. According to Paul Maccabee's research, this family bought the *Alamo* from her in June 1933. According to what she said to the FBI in her confession, she sold her share in the place to Harry Sawyer and Jack Peifer. She did not tell the FBI authorities or Alderson how she disposed of this "honest" establishment.

While Beth and Eddie were living together, son Leonard believed that Eddie and his mother were married. He also believed that Eddie was an ironworker as Eddie had initially told Beth. Eddie had indeed been employed as such and worked on the First National Bank building and several others in St. Paul. But he was also an associate of Harry Sawyer and Tommy Carroll. Nope, you couldn't trust what either Beth or Eddie said.

Beth was under no obligation to tell the truth to the FBI or to the prison authorities or to her family about Eddie Green. When in doubt, this current narrative uses the FBI account. Beth obviously had few qualms about squealing on all sorts of mobsters, lying to friends, lying to family and especially lying to the authorities but through her many twists and turns she remained faithful to the version of "marriage" that she and Eddie had concocted.

So, the story that Bessie told to the prison authorities, in 1934 made out that she and Eddie were the equivalent of a married, and loving couple. This may be true but the history around their relationship was considerably different than she painted it when she was defending Eddie and family.

What really was going on was that, in early 1932, Harry Sawyer was using Eddie Green as a "jug marker" and as an occasional stick-up man. Beth was also helping out with bank robberies as a "jug marker," a person who scouted the banks and bank employees before a robbery. Beth and Eddie also scouted out roads into and out of the towns where the banks were located. Beth also scouted out and rented "safe" apartments for bank robbers and kidnappers coming into St. Paul and Minneapolis, and helped them with finding clean cars, when the vehicles they were driving became "hot." Beth, long a hostess as Bessie, became a person who provided the greatest gangsters of an era with concierge services.

Eddie was introduced to Harry Sawyer by Eddie's brother Jimmy, who was a gofer for Harry. Because of Eddie's prison record, eight years in Stillwater for the Crane Ordway holdup in 1922, Eddie, although a skilled ironworker, was not very employable. Harry helped him get jobs through Harry's union contacts.

Beth stated, for her prison record, that while she and Eddie were living together, she did not know that he was engaged in any illegal activities until the Dillinger days. When she pointed out the gangster hangouts in Chicago to Melvin Purvis, she was telling a considerably different story. She confirmed the story that Alvin Karpis later told in his autobiography. Her story and Alvin's story showed that her life was a little wilder than she told the prison authorities.

Besides being associated with John Dillinger, the most famous gangster of the thirties, Beth and Eddie were associated with the next most famous gangsters, the Barker-Karpis gang.

There was lots of history (or a three-year version, thereof) behind the Barker-Karpis gang when they celebrated New Year's Eve with Harry Sawyer in 1932. By then the gang had participated, collectively and individually in all sorts of crimes across the middle Midwest. They were not really big in the upper Midwest.

That they were not given much thought by the resurgent FBI in 1932 was not for lack of trying on the part of Alvin Karpis and Freddy Barker. Alvin Karpis himself has said, however, that at this time they were still on the make, and he was impressed by more experienced gangsters, and excited to be working with Harry Sawyer in St. Paul.

The Barker-Karpis gang, like the contemporaneous Dillinger gang was a thing often made up on the spot. Fred and Doc Barker, and Alvin Karpis were its core members but other hoodlums joined on for longer or shorter times. Fred Barker had had a long history of being the principal in crimes of burglary and murder, but he seems to have been a bit of a loner, despite what Alvin Karpis says in his book. When Alvin Karpis, Freddie's friend, was introduced to Ma Barker and Freddie's brother, Doc, there was instant rapport and Karpis says that he was accepted as a "member of the family."

Karpis had worked with many other crooks besides the Barker brothers, and discusses them all in his autobiography. He began his life in crime at about 11 years of age and appears to have been something of a child prodigy in his chosen field. In 1926, when he was 18, he was arrested and jailed for the first time and it was the contacts that he made in prison that were to help him reach the exalted position of "Public Enemy #1" by 1935.

Larry "The Chopper" Devol was his earliest partner. Karpis met Devol in prison in Hutchinson Kansas. Devol moved to Minneapolis in 1930, where Bessie Skinner first met him at the *Alamo*. She was later to help him find a place to live.

Devol, under Harry Sawyer's tutelage had a reunion with Karpis, and together with the Barkers and others, they pulled one of the bloodiest stick-ups in Minneapolis history in December, 1932. They robbed the Third Northwestern National Bank, escaped with $20,000 in cash and another $100,000 in securities. During the robbery, Devol killed two policemen with machine gun fire (thus his nick-name). A Swedish immigrant was shot by Freddy Barker when the poor newly-wed man looked too long at the robber's getaway car that had broken down in Como Park after the robbery. Devol was arrested by Tom Dahill, later to be a reforming Chief of Police in St. Paul. The police, after questioning Devol about the job, let him go for lack of evidence. It is interesting to note that during this investigation Dahill was working closely with Tom Brown.

Corruption in St. Paul, "Dapper Danny" Hogan, "Aunt Grace" and Tom Brown, even various bootleggers and hold up men, were all part of Beth Green's history. But psychotic killers, at least up close, were something new. Beth did not like to deal with these people. She had to deal personally with Larry Devol and Freddie Barker and these two were not the only psychotic killers that Bessie was to meet in the next few years because of her partnership with Harry Sawyer.

In Reno, Nevada, in December 1932, shortly after the Third Northwestern robbery, when Karpis had gone to hide out, Alvin made contact with an ardent, young and married gambler, who was on the lam from prison in Illinois where he was convicted of a very brutal, indeed sadistic, crime. This young man had earlier made contact with Harry Sawyer while hiding out in St. Paul. This kid, Lester Gillis, loved his wife. Tommy Carroll's girlfriend from November 1933 until his death, Jean Delaney, told the authorities how faithful and attentive the baby-faced kid was.

Karpis, upon meeting him, figured that Gillis could be someone useful at some point in the future and took dinner with "Baby Face" Nelson and, his wife, and their two young children. Karpis, however, had no doubts about the sociopath side of Nelson's nature. Nelson did several criminal favors for Karpis that Alvin describes in his book. Alvin reciprocated by "get[ting] him into an outfit [gang] in St. Paul" (p.71 TAKS). Lester was to go back to Minnesota in early 1933 and find further career opportunities working with Tommy Carroll and John Paul Chase, reporting to Harry Sawyer.

Beth implies that this was the time that Eddie Green met Nelson, whom they called "Jimmy." In any event, Eddie Green was associated, as a jug marker, on several jobs with "Baby Face" Nelson in early 1933. It is unlikely that Beth was along on all of these. She went on some and she did travel to Chicago with Eddie during very early 1933, while Eddie was representing Harry Sawyer to the Chicago mob. In Chicago, they lived on 271 South Kedzie, which was also a hideout for the Barker-Karpis gang.

In the early spring of 1933, Eddie and Beth also found time to travel to Kansas City on business. They stayed in Kansas City for about two weeks, but Eddie spent much of the stay on the road, driving many times by several routes about 175 miles back and forth to Fairbury, Nebraska, which was close to Harry Sawyer's old home town, Lincoln. Eddie went to Fairbury to check out the First National Bank.

When he reported what he had found to the Barker-Karpis

gang, they also toured escape routes and set out stocks of gasoline along the routes. On April 4, 1933, the Barker-Karpis gang plus extras, i.e. Fred and Doc Barker, Alvin Karpis, Volney Davis, Jess Doyle, Earl Christman and Eddie Green robbed the Fairbury bank of over $74,000 in cash and bonds.

Fairbury was a sleepy town with one, well stocked, bank. The gang went into town armed to the teeth. This robbery, however, did not go smoothly. A woman observed the gang running into the bank with their guns and shouted "Bank robbers!" She continued to scream until the scene outside the Fairbury bank, began to resemble a scene eighty years earlier, outside the First National Bank of Northfield Minnesota, when an enraged civic population took up weapons and fired back at bank robbers. In the case of Northfield, the robbers were the James and Younger gangs.

ARTIST'S RENDITION OF EDDIE GREEN ABOUT THE TIME OF THE FAIRBURY JOB. (*LIBERTY MAGAZINE*, NOV. 26, 1939)

The gang got the money and bonds, but as they ran out shots

were coming at them from both ends of the street. Alvin Karpis fired a Tommy gun and other robbers sprayed the area with small arms fire. Earl Christman was shot and died somewhat later. Eight townspeople were wounded, two critically, but no townspeople died in the raid. The gang members headed back to Kansas City and hid before going north. The gang members, and Beth and Eddie, soon went back to Minnesota, where Harry Sawyer helped them dispose of the bonds.

Early in May, 1933, and for a brief period of time thereafter, Beth and Eddie lived with Eddie's mother. They also spent time at the lakeside house of Danny Hogan's widow, Leila Hogan, resting, fishing and hiding out during the summer of 1933. Beth told the prison authorities that she and Eddie lived at the Alamo during this time. If so, they were very busy moving around.

There may have been a reason, "jug marking," that Beth and Eddie stayed with Leila part of the summer. Tommy Carroll, Homer Van Meter, John Paul Chase and Baby Face Nelson all stayed in the same area in early fall, when they robbed the First National bank of Brainerd, Minnesota in October, 1933. All were Eddie Green's associates, and Beth and Tommy's girlfriend, Jean Delaney were to room together shortly thereafter.

Beth was not only friendly with the widows of capos and the mistresses of hoodlums. She was well got up with the rising lights in the inner mob in Minneapolis. A friend of Beth Green's during her days with Eddie was Florence Josemich Taran, the wife of Sam "the Tailor" Taran.

Taran had started out as a boxer, but by the mid-twenties he was also a bootlegger. In 1925, Taran's distillery was raided as part of the crackdown that surrounded the Gleeman-Gleckman case. For some reason, no one could be found to testify against Taran in that first round and the case was dismissed. Later he was an associate of Harry Sawyer, and according to Beth Green's FBI statements, Taran actually handled the hot money from the

Fairbury, Nebraska, bank job carried out by the Barker-Karpis gang in April 1933. In late 1933, Taran was put away for extortion in the prison in Stillwater, Minnesota. At this time, he was moving into control of aspects of the mob, which control he would later exercise.

While Sam was away, according to Beth, Florence "dated" Eddie Green's brother, Jimmy. At this point, Beth and Florence both partied with Francis Keating, Tommy Holden, Frank Nash ("the Gentleman Bandit"), and Harvey Bailey.

The male contingent of this group of friends accounted collectively for million-dollar bank, train and mint robberies, and several killings. (Harvey Bailey was the dean of bank robbers in the United States, at that point, and was a regular at the Green Lantern where he would offer master seminars in bank robbing techniques with occasional field trips and demonstrations. Holden and Keating held adjunct professorships starting in 1930 and included bright young students into their classes, for example when they took along the young "Machine Gun Kelly" to rob a bank at Wilmar, Minnesota in July 1930. Nash was unfortunately gunned down by accident by his colleagues when they were trying to rescue him: the "Kansas City Massacre.")

Sam Taran was to resurface as a member of the Twin Cities underworld and hang around for a long time. In 1952, he was one of the bosses named in *USA Confidential.* In 1989, he was living as a 93-year-old man in Florida. When Paul Maccabee got in touch with Florence, seeking an interview. Sam was not available to talk.

Beth was under no personal or moral obligation to tell these things to the prison authorities at Alderson once she was there. She was under extreme pressure but, had no absolute obligation to tell the FBI the truth. So, what were Beth and Eddie Green really doing from November 1932 to January 1934?

We don't know. It is a reasonable surmise that they were helping the Barker-Karpis gang, and the Chase, Nelson, Carroll gang rob banks and shoot law officers and inconvenient citizens. The direct evidence of this, on the part of Beth, is slim, although there is plenty that implicates Eddie. Many of her notes and pictures and the background of her life were burned by her in a barrel in Garrison Minnesota in 1973. But the indirect evidence, in part in the FBI files, is overwhelming.

The Barker-Karpis gang, of course was often engaged in activities that Beth did not participate in and only knew about because she was just a "fly on the wall." She sat and listened to Harry Sawyer, and to the gang members bragging and talking to their girlfriends. She also shared everything with Eddie, and he told her what other hoodlums were saying and doing.

It is also a reasonable surmise that she and Eddie did not participate in the two crimes for which the Barker-Karpis gang gained its most lasting notoriety. From all indications, and from their ages, backgrounds, feelings and statements there were levels to which Beth certainly, and Eddie probably, would not sink.

During the period of time from April 1933 to February 1934, the Barker-Karpis gang pulled its two most profitable jobs. These were not robberies. They were kidnappings. The first kidnapping was carried out by the gang in early May 1933, was the kidnapping of William Hamm, Jr., "39-year-old multimillionaire St. Paul brewer" (St. Paul Dispatch June 17, 1933). This job was orchestrated by Harry Sawyer and Jack Peifer; and the gang had rehearsed it in April.

The second kidnapping, in January 1934, was of Edward Bremer, banker and son of the owner of the *Schmidt* brewing company; Alvin Karpis says that this job was also planned by

Jack Peifer. However, Harry Sawyer, in addition to Jack Peifer, was later arrested for planning the Bremer kidnapping.

Kidnapping was not new to St. Paul but usually it was an intramural activity for the gangsters. Leon Gleckman was kidnapped in 1931. But apparently to Beth and Eddie kidnapping had none of the "romantic" or "adventurous" aura of bank robbery. It was, as Leon Gleckman had said after his daughter Florence was kidnapped and ransomed in 1932, "the lousiest crime in the world."

In 1934, the recent kidnapping of the Lindbergh baby outraged the American people. Beth still talked about this crime to her family late in her life as if it were something very beyond the pale.

The American public, thanks to the media, was outraged and titillated at the same time. The federal government was moved to make kidnapping a federal crime and the nation mourned innocent victims. The country agreed with Leon Gleckman's dictum. It was a lousy crime.

In this context, when Harry Sawyer's murderous, rapacious and disloyal nature came through in the Hamm kidnapping, this nature may have finally been too much for Beth to stomach. Beth and Eddie were well known about the Twin Cities, and had close family ties there. They were not prone to violence. Even more telling, Beth had ties to people who worked with the Bremer family.

The FBI was told that "Beth Green was on the outs with Harry Sawyer" when they talked to the Madame, "Aunt Grace," in April 1934. She implied it may well have been the kidnappings that caused the rift between the patron and his helper. Both

A FULL CONFESSION

the Hamm and the Bremer kidnappings represented forays into areas that were off-limits geographically and socially under the old "O'Connor layover system" rules, the rules that Danny Hogan had observed.

There is another indication of how much Beth wished to distance herself and Eddie from these crimes. In her various confessions, testimonies, and biographical statements she made sure to say that she and Eddie, the Greens, were not around town for the Bremer kidnapping. They were also working on other jobs while the Hamm kidnapping was planned.

There are later indications that Beth was grateful for these "absences." She told the FBI that in January 1934, Eddie was away again casing banks in Kansas for Harry Sawyer. She assured them that Eddie could not have been in on either crime.

Although Eddie and Tommy Carroll had left Beth and Jean to keep each other's company, in late January, Beth told the FBI that she got lonely. She went to Topeka, Kansas, to join Eddie and they lived for two weeks there in the *Senate Apartments*. They used the alias of Mr. and Mrs. J.S. Makley. Eddie and Beth were gone. How could they have been involved with the kidnapping?

The fact that she was not in St. Paul did not stop Beth from gaining considerable knowledge of the kidnappings, however. When she came back, she listened to what her friends, and Eddie's friends, were saying and she later gave this information to the FBI.

PART III

Here We Have the Wild Beth Green

ILLUSION: ON RONDO STREET

The new Essex Terraplane slowed to a stop near a wood frame house on Rondo Street in St. Paul Minnesota's Negro district. It was 5:30 in the afternoon, April 3rd, 1934. There were two people in the Essex, and they almost looked like they belonged in such a classy car.

The woman in the car had a gray shearling coat, and her hennaed hair was tastefully done. You could tell that in summer she would be stunning, an auburn like Katherine Hepburn. She had a strong face, a wide smile and, it appeared, a strong personality; she was willing to argue even with her lover, and she turned toward him, the driver, her lover, and argued.

The man in the car looked like a stevedore, but one who had found money. He was ropy, of medium height and wore his clothes very well. He had a slightly lop-sided smile that charmed with a charm that you did not quite trust. As was the woman, he was also well dressed.

When they stopped, they left the motor running. God knows what they talked about as they sat in the car, but the woman, who cared about the man, knew that he was going to pick up "evidence" from the house. She knew that if the "evidence" was anything heavy, his old rupture, diagnosed during his time in Stillwater Prison, might come back. Probably, she was telling him that **she** should walk up and get the bag containing the gang's belongings from the women in the house.

In the event, he demurred. He got out of the car, turned and leaned back in through the door, and said something else to her. Then he shut the car door, looked around, carefully scouting the familiar territory, and walked across the street and two steps up to the kitchen door.

Eddie knocked at the door and a handsome middle-aged African American woman came right away in response to his knock; she already had the duffel bag in her hands. Like Eddie, she was looking around, more nervous than he was. She did not respond as he started to talk and they had no conversation. She practically threw the bag at him.

She pushed the door shut quickly, almost slammed it, closing her visitor out. Then she leaned her forehead against an inside window panel for a second.

"Well?"

The question came from the man who was standing out of sight in the kitchen, Agent Gross.

"That's him." She said.

Eddie Green hefted the bag, and quickly began to walk back across the street to the car. As he did, a muffled shout came from the house. The words shouted, which neither Green, nor the woman in the car heard, were, "Let him have it, boys!"

Gross, fired his rifle through the living room window, and other agents joined in the shooting from another window in a small pantry off the kitchen.

Eddie Green, struck in the shoulder and back of his skull, fell on the grass between the sidewalk and the pavement.

Oddly enough, the woman said later that she had not heard the shots nor did she hear the glass breaking on the window of the house. Her concern when she saw Green crumpling up was that his inguinal hernia had not been able to take the weight of the duffel bag that he was carrying, and that he had collapsed because of the pain. Her immediate reaction to Eddie's distress was to get out of the car and run to help him.

It was only a few steps. Two things happened as she knelt down next to Eddie. First, she saw the blood seeping from the left front side of his forehead where a bullet had exited. She did not know what had happened but she unwound the white silk scarf from her neck and began to bandage his wound with it. At the same time, another FBI agent, armed with a Tommy gun, came from behind 778 Rondo, and fired a burst into a rear tire of the Terraplane, making it undriveable.

Beth Green certainly heard this noise, and she heard the Federal officers demand that she stand up and get away from Eddie. She heard several cars drive up, and she saw the Saint Paul police get out of one. Although she must have been confused, she may have recognized one of the local cops who came up to grab her arm as a long-time frequenter of the *Green Lantern* saloon.

The cops took her across the street. She was pushed into a police car by an FBI agent. In all of this, it is unlikely that she heard the wounded Eddie say, as he was placed in a police ambulance, "Honey, back the car up to the door!"

The duffel bag which Eddie and Beth had tried to retrieve contained only what the FBI allowed: a man's and a woman's dirty clothes and underclothes, an overcoat, a clip for an automatic pistol and a loose supply of ammunition, the stock of a machine gun, and miscellaneous small silver and silver dollars totaling about $30.00.

CHAPTER 10

Bessie Skinner/Beth Green: A Wild Time

Let us dispense with the tabloid stuff here, in this section: Bessie Hester Hinds, Bessie Skinner, Beth Green was no better than she should have been. But for a time from about 1924 to 1934, she lived in a really exciting atmosphere; a time that novels and movies and magazine articles have portrayed and still portray.

When the FBI arrested Beth Green on Rondo Street in 1934, she had been living outside the law for at least ten years. She was, by her own admission, well acquainted with many members of the St. Paul and Minneapolis mobs. In fact, from 1924 to 1928, she was a student, and then colleague of Danny Hogan, the person who consolidated St. Paul's corrupt and effective criminal protection system, and one of its main characters.

It could be assumed from a look at Bessie's associates and the places that she worked from 1924 to 1934 that she lived a wild life, there in St. Paul, and she may have. She did not have an arrest record, however, and many of her friends who survived the gangster era remained her friends until the end of her life. Despite the fact that Hoover mentioned her by name, she was not really in the public eye, ever. She was not like Danny Hogan who seemed to enjoy his racy reputation. Beth did not want any reputation, except, perhaps, a solid one. Even under arrest, with the press dogging her, she kept out of the way of publicity. She was circumspect. She had a family, friends, and partnerships with gangsters, and a good time sometimes.

She seems to have learned her circumspection early. Since she was 15 years old, she had defied convention <u>and</u> kept her head low. Photos taken of her from age 15 through to her old age always show the front she put up; whatever her profession and associates, she tried to look respectable, and succeeded.

She went to prison in 1934 and came out in 1935 to live a more or less normal existence to an old age where tragedy or perhaps just bad luck marked her end. In 1934, however, she was involved in a public and dramatic situation.. It is only due to this brief time that there is a public record of Bessie's life in some detail.

This scene only starts in late 1933 or early 1934, the first months of 1934, before John Dillinger came to St Paul, and then left in a most spectacular manner. Before Beth Green was arrested by the FBI for harboring Dillinger, and Eddie was ambushed, Beth was "on the outs" with Harry Sawyer, although Eddie was working for this boss. The reason for the split between Beth and Harry seems to have been Harry's increasingly risky undertakings.

Sawyer was abandoning the patterns that kept St. Paul bosses safe; he was willing to let the new, even more violent gangsters, rob and murder in town. While Beth was closely connected to gangsters who were making headlines when she was with Danny, and these gangsters killed people, the rule was that they kept the violence away from St. Paul and Minneapolis. She knew the gangsters but lived in a city that was protected by a strange sort of NIMBY principle.

Beth, from 1924 to 1934, was protected first by Danny Hogan's rules, and then Harry Sawyer's need to consolidate his powers. After that she became associated with the most dangerous and violent bank robbers and kidnappers, and their molls, while they were robbing and killing within city limits. Even during that time, she managed to avoid police and press scrutiny; from 1924 to 1934, she was known in the demimonde but not in public. When Beth associated with Harry Sawyer from 1932 to early 1934, Harry wasn't playing by the same rules.

Beth and Eddie Green's connection to John Dillinger brought her only bad things, negative attention and Eddie Green's death. During the early thirties she had known and was known by Fred and Doc Barker, Alvin Karpis, and other denizens of the Most Wanted list. The Green couple were active in bank robbery and harboring criminals. But they were caught, and Eddie Green shot, in the FBI ambush intended to kill their most infamous recent associate, John Dillinger. Dillinger came to St. Paul along with "Baby Face Nelson," Jack "Red" Hamilton and other crooks in early March 1934, and Beth and Eddie helped them find a place to stay. They also helped them rob banks.

Before that, during part of January and February 1934, while Eddie was out on the road, she had shared an apartment with Jean Delaney, the girlfriend of Tommy Carroll. Tommy, a relatively successful bank robber, was an associate of "Baby Face" Nelson," as well as of Eddie Green.

Tommy and Eddie, according to Beth, "thought it best for the two girls to live together while they [the boys] were away from home so much." [Alderson case history.] Tommy and Eddie were away so much at that time because they were robbing out-of-state banks. In this they were still following the Danny Hogan rules and keeping well away from the Twin Cities.

Before Dillinger, and before Tommy Carroll and "Baby Face" Nelson, Beth and Eddie were associated with the Barker-Karpis gang. For many reasons, however, the law seems to have paid little attention to Beth. The primary reason was that the wonderful system to keep gangsters safe in St. Paul, the "O'Connor layover system," still more or less worked. Because she was a close associate of the main operators of the "O'Connor" system, she was untouchable, at least until Harry Sawyer's greed broke the system.

The system's major goal was to keep malefactors safe in St. Paul. This helped Beth when she was engaged in illegal activities. Beth also avoided scrutiny however because she simply did not look or act as a typical gun moll might. She looked like what she knew that she was, a mature businesswoman. She had a wide circle of friends, of all colors and religions and types. She had many acquaintances. Some were whores and fixers, it is true, but some were businessmen and politicians, and some were porters and cooks.

While she was circumspect regarding her illegal activities, she talked to her friends and acquaintances about her "personal," i.e. non-criminal, concerns. Many of her acquaintances knew her to be an active mother, and that she had a son who was enrolled in a good local school. During the time she worked with Danny Hogan and Harry Sawyer, she kept contact with her family. Some family lived in Canada and some close by, and she was a regular visitor at the homes of her nearest two brothers.

She was circumspect from her earliest to her latest years. While she had a raucous sense of humor, she never had any desire to be notorious and when notoriety was thrust upon her, because of Eddie Green's association with the Dillinger gang, she did her best to avoid it. Her period of unavoidable notoriety started exactly one month before Eddie Green was ambushed on April 4, 1934. It lasted only until the end of May 1934. Even when she was making headlines as "the red-headed woman," she managed to keep close members of her family confused about her illegal life.

The public loved a good story in the papers, especially a good story involving criminals and their molls, a story of sex, thievery and violence. Beth's story had all those elements. If Beth had taken advantage of available publicity immediately after she was arrested, she could have claimed a minor place in American criminal history. After all, it is clear from both FBI files and from stories published in the local papers- the *St. Paul Dispatch*, the *Pioneer Press*, the *Minneapolis Star* and the *Daily News,* and the much more comprehensive FBI files that she was instrumental in ensuring the demise of America's favorite bank robber, John Dillinger, and the capture or death of more than 20 hoodlums.

Beth chose to keep away from the public and press. She chose, instead, to hide this part of her life to the extent that she could and for as long as she could. She chose to lie to the press, authorities and her family, and to pull her hat down over her eyes when she entered the courtroom to testify. Through her insistence, the FBI covered up her role in Dillinger's story. For their own reasons, and hers, they also covered up her role with the Barker-Karpis gang and her close association with the mob chieftains that ran St. Paul. The cover up lasted beyond her death in 1983.

CHAPTER 11

March 3-March 30, 1934: John Dillinger Comes to St. Paul

In late winter, 1934, John Dillinger was approaching his apotheosis into an American folk hero. His infamy and fame were pushed to their height by media accounts of Dillinger's escape on March 3 from a Crown Point, Indiana, jail using, according to newspaper stories (almost certainly provided to the press by Dillinger himself), a pistol that Johnny claimed to have whittled out of a washboard and coated with boot blacking. Probably the real story is that Dillinger escaped the heavily guarded jail as result of payoffs totaling $15,000 from his associates to local authorities.)

Nonetheless there was a real wooden pistol although this was a wooden pistol carved by a German woodworker in Chicago ,and given at some time to Johnny by his attorney. A few days after his escape, Dillinger carried the wooden gun to St. Paul as a souvenir. Johnny showed it to Beth Green in St. Paul less than a month after he made it and long before it was in J. Edgar Hoover's hands. Thirty years later, it was displayed at FBI headquarters in Washington.

During his breakout, Dillinger invited fellow gangster, the African-American Herbert Youngblood, to escape with him.

Youngblood took him up on the offer. According to the accounts in the press, they stole a car parked in the police garage near the jail. But it was not just any car; it was an unmarked Ford V-8 sedan, with keys in the ignition, which were given to the lady Sheriff, Lillian Holley, by local supporters. Holley had received Dillinger in Crown Point after he was arrested in Tucson, Arizona, and he was flown back for trial from there. Sheriff Holley and the man who was to prosecute Dillinger in Indiana could not resist posing for pictures with their prize capture.

Dillinger and Youngblood drove the car to Chicago, where Dillinger dropped off Youngblood. Up to this point, the FBI lacked jurisdiction to pursue him: Dillinger had committed no Federal offenses, and the FBI could only act as a clearing-house for information from various States' law enforcement agencies.

The FBI had, however, accumulated considerable information on Dillinger. When Dillinger and members of his gang were arrested in Tucson, J. Edgar Hoover had forwarded information that the gangsters were wanted by local authorities throughout Indiana and Illinois. This was all he could do, there was no Federal warrant out for Dillinger's arrest.

So, it is not surprising that, when Hoover was told of Dillinger's escape from the Crown Point jail early in the morning on March 3, the Director believed that the FBI's involvement would have to be limited. Dillinger seemed not to have even committed a federal crime in escaping from this lockup.

Dillinger, however, by driving the lady sheriff's stolen car across state lines, from Indiana to Illinois, had given Hoover an opening; Johnny had violated the *National Motor Vehicle Theft Act,* and thus he became a criminal under a Federal law. Hoover was aware of this at first, and he was unable to take full advantage of this opportunity for three days. After three days, however, the car was located in Illinois, and the federal authorities could presume that Dillinger brought it there from Indiana. A

Federal complaint was sworn out and a Federal grand jury indicted Dillinger for taking a stolen auto across state lines.

Even at this point, federal law had limited authority to pursue Dillinger, and state and local cooperation was essential. One may disregard the fact that Dillinger and his gang had robbed eight banks, raided two police stations for machine guns, bulletproof vests and ammunition, and shot several bank guards, policemen, and ordinary citizens since May 10, 1933. One may ignore the fact that he was sought in eight different states for robbery and murder. This was nothing except information to the FBI. Inter-state auto theft was Johnny's mistake, and now the FBI was to get on his case, with all the magnificent force of the Federal government.

To be fair to Hoover, from a vantage point of history, the Director was looking for an opportunity to get after Dillinger, and did that as quickly as he felt that it was legally possible. He wanted to use any Federal statutes available and had also used the transport of stolen cars act to pursue and capture Dillinger gang member Harry Pierpont, who was on trial for his life in Ohio. Where more serious federal crimes were violated, for example kidnapping (and two recent cases in St. Paul had received national attention), the FBI was quick to investigate.

At the request of local authorities and congressmen, starting in October 1933, the FBI had kept copious files on Dillinger along with ten other gangsters. (Dillinger had gained this recognition following a breakout from Indiana State Prison in Lima.)

The FBI, at this point, did not have an unsullied record. It had not caught Capone, it frequently found that people it arrested were acquitted, and Hoover was viewed with suspicion by many in Roosevelt's administration. Perhaps for this reason, Hoover had publicly expressed his eagerness to kill or capture midwestern desperados. His lists of the most wanted included Dillinger, the Barker-Karpis gang, and those, as yet unidentified, gangsters who had killed Verne Miller, as well as those that killed the law enforcement officers in the "Kansas City Massacre" on June 17, 1933. Hoover also had decent sources in the underworld and, according to Alvin Karpis, many of these sources were willing to rat on Dillinger and turn him in, not only for the rewards offered, but because wherever he went the heat was turned up on local hoods.

Not until April 1934, however, when Beth Green confessed, did Hoover and the FBI have detailed intelligence on Dillinger's goings and comings. They would have had a hard time finding such copious and up-to-date information elsewhere. The FBI also got a great deal of information from Beth about the Barker-Karpis gang. From her they learned which gangsters associated with what gangs were earlier involved in the "Kansas City massacre."

In just one conversation, when Beth talked to Melvin Purvis in Chicago in the spring of 1934, the FBI was able to learn from what car dealers, safe houses and apartments and contacts in Chicago would be sought out by gangsters on the lam. She described steps that Dillinger might have taken after he arrived in Chicago on March 3, 1934. There, according to Beth, if he contacted either Jack Svoboda Liberty, or Bill Davis of the "Terrible" Touhy gang, John would have found a place to bed down.

Hoover's opinions of female criminals have been well documented. In the case of Beth Green, "Bessie Skinner" as Hoover called her, he was almost polite in his expressed opinions. Perhaps this was because of the depth and breadth of information that Beth Green provided, but in any event, Hoover treated her relatively gently in his first stories on the era, published over the next several years. To Hoover, "Bessie Skinner" was a cut above the ordinary gun moll.

Immediately after his escape from Crown Point, John found a place to hide. Calling from his hideout on March 3, Dillinger talked to the young woman, his lover since November 1933, who was the most recent in a series of girlfriends. This was Evelyn "Billie" Frechette. She was staying at her sister's Halstead Street apartment in Chicago.

On March 4, Johnny and Billie saw each other for the first time in several weeks and when they met, the meeting was a reconciliation of sorts. On the previous Christmas day, Dillinger had told Billie to go home to Wisconsin, to the Neopit Menominee Indian Reservation. According to her story he was concerned for the two of them. He thought he was too hot to have her near. She took this advice and went back to Wisconsin for a while, but she missed him a lot. She soon went back to Chicago, where she waited for news of what he was going to do.

Her impatience to effect reconciliation showed, however. Despite Johnny's warnings to stay away from him, Billie traveled to Tucson with him in late January, where she posed as Dillinger's wife. There she was arrested along with Johnny. Perhaps Dillinger had kept her devotion in mind, for he later reciprocated, and showed up when she was a prisoner on trial in St. Paul.

Billie went back to Chicago from Tucson. She and Johnny kept in touch through coded letters. On March 4, upon hearing of Dillinger's escape from Crown Point, Billie again made herself available in Chicago. He picked her up at her apartment on Addison Street and the two did as many crooks had done before, they headed for St. Paul, Minnesota. The town was not as warm as Tucson, but it was safer.

(While the relationship between Dillinger and Frechette has been belabored and romanticized in books and magazines of the period, Beth Green was not terribly impressed with either Billie or Johnny, or with the two together. She described Billie, as small, dark, and dumb, with a bad complexion. Billie had indeed had a difficult upbringing and although devoted to Dillinger, she was married at this point to a felon serving time in a Leavenworth. Some other man had abandoned her, pregnant and with syphilis when she was sixteen. Her baby had died of a syphilitic infection shortly after birth. Beth's descriptions of Dillinger were less personal, she said that she told Eddie Green not to get involved with him. But it is obvious from her comments in the FBI files that she hated Dillinger and held him responsible, in large part, for Eddie's death.)

The first thing that Dillinger needed after his escape from the Crown Point jail was money. He also needed a new gang if he was to get the money utilizing his previously honed occupational skill of bank robbing. Through aid from the Chicago mob, Dillinger got in touch with two gangsters who were hiding out not far from Chicago, in Wisconsin. These were John "Red" Hamilton, and Lester "Baby Face Nelson. Dillinger knew Hamilton well, having been associated with him in two bank robberies the previous fall. He did not know Nelson as well but knew that he had a reputation as a killer who would dare practically anything. Dillinger, Nelson and Hamilton formed the core of a new gang.

These three agreed that Dillinger should go to St. Paul before they began to pull stick ups to get the needed front money. All needed to keep at least one step ahead of the cops. Chicago was much too hot for them; the most effective of the FBI gangster hunters, Melvin Purvis, was based there. J. Edgar Hoover was setting up the "Jodil" (John Dillinger) task force in Chicago under agent H.H. Clegg. The robbers did not need Clegg or Purvis around, and they did need safe money, safe houses and safe cars.

On March 6, the FBI received a tip that Dillinger was in Chicago. He had gone to Minnesota two days earlier. After informants told the FBI that Dillinger was gone, and could not say where, Hoover took Purvis to task for not having better underworld information. A look at the timing, however, would indicate that Johnny was moving too fast for this to be a justified criticism.

As he moved toward St. Paul, Dillinger touched down in places that Beth and Eddie Green knew well. For example, Dillinger's first stop outside of Chicago was with Louie Cernocky at his restaurant, *Louie's Place,* in Fox River Grove, 45 miles north of the city. This may have been where he met with Hamilton and Nelson.

The joint had the elaborate real name of *Louie's Crystal Ballroom*, and the FBI was to search for Dillinger there in April after his next great escape. Hamilton had spent many evenings there. Beth Green gave an acerbic description of the owner, underworld character, Cernocky in her Alderson confessions. She said that Louie weighed 300 pounds and went wheezing from table to table. His wife, who "weighed only 200" did all the work. Louis, a fixer for the Chicago mob, had earlier helped out the Barker-Karpis gang. That was probably when Beth Green had met him. Dillinger also knew him from six months before, after Johnny's breakout from the Lima, Ohio jail.

Louie ran the "underworld railway" which ensured the delivery of crooks among cities in the Midwest. Chicago, or perhaps Cicero, Illinois, was the heart of gangster-land in the Midwest. But there was a real flow of criminal information and gangsters along the Milwaukee Railroad's "400" line going north to the Twin Cities. Chicago was linked solidly to St. Paul.

Although Johnny may have visited St. Paul earlier, it is likely that Dillinger had first become well acquainted with the lax law enforcement standards in the Twin Cities from his prison friend, Frank Dennis Carpenter. Carpenter, under Harry Sawyer's tutelage, had robbed the State Bank of Byron, Minnesota in March 1933. Carpenter and Dillinger looked much alike and early reports on the Byron robbery put it down to Johnny.

Homer Van Meter, Dillinger's old prison companion from the

Michigan City and the Pendleton, Indiana prisons, was robbing banks in the upper Midwest since the fall of 1933 and was hiding out in St. Paul. The Barker-Karpis gang after making themselves very rich in the Twin Cities through kidnappings and hold-ups had just left. "Baby Face" Nelson's bank robbing confederate, Tommy Carroll, was headquartered in Minneapolis. 'Baby Face" Nelson went there again; he had already worked in Minnesota with Tommy Carroll.

Lester Gillis, whom the press dubbed "Baby Face Nelson," was very sensitive about his short stature and teenage appearance; this touchiness showed itself most fully in his willingness to shoot people that he didn't like. He preferred "Big George Nelson" as his alias. Nelson had earlier been associated with the Barker-Karpis gang but even "Creepy" Karpis worried about Nelson/Gillis's sanity.

Nelson arrived in St. Paul before Dillinger and the rest on March 4, with a companion, John Paul Chase. Once there he contacted Van Meter telling Homer that he was joining the new gang. First, to prove his bona fides, "Baby Face Nelson" killed someone. This was Theodore Kidder, a house painter. Kidder's offense was that he cut off Nelson and Chase's car in downtown Minneapolis traffic. Nelson followed Kidder to his suburban home and expressed road rage by shooting him to death on the front step as Kidder's wife watched.

Dillinger arrived the next day, in a less spectacular manner. He and Billie just drove into town. Shortly after arrival, on March 5, they rented an apartment at the *Santa Monica* in Minneapolis under the name of Mr. and Mrs. Olson. This apartment was just around the corner from that of Beth and Eddie Green. A year earlier, Beth had looked over this building and told Harry Sawyer that it could be a good hideout. The building was subsequently used by members of the Barker-Karpis gang.

Immediately after arriving in town, John checked in with

Harry Sawyer. Sawyer was not only an underworld real estate magnate; he was a mob boss and the successor to "Dapper Danny" Hogan as chief fixer in the city. In this role, Harry was now the chief connection between the St. Paul underworld and the St. Paul police. If Dillinger wanted to avoid police scrutiny, he would have to pay off Harry Sawyer.

In March 1934, Sawyer was operating out of *McCormick's Town Talk Sandwich Shop* on Wabasha Street in St. Paul. Sawyer's usual principal place of business, the *Green Lantern* saloon, two doors down from *McCormick's*, was closed down by police after the kidnapping of Edward Bremer, a scion of St. Paul society.

Harry Sawyer had recently been under intense FBI and local police scrutiny. They suspected that Sawyer was instrumental in planning Bremer's kidnapping, as was true. While Bremer was back home safe at this point, Harry was in trouble with the St. Paul power structure as well as with the FBI. It has been speculated that Bremer, prominent banker and most prominent member of the family that owned *Schmidt Brewing*, or his dad, Adolph Bremer, knew about Harry's involvement with the kidnapping and had the *Green Lantern* closed down. They could do this because *Schmidt* owned it in part, and the Bremer family was fed up with Sawyer.

Albert "Pat" Reilly was Harry Sawyer's front man at McCormick's as he was earlier at the *Green Lantern*. Reilly was an ex-mascot of a professional baseball team in St. Paul and connected by marriage and inclination to the mob.

Harry Sawyer, when he met John Dillinger just after Dillinger arrived in March called a brief meeting where he put Dillinger in touch with Harry's favorite "jug marker" Eddie Green. Sawyer was a patron of Eddie Green for two years at that point. Sawyer, also the patron of Beth Green. Beth, Eddie's common law wife, was valuable in keeping Danny Hogan's team together after 1928, and Beth passed into the hands of Harry. Among other activities since then, Beth was a hostess at a club Harry owned, and part owner of a mob financed joint that was under Harry's protection.

Eddie Green and Beth were living well, working together for Harry Sawyer. But they, like Dillinger, were in constant need of money to support their life style. In early 1934 something went wrong with Beth's relationship with Harry and, according to FBI files by March 1934 Beth and Harry were "on the outs."

Dillinger already had an experienced "jug marker" joining the gang that he was forming. This was Homer Van Meter. In that role, Van Meter had cased banks ("jugs") before robberies and mapped routes into and out of town. And Homer Van Meter knew Green, who had served the same function admirably when Eddie worked with the Barker-Karpis gang and other marauders.

Eddie seems to have been brought on board by Dillinger as a favor to Sawyer. Sawyer liked to have local talent on out-of-town teams that he was managing. Eddie was valuable as a person who knew the St. Paul underworld. Eddie also had done considerable research and had hard information about the ways in and out of towns where there were banks with potential. (Not all banks had a great deal of money on deposit during this time of the Depression.) Last, but not least, Eddie had shown that he had general utility as a stick-up man, when he had worked with the Barker-Karpis gang.

In Beth Green's confession to the FBI, she first stated that it was Van Meter who introduced Green to Dillinger; she said that Eddie had not known Johnny prior to his escape from Crown Point. She implied that Eddie had not been involved with anything illegal prior to Dillinger's arrival. This was deliberately misleading, but it is possible that Beth did not know all of what Dillinger and Eddie did together during the days before March 1934. In any event, Eddie had not only scouted banks, but robbed them with the Barker-Karpis gang. Beth certainly knew this.

Eddie Green was working freelance for two rival crime chiefs in St. Paul, that is for both Harry Sawyer and Jack Peifer. He started working for them before he met Beth and may not have told her everything he knew.

He told her plenty, however, and one thing he said was that he did not like to get involved in violence. He never killed anyone, and as far as can be ascertained, only shot at someone once. This is not to say he was an innocent. From age 16 to age 34, he had spent as much time in prison as out. Eddie was released from Minnesota's Stillwater prison in 1930. For two years after that, he was engaged, mostly by Harry Sawyer, in a series of largely non-violent, and usually profitable, roles.

One of Eddie's jobs for Harry Sawyer may have led Eddie to an earlier association with Dillinger. Despite what Beth told the FBI that she believed, Dillinger may have first met Eddie Green about September 15, 1933. Eddie was in Chicago then doing business for Harry Sawyer with the Barker-Karpis gang. Beth was living with him but may not have been informed of what was happening all the time. In any event, there are FBI and police files that indicate that Eddie and John might have been introduced by Louie Cernocky. On his deathbed, Eddie said this also, but you cannot trust what Eddie said then.

Eddie was both smooth and amusing despite his rather rough appearance. He was well liked by the people who counted. He had several aliases and had shown himself cool under difficult circumstances, and a loyal son and brother. By 1934, he was always impeccably dressed as was his inamorata, Bessie Skinner, who called herself his wife, Mrs. Beth Green.

Eddie was also more mature and calmer than your average gangster. In 1934, Eddie and Beth were both 36; Beth was Eddie's elder by five months. For almost two years, Eddie and Beth as a team were earning at least a good portion of their crooked money without pointing guns at people, unlike the younger hoodlums. Their specialty, at its most sophisticated, worked this way: Eddie and Beth would drive to a small Nebraska or Minnesota or Iowa or Wisconsin town, park their new car and walk into a bank; one that Harry Sawyer had identified as having lots of available cash. Once inside they would tell the bank officials that they were moving to town and had over a thousand dollars that they would deposit shortly, but with the rash of robberies, they were worried about how safe the bank was. The manager would frequently take them on a tour of the bank, pointing out alarms and how the vaults worked. The Greens took notes.

Beth and Eddie would also tour the town and roads, plotting out escape routes, drawing routes on maps and showing where roadblocks were most likely to be set up. The Greens kept notebooks. They would take this information back to St. Paul.

There, Harry Sawyer would sell the information to the highest bidder along with other notes that Harry had collected on the deposits in the town's banks. Eddie also sold his expertise as a cool character through Harry Sawyer and went along on the stick-ups. He carried a gun then, and neither Beth, nor Eddie's mother Margaret, liked him doing this,

It is likely that Beth and Eddie had recently cased banks in Sioux Falls, South Dakota, where Eddie had marked the Securities National Bank and Trust Company as a possible target, even before Dillinger arrived in St. Paul.

Beth had another, more legitimate and more steady occupation. Her jug marking activities, and fronting for the mob for apartment and car deals, were not really what she did for a living. Rather she was a restaurateur and nightclub operator. (She may also have been a brothel manager. In later times, she was.) Beth had started her real career in the mid-1920s, and over time she worked as manager and hostess at bars and nightclubs owned by Danny Hogan, Harry Sawyer and Jack Peifer. She advanced in this occupation and appears to have ended up co-owning the popular *Alamo* nightclub. During the late twenties and early thirties, she was one busy lady.

CHAPTER 12

Midwestern Madness

On March 5th in the evening, a meeting was held at Dillinger's Minneapolis apartment. The subject discussed was the Securities National Bank of Sioux Falls in South Dakota. All but one of the members of Dillinger's new gang attended the meeting. These people represented an almost entirely different group than Dillinger's regular team of hoodlums, with whom he had robbed banks across Illinois and Indiana. Most of his "regulars" were in prison or dead. Nonetheless, Johnny knew the group gathered in Minneapolis by association and reputation and its members were to constitute the last "Dillinger gang."

The people present in the apartment, in addition to John Dillinger, were Eddie Green, Homer Van Meter, and "Baby Face" Nelson. John Hamilton, who was supposed to be there and who had worked with Dillinger more regularly than the others present at the meeting, had not yet come up from Chicago. (Hamilton may have made it to Sioux Falls.) Also present that evening in Minnesota was Nelson's acquaintance, Tommy Carroll, a Minnesota boy and free-lancer for whom both Green and Nelson could vouch. Green, following Harry Sawyer's suggestion, and showing his own get-away maps, proposed that the gang hit the Sioux Falls bank.

Utilizing the Greens' notes and penciled in marks on escape routes, Dillinger talked about a particular way in and out of town and suggested that the gang use the same technique that he had used successfully to rob the American Bank and Trust Company in Racine, Wisconsin the previous November. This methodology had gained Dillinger's previous gang $27,000 and no civilians were killed; a police officer was wounded. Eddie, in all likelihood, agreed immediately to the proposal. There is good evidence that Eddie Green was in on the Racine job, his first with Dillinger; but if so, Beth did not know, or was unwilling to speak to the authorities about it.

Beth later reported that during this meeting "Baby Face" Nelson was not impressed with the plan to rob the Sioux Falls bank and argued for the gang shooting their way in and out. In any event, Dillinger's plan was the one adopted, although once on site in Sioux Falls, "Baby Face" was to improvise around John's theme.

The Greens, working through the good offices of the Federal Acceptance Corporation, had provided the mob with a large green Packard touring car. On the morning of March 6th, only three days after Dillinger's escape from Crown Point, the gang set out for Sioux Falls. The 255-mile trip took them over five hours. They arrived at the bank shortly before it closed and parked in front.

The two free lancers, Green and Carroll took up the most dangerous positions outside the bank, an imposing brick edifice of several stories. Green was stationed by the car and was to keep traffic moving along while Carroll, with a Tommy gun, guarded the entrance to the bank. Dillinger, Nelson, and Van Meter went inside. The robbery went according to plan, fairly smoothly at first, and only the expected "unexpected" happened when an employee set off the burglar alarm which rang outside the bank. There was a delay when the head teller refused to open the vault, but Dillinger with a combination of threat, and beating the teller with a pistol butt, persuaded him to cooperate. The robbery was going better than expected and during their time in the bank, the gang confiscated about $50,000 in cash and negotiable bonds.

But as the gang was ready to leave, an off-duty policeman came over to investigate the people gathered outside the bank and the commotion. From within the bank, Nelson looked out through a window and saw the policeman who was still in uniform. "Baby Face" then climbed from behind a railing that separated the tellers from the public lobby and fired his Tommy gun through the window wounding the officer.

This officer, however, summoned his colleagues. First, Police Chief Parsons, and then a carload of officers arrived. As they drove up, Tommy Carroll, waving his machine gun invited the Chief and his minions out of their cars and had them unholster their pistols and lie down on the sidewalk.

Thus, the scene: In front of the bank were the captured police, lying on the ground. Milling around outside the bank was a large number of citizens and at least one photographer. The onlookers provided not only witnesses to what was going on but problems to the gang if any one of them might wish to be a hero.

To ensure their own safety, Dillinger, Nelson and Van Meter selected four female bank employees and one male, and using them as a shield, went to the car through the crowd; the hostages were shoved inside. Carroll fired his machine gun in the air, Eddie Green got in the car to guide the route and Carroll to drive, and the bandits and hostages rapidly left town. They were followed by a large posse got up by the Chief once he got up from the sidewalk, and consisting of county and state lawmen. The gang released the male hostage unharmed just outside Sioux Falls. it was obviously crowded in the Packard some miles further on they stopped a farmer and stole his car. When the radiator of the farmer's car started to steam, however, and the police began to draw close, the female hostages were abandoned and the robbers took off again in a single car.

All these activities slowed down the gangsters in the car and the police came close enough to exchange shots with the gang. The gang drove the short way to the South Dakota-Minnesota border and the gang lost the Sioux Fall's police just across the Minnesota border, at Luverne. However, South Dakota and Minnesota authorities launched a large- scale hunt, also using airplanes. The gang zigged and zagged along small roads on Eddie's map, being chased closely and then losing their pursuers several times. According to some reports they went down into Iowa before approaching Minneapolis from the south. In any event, they were unharmed and in the Twin Cities and in Green's apartment before midnight. Beth Green was there when they arrived, but at Eddie's urging, she stayed in the bedroom while the boys divided up the loot. She was able to hear what was said in the next room.

The division of booty apparently caused dissension among the gang. Eddie Green took his prerogative as host to arrange the money and bonds in piles on the table so that the whole gang could help count. Pushing Green aside, Nelson told him that he, "Big George," was the one who shot the cop and Green was just a "jug marker." Dillinger intervened and softly suggested to Eddie that Nelson count the money since all knew what proportion their shares should be anyway. Green was not interested in asserting himself, and getting in the face of a psychopath. He had no problem agreeing to John's suggestion.

This robbery, which went more smoothly than many, resulted in no deaths or serious wounds. It nonetheless became the stuff of legend during the Thirties. Reporters, magazine writers and an apologist for J. Edgar Hoover wrote about the Sioux Falls job at length. The *True Detective Mysteries* magazine for February 1941 cover story contains an amusing addition to the standard versions of the robbery in Sioux Falls. According to "Baby Face Nelson's" self-proclaimed "associate," Fatso Negri, prior to the Sioux Falls job, Negri had purchased a used gasoline truck. Using a blowtorch and hacksaws, the truck was turned into a "tank" with gun slits in the back and sides and machine gun rests inside the converted body. Steel plates were installed that would protect the driver. Members of the gang, including Negri drove this result of enterprise to Sioux Falls where it was used in the getaway. The truck was later used in an Iowa robbery.

This story is not true. While Negri had met Lester Gillis in California several months before Gillis, now famous as "Baby Face" Nelson, joined Dillinger, he did not see Nelson again until after this job (and the Iowa one) when Nelson was in Las Vegas.

Except for his own account, there is no indication that Negri was around the Midwest until June 1934, and even then, he was not associated with Dillinger. He has many of the facts wrong, even if he heard them from Nelson. For example, he places the gang in Sioux Falls (and Mason City) on a date before Dillinger broke out of the Crown Point jail. But he does tell an amusing fiction, with a sprinkling of fact, and his story helped to keep alive the legend of Dillinger and the time.

At the time, the robbery in Sioux Falls convinced some law enforcement agencies that a new gang was operating in the upper Midwest, but also at that time, it appeared unlikely that Dillinger was with the gang. In fact, Werner Hanni, who was in charge of the St. Paul FBI office, was quoted in the *Omaha World Herald* on March 7, as speculating that a Sioux City or Omaha gang had hit the bank. The fact that Hanni spoke to the press at all irritated J. Edgar Hoover but Hoover seems not to have disagreed with Hanni's opinion. The various authorities, including Hoover, had, at the time, two reasons for doubting Johnny's participation:

When Dillinger had escaped from Crown Point, he was accompanied by the murderer, Herbert Youngblood. These two fugitives were thought by many to be together still. Youngblood went on a robbery and killing binge in Michigan in early March and witnesses placed Dillinger with him. When Youngblood was shot and dying on March 16, 1934, he told the police that Dillinger was also in Michigan, hiding out.

From March 6 to March 13, Dillinger's former partner and longtime gang member, Harry Pierpont was standing trial in Lima, Ohio, for a murder he had committed when he helped Dillinger escape from the Lima jail in October 1933. It was believed by other police agencies and General Bush of the Ohio National Guard, who was charged with guarding Pierpont, that Dillinger was in Indiana, Illinois or Ohio, preparing to rescue Harry, as Harry had earlier rescued him.

"Oh We've Got Trouble, Right Here In River City..."

On March 7, Eddie Green took a share of the loot from the Sioux Falls job to McCormick's to pay off Harry Sawyer for the gang's protection and for Dillinger's continued anonymity in the Twin City area. Sawyer made another suggestion to Green. The First National Bank of Mason City, Iowa, was very wealthy and could present an easy target. Eddie took this suggestion back to Dillinger, who asked Green and Homer Van Meter to scout out Mason City. (March 7 also marked the day that the FBI formally entered the search for Dillinger as a result of Dillinger's violation of the Dyer Act, which forbade interstate transport of stolen cars.)

Eddie learned that there was about $240,000 in the vaults of the Mason City, Iowa bank from Harry Sawyer; therefore, each gang member could haul about $35,000 home after expenses. Beth and Eddie had talked about what they would do with a large amount of money and thought they would purchase a really class establishment such as Jack Peifer's *Hollyhocks Club* in St. Paul, or a resort on one of Minnesota's big lakes that tourists frequented. Dillinger, according to John Toland's *The Dillinger Days,* planned to flee to Mexico or South America *a la* Butch Cassidy.

John Hamilton had joined the gang in St. Paul at this point and the group required several vehicles both for their own transport and for placing along escape routes along with extra gasoline. Again, Beth aided in obtaining these cars. Green and Homer Van Meter left the Twin Cities for Mason City on March 10 to mark the jug.

Mason City, then a town of about 25,000 people, was the hometown of the young Meredith Wilson. (Wilson later wrote a musical about a crook, the much more benign mountebank, "Professor" Harold Hill.) When the gang arrived, they put up in the local YMCA and visited the bank, to take a look around. They planned to meet the gang again in three days.

The day after their arrival, they mapped out get away routes and found a place in a sand pit outside of town to stash an extra vehicle, so that the gang could switch cars after the robbery. On March 12, at 7 p.m., Eddie paid a visit to Harry Fisher, assistant cashier of the First National Bank, at Fisher's home. Eddie peered in from the front porch and knocked, and Fisher's wife sent Fisher to answer the knock. Eddie asked whether the house was number 1228, Fisher told him that 1228 was a few houses down; Fisher noted that when Eddie walked away, he turned in the wrong direction. Green was making sure that he would recognize Fisher at the bank the next day. But Fisher was also alerted and was able to identify Green's photograph much later.

FIRST NATIONAL BANK, MASON CITY, IA (PHOTO: PRIVATE COLLECTION MHO)

At about 1 p.m. on March 13, Dillinger, Tommy Carroll, "Baby Face Nelson" and John Hamilton arrived at the sand pit outside Mason City, and met Van Meter and Green. All the gang transferred to a single car to go into town. At 2:40 p.m., the gang parked in front of the bank and went to work. There are several versions of how the hold-up went.

The most coherent story about the robbery and the problems which Dillinger's gang ran into as they attempted it, is told in John Toland's *The Dillinger Days.* Toland states that the officials at the bank, although forewarned of the possibility of a robbery by their holding company, Bancorporation, were not worried that their bank would be held up. They had a guard inside the bank, stationed in a raised steel cage above the floor. They also had electric locks on their vaults, and these could be tripped by the cashiers.

There is a difference of opinion among the various writers who have chronicled Dillinger's exploits, as to who went into the bank. Tommy Carroll was driving and stayed with the car and someone guarded the back door while someone else took up a position as a lookout in the door of a drugstore across the street. Toland says that Eddie Green, Van Meter and Hamilton went in. Green was an "outsider" both in the sense that he was a Minnesota boy, and not a longstanding colleague of Dillinger or

Nelson, and because his usual tasks kept him outside the banks while they were being knocked over. But because Green had to point out Assistant Cashier Fisher, and Van Meter was to identify the bank's president, who could open the vault, it is very probable that they both went into the bank in Mason City.

In the event, the bandits burst into the room waving guns and shouting, "This is a stick-up" and various other traditional phrases. Van Meter grabbed the bank president, Willis Bagley, right away, but Bagley twisted free and went into his private office. When Van Meter stuck his Tommy Gun barrel into the crack in the door as it slammed, Bagley trapped the barrel and Van Meter had to pull the gun back out. The bank president then locked the door and went immediately to his telephone. The bank switchboard operator had had the presence of mind to open the lines to outside and Bagley raised the alarm.

Hamilton went behind the cashiers' cages and ordered the employees to open their cash drawers. He grabbed the money in the drawers and went to join Eddie Green who was waving a machine gun at the people in the lobby.

On the balcony overlooking the lobby and built into the wall over the bank's entry door was the steel cage with a steel floor and gun slits. Inside this cage was a bank guard. Although he had a very good view of the robbery below, the guard did not dare to use his shotgun or pistol on the gang for fear of hitting employees or customers. But when he saw Eddie Green pointing a Tommy gun at the staff, he stuck his teargas rifle through the slot and fired an eight-inch long canister. The projectile hit Green in the back and went off. Seeing where the danger came from, Hamilton told Green to shoot the guard in the cage, and Eddie fired his machine gun toward the steel. A few bullets went through the gun slit and one wounded the guard slightly.

With the Bank's president locked in his office, most of the vaults closed and the place filling up with tear gas, Dillinger's gang had to settle for what they could grab from the cash drawers and one open vault where the lock failed. Their take totaled about $50,000, as at Sioux Falls, but this time the escape did not go so smoothly.

As at Sioux Falls, the gang took bank staff members hostage; and they herded them into the street, toward the car. As the gang and hostages were leaving the bank, a policeman on the roof of a building across the street shot Dillinger in the shoulder, and John Hamilton was also wounded as more gunfire broke out.

The robbers, under fire, forced the bank employee hostages to stand on the running boards of the getaway car and they were not fired at again as they made their escape. Once clear of the town the gang made the hostages jump off while the car was still moving. The gang then drove by circuitous paths back to the sand pit. The wounded Dillinger and Hamilton continued to travel with Tommy Carroll in the hold-up car back to Minneapolis. The rest of the gang used the remaining vehicle hidden at the pit to affect an escape. It probably really wasn't Fatso Negri's "tank."

※ ※ ※

While Dillinger was in Mason City, Beth Green was trying to find a new apartment for Dillinger and Billie Frechette. Because Dillinger was so hot, he had to keep moving from place to place, and move regularly. But Beth had her own reasons for helping Johnny and Billie to move: Beth was earlier complaining to Eddie that living in the Minneapolis neighborhood of the Dillingers was making the area dangerous for them.

More than a few of the crooks who were in on the crime spree in March were living in a tight geographical circle in Minneapolis. While Dillinger and Billie were on Fremont Avenue, Eddie and Beth were living a block away at 3252 Girard Avenue.

Johnny and Billie had disturbed their first Minneapolis neighbors because of the constant comings and goings of all sorts of tough types at all sorts of hours. In addition, according to Beth Green, shortly after John Hamilton had moved in with Dillinger and Frechette on March 7, someone dropped a pistol on the floor of the Minneapolis apartment and it went off. Because of this, Dillinger told Eddie that he was worried that they would shortly either be identified or asked to leave.

Homer Van Meter lived at the *Josephine Apartments*, 3310 Fremont Avenue, close to this building. Also in the neighborhood was a "safe house": apartment 207 at the *Charlou Apartment*, 3300 Fremont. (This was Beth's address on the fake driver's license that the FBI found in her purse.) The previous September, Eddie Green and Beth had rented this Freemont Avenue apartment under the aliases "Mr. and Mrs. Theodore Randall," and it was used to store weapons. (In all likelihood, even before the "Randalls" had it, Beth had arranged the rental of this place for the Barker-Karpis gang, so that the gang could drop their weapons there.)

The new apartment that Beth found was at 93-95 Lexington Avenue at the Lincoln Courts Apartments in St. Paul. The Beth Green had earlier rented apartments in this building as hideouts for other associates of Harry Sawyer, and the Greens had occupied apartments here in 1932. On March 19, Beth and Billie packed up the guns and clothing in a duffle bag at the *Santa Monica* and took them to the "U" shaped building in Minnesota's capital.

John Dillinger and John Hamilton did not get back to their apartment from Mason City until the morning of March 14. Both men were bleeding from shoulder wounds and they had to find a doctor. The two men went first to see Eddie Green to find out how they might get medical help. Then, the three picked up Van Meter and went to Harry Sawyer's front man at *McCormick's* café, Pat Reilly. Towards midnight on the 13th, Pat took Dillinger, Hamilton and Van Meter to the private home of Dr. Nels Mortensen. Eddie drove.

Dr. Mortensen was a distinguished member of the St. Paul medical and political establishment and President of Minnesota's Board of Health. Mortensen was also an ex-Post Commander of the American Legion, President of the American Legion Hospital of Minnesota, City Health Commissioner of St. Paul and preparing to announce his candidacy for County Coroner. Such was the level of Sawyer's legitimate associates in St. Paul, a good indication of how ingrained corruption was in the town.

As well as having a range of civic positions, Mortensen was a good doctor, and he and his family were well liked in the community. He was also, to his lasting sorrow, a doctor who had as regular patients both Harry Sawyer and Pat Reilly. When Reilly brought the wounded robbers and their drivers to Mortensen's home late in the evening of March 13, Reilly told Dr. Mortensen that two of the men with him were wounded in a gunfight in the Twin Cities. Reilly also told Mortensen that Harry Sawyer knew the men and did not see any reason to involve the police. Reilly further told him that neither man was at fault in the fight. While Mortensen was not legally required to report this episode, his ethical position was more than shaky.

Mortensen patched them up as best he could at home without adequate equipment and told them to come to his office the next day. Neither man did. As the men left, Mortensen noticed that the unwounded man, Van Meter, had a sub-machine gun under his coat. Mortensen later claimed to be too frightened by the episode to call the police.

Van Meter recounted this story to Eddie Green, who had waited in the car, and Green revealed it to the FBI in his delirium after being wounded. The FBI
indicated to Beth that they knew who the doctor was from Eddie, and Beth was fooled into revealing Mortensen's name in

her confession.

The FBI later discovered from that Mortensen had also treated members of the Barker-Karpis gang and was a friend of Harry Sawyer. From that point on, the FBI was all over Dr. Mortensen like a cheap suit. Mortensen carried the stigma of these associations to his grave, some 37 years later.

CHAPTER 13

Cruel April

The FBI as an organization was chasing a variety of crooks that hid out in St. Paul since the mid-twenties. They had arrested Danny Hogan in the mid-twenties to no avail, but they knew in some detail how the "O'Connor layover system worked. The FBI, U.S. postal inspectors, and some honest Minnesota investigators, were well aware that Harry Sawyer had inherited Danny Hogan's mantle. From 1929 onwards, they had haunted Harry Sawyer, the man who, through his connections with St. Paul authorities, made many crooks "invisible" to the law. The FBI watched Sawyer, and his family, at their home and on their farm some 20 miles outside St. Paul, where Harry would go to relax.

Sawyer had acquired the farm through a typical crooked maneuver: Alvin Karpis and the Barkers were cheated out of money that they gave to Sawyer to launder; shortly thereafter Harry bought his country retreat with that money. Harry had no shame at all, and later entertained members of the Barker-Karpis gang and many others on the "Most Wanted" list at the farm as well as in St. Paul, at his home and at his bar.

In early 1934, the FBI was aware that Sawyer might be connected both to the Hamm kidnapping and to the Bremer kidnapping, (as indeed he was), and had warrants for his surveillance including wire-tapping under the "Lindbergh Law," which made kidnapping a Federal offense. They watched Harry even more intensely for this reason, but in late March and early April 1934, the agents were not aware that Sawyer was involved with Dillinger. The "Jodil" task force was seeking Johnny in other locations.

John Edgar Hoover, Director of the Justice Department's Bureau of Investigation, however, only named Dillinger "Public Enemy Number One" in June 1934 when the robber and his gang were completing this spree of killings and Midwest bank hold ups. These activities had netted Dillinger and his hastily appropriated funds, and cost the lives of at least ten lawmen and ordinary citizens. However, "ordinary citizens" also helped Dillinger as his fame grew, and *True Detective Mysteries* and *Startling Detective Adventures* and other magazines, the radio and the press painted Dillinger as intelligent, cunning, daring and witty. There were other bank robbers, such as Harvey Bailey, who were more successful and had less notoriety.

Dillinger had a cult following, especially in the upper Midwest. More than two-dozen people who did not have any previous criminal records were to go to jail for "aiding and abetting" or "harboring" Dillinger or members of his gang. Well before Crown Point, and before Dillinger was declared "Public Enemy Number One," he had embarrassed and damaged Hoover's agency and its reputation.

A national movie audience survey by *The Detective* magazine in May 1934, showed that Dillinger led both Colonel Lindbergh and President Roosevelt in name recognition and popularity. Admittedly, the methods used for this survey were flawed at best, but Hoover paid attention to this and other indications that the public perception was that he was not doing his job.

On March 7, 1934, after the Federal warrant was issued for John Dillinger's arrest, J. Edgar Hoover had ordered that all male hoodlums associated with the gang be shot on sight. This order seemed to many columnists and editors to take the American judicial system back a step, to the days of posses and frontier justice. The popular press played up this order as almost a personal struggle between Hoover and Dillinger.

There was no doubt that law enforcement and financial institutions saw Dillinger as a threat to life and property. Dillinger, however, was not "organized crime." He was more a progeny of the robbers and psychopaths of the old West, than he was like Alphonse Capone in Chicago, Isadore "Kid Cann" Blumenfeld in Minneapolis, Leon Gleckman in St. Paul, or the later Benjamin "Bugsy" Siegel and Meyer Lansky coast to coast. "Frontier justice" may have been the best kind for the way Dillinger wanted to live.

That being said, an organized crime connection remained: Dillinger paid off and relied on the big mobsters, he needed them to launder the results of his frequent large and illegal withdrawals from banks. The Barker-Karpis gang needed the likes of Harry Sawyer to clean the wealth they had made kidnapping prominent Minnesotans. But Dillinger and "Creepy" Karpis were tied, at best, only to the upper middle management of the mobs. For example, they went to Harry "Dutch" Sawyer or Jack Peifer in St. Paul for help, it is most likely, indirectly through local gangsters.

The big mobsters did not seem to worry too much about gangsters like Dillinger. Dillinger could not directly approach Leon Gleckman or a police chief in St. Paul, but as long as he did not call too much attention to the steadily profitable rackets of bootlegging, prostitution and especially gambling and drug dealing, the big guys only expected respect and tribute in the form of cash from the Dillinger or the Barker-Karpis gangs.

There has been considerable speculation about why Hoover's FBI was more interested in pursuing bank robbers than the chiefs of organized crime. For example, Anthony Summers in his muck-raking tome, *"Official and Confidential- The Secret Life of J. Edgar Hoover"* (G.P. Putnam and Sons, 1993, New York), suggests that the mob had photographs or other irrefutable evidence of Hoover in a compromising position with another male. The mob's threat to disclose this evidence kept Hoover away. This, however, seems to be "unproven."

Nonetheless, the FBI devoted considerable resources to catching Dillinger. Shortly after the new Dillinger gang held up the bank in Mason City, the FBI determined that Dillinger was in on the Sioux Falls, South Dakota, robbery based on a positive identification of his photo by witnesses to the robbery. By March 17, the FBI had found latent fingerprints of Dillinger at the Mason City Bank. What the FBI did not know was where Dillinger was hiding, and what was the extent of his new gang.

Since he was fairly safe in Minnesota, after the Sioux Falls and Mason City robberies, one might expect the Dillinger gang's chief would take a little time off. But Dillinger seems to have been both foolish and restless. His "recuperation" in St. Paul from his shoulder wound lasted only one day. Then Dillinger took Billie Frechette to Chicago. His goal there was to see his lawyer Louis Piquett, and talk about Billie obtaining a divorce from her first husband who was in prison, so that Johnny and Billie could be married.

Piquett was not available and in any case was not a divorce lawyer, and Art O' Leary, his partner, met with the two lovers and pointed out that they should seek a divorce lawyer elsewhere.

While he was in Illinois, and nearer to his family home, Dillinger decided to get in touch with his father. John knew that it would be dangerous for him to go near the farm. So, on March 19, he sent Billie to Mooresville, Indiana to see the senior Dillinger. Billie showed Johnny's dad the wooden gun from Crown

Point, and gave him some money and news of John. Dillinger entrusted to Billie a letter he had written to his family assuring them that while he had been wounded, the wound was getting better; he was in little danger!

Billie returned to Chicago late at night on the 19th, and then she and Johnny went up to St. Paul and back to the furnished apartment that Beth Green had rented for them a few days earlier. This was on the third floor of Lincoln Court Apartments. They were identified (in Beth Green's handwriting) in the landlady's records as Mr. and Mrs. Carl T. Hellman. On March 13, Beth had paid the $60 rent for a month in advance and also given the manager these names.

As Alvin Karpis has written about this time, the bank robbing business was beginning to suffer a decline, as did others in the Depression. There were too many out-of-work amateur crooks, many of whom were bootleggers whose source of income was about to dry up. Karpis said that these people were willing to dare anything for dollars.

In addition to the problem of a crowded and inexperienced supply of bank robbers, communications were improving among law enforcement officers and there was an aroused citizenry. It was getting tough to rob a bank without killing someone. But the members of the "new" Dillinger gang had not accumulated enough money from the jobs in Sioux Falls and Mason City to, in Beth and Eddie's case buy a nightclub, and in Dillinger's, to go to Mexico. It can be safely assumed that the gang was planning further bank jobs, using information from Harry Sawyer and Green. But even so it would have been wise to lay low for a while.

One restless member of the gang did not want to hang around the Twin Cities; "Baby Face" Nelson and his wife had left Minnesota about March 13 and gone to Reno to blow the $12,000 or so that was Nelson's share of the loot from the first two bank robberies. John Paul Chase went along with "Baby Face." In Reno, Nelson made contact with a minor hoodlum whom he had earlier known in California. This was "Fatso" Negri, who did not come to the Midwest until several months later.

As far as can be determined, Dillinger and Frechette did nothing crooked nor did they travel between March 21 and March 23. On March 23, Dillinger went to Leipsic, Ohio, perhaps to visit Harry Pierpont's mother who lived there. From Leipsic he went to Lima, Ohio, to judge for himself whether there was any chance of breaking Pierpont out of prison. On March 24, the same day Dillinger came into town, Pierpont was sentenced to death. Dillinger soon concluded that there was no chance of pulling off a raid on the heavily guarded jail, and that other means would have to be used to save Pierpont. Events were to intervene, assuring that nothing could be done to save Harry. (Pierpont was executed on October 17, 1934.)

Billie had gone down to Chicago with Johnny when he set out for Leipsic and Lima. Late on March 24, he came back to Chicago and together they returned to St. Paul and their place at the Lincoln Courts. They were joined at the apartment by John Hamilton, Hamilton's moll, Pat Cherrington, and Pat's sister, Opal Long, all of whom moved in.

The time between March 25 and 30 seems to have been a quiet time for Billie and Johnny. At a visit to the Green's apartment, during that period, Billie complained to Beth about how boring her life was when they were hiding out. But she and Dillinger went to see the movies "Joe Palooka" and "Fashions of 1933." He mentioned both of these movies to Eddie and Beth on March 29 when they returned Johnny's visit of a few days earlier. (In fact, Beth took umbrage at the fact that Dillinger advised Eddie not to take Beth to see "Fashions of 1933" as it might "give Beth ideas.") In her confession to the FBI Beth had some trouble with exact dates, but she could remember the date of their visit to this couple because there was a late winter snowstorm; she and Eddie had a hard time getting home.

While visiting Billie and Johnny, Beth also saw mounted photos of Dillinger as a boy, one showing him in a sailor suit and one showing him climbing a tree. Johnny also showed her the famous "wooden pistol."

Notebooks and plans that turned up later indicate that Dillinger and Hamilton were planning another job with the aid of Harry Sawyer and Eddie Green during the late part of March, but Dillinger had reason to continue to keep his head low, even if Billie was bored. After all, although he was sought like the Scarlet Pimpernel and was identified as a participant in the South Dakota and Iowa robberies, he seemed relatively safe as long as he kept quiet in St. Paul.

Johnny was unable to keep quiet. His actions already were arousing the suspicions on the building's manager, Mrs. Coffey. Nonetheless, he let Billie throw a party on the evening of Friday, March 30. While the guest list appears to have been small, consisting of Opal Long, Pat Cherrington, John Hamilton and Dillinger, the party lasted all night and it was under close observation.

Even before this party, Mrs. Coffey, the manager of the Lincoln Courts had sensed something was amiss. While other criminals, including Larry "The Chopper" Devol, a partner of Alvin Karpis, had lived at the Lincoln Court Apartments, they must have been more circumspect around the landlady. Johnny was careless.

Maybe it was (as reported by Paul Maccabbee) that Billie Frechette took wet clothes out to the line in back to hang them to dry, clad only in a red halter, shorts and high heels. For Minnesota in late March, this was highly irregular behavior. Maybe it was the people with bulging overcoats going up and downstairs at all hours. Maybe it was that the shades on the apartment were drawn all the time. Maybe it was that the apartment was rented for two people and five were actually living there. Whatever it was, the landlady got in touch with the police, who passed her suspicions on to the FBI.

On March 30, the FBI went to the apartments and talked to the lady manager who informed the agents that the tenants acted nervous. The FBI was told that the people living there had refused to let a maintenance man come in on the excuse that "Mr. Hellman" was in the bath. So, the FBI set up a surveillance of 95 South Lexington Avenue that began the evening of March 30. The FBI was searching for Johnny in Indiana and Michigan, and did not expect to find him in Minnesota. But they were convinced that something criminal was going on at the Lincoln Courts.

Although the FBI thought that the place should be watched and did not trust the St. Paul police, the stake out seems to have been somewhat haphazard. Later, in memoranda meant to be read by J. Edgar Hoover, two FBI agents responsible for handling the events at Lincoln Court review traded charges as to which one was the most incompetent in this initial investigation.

On Saturday morning, John Hamilton left the apartment building at 9:45 and walked past the FBI agent who was sitting in a car outside the Lincoln Courts. About 10 o'clock, Opal Long and Pat Cherrington also left the apartment. Hamilton had gone to pick up his car and shortly thereafter he met Opal and Pat who got in the car with him. The three were apparently on their way shopping and went unrecognized by the FBI observer.

That morning, J.M. Ladd, the acting chief of the St. Paul FBI office dispatched Special Agent Rufus C. Coulter, to talk to the people living in Apt. 303 at the Lincoln Courts; and to find out whether Coulter's partner Rosser Nalls who was sitting outside the building on stakeout had seen anything. Sent with Coulter, was Detective Henry Cummings of the St. Paul police department. The FBI wanted to ensure that there was a local cop there initially to approach the tenants who were behaving peculiarly. Ladd had specifically asked for the most honest St. Paul cop available, and Cummings had a very good record and did not seem corrupt. (The fact that his family said that they found some $60,000 in cash in his safe-deposit box after he died casts some doubt on his incorruptibility.)

Coulter and Cummings arrived at the building at about 10:15. Agent Nalls remained staked out in front, and Cummings and Coulter went up to Apartment 303, where Billie and Johnny were still in bed. Cummings knocked on the door.

Dillinger had arranged with Billie that should someone unexpected knock, she would go the door and try to find out who was there. Billie opened the door on the chain and saw someone she didn't know.

"Who are you?" she asked.

"St. Paul police," answered Cummings, "Is Carl Hellman home?"

"Who is that?" asked Billie, never too swift on the uptake, and forgetting her alias.

She thought for a moment and it dawned on her: she and John were in trouble.

"Oh Carl..." she continued. "He just left and won't be back until this afternoon. But you can talk to him then."

"I'd be happy to talk to you," said Cummings, "If you are Mrs. Hellman."

"But I'm not dressed." Billie stated, and indeed she was still in her negligee.

"We'll wait," said Cummings, emphatically.

As soon as Billie shut the door, Coulter and Cummings could hear a man and a woman talking inside the apartment, although they could not hear what they were saying. Dillinger was telling Billie to get dressed and pack up, they were getting out. Anticipating an escape attempt, Cummings drew his revolver and went to one side of the door.

Coulter thought that there could be several people in the apartment, as indeed there had been a short time earlier. He went down the steps quickly to ask Nalls to call for back up. Moments after Coulter came back toward the apartment, another man came up the stairs. It was Homer Van Meter who had parked outside and was paying a morning call on John and Billie. He caught up with Coulter. When Coulter asked him who he was --he seemed on his way to Apartment 303-- he said that he was a soap salesman. When Coulter asked him where his sample case was, Van Meter said it was in the car, and offered to show it to Coulter.

As they went back down the stairs, Van Meter brushed ahead of Coulter and going out the door, he drew his pistol. "You want it! You bastard! Here it is!" he shouted and shot at Coulter. Coulter was not hit and getting his gun out, shot back at Van Meter. Agent Nalls who was still waiting outside, heard the shots and pulled his gun. He also fired at Van Meter. The two FBI agents chased Van Meter around the lawn and back up the driveway next to the building. They approached the building's alley carefully; they believed the gunman was hiding; there but he had disappeared. And behind them they could hear gunfire.

Van Meter, given a brief time alone in the alley, had climbed up into the seat of a garbage truck, which was standing there with two men inside. He exchanged hats with one of the men, and forced them to drive at gunpoint. Several blocks away he got out of the truck, and gave the workers $10, and wished them good luck.

While Van Meter was being chased up the alley, Billie and John were still in the apartment. They had packed a suitcase with money and clothes and Billie could see that John had the butt off the Tommy gun so he could shoot it like a pistol. She was begging him not to shoot. Dillinger opened the apartment door a bit, stuck the barrel out through the crack and began to spray the hall with .45 caliber bullets. This shooting brought the FBI back to the front of the building.

Upstairs, Detective Cummings jumped back around a corner and fired at his assailant until he ran out of bullets. As he withdrew farther to reload, Dillinger and Billie, each carrying a suitcase, came out of the apartment and ran down the back stairs. While Dillinger stood by the back door ready to shoot anyone who followed, Billie ran to the garage to get the car. She backed out and drove toward Dillinger, the car facing downhill toward Lexington Avenue.

"Not that way, stupid!" shouted Johnny, "Turn it around."

She pulled back into the garage and turned the car so it faced the other direction.

"Why don't you drive?" asked Billie.

"I'm shot." was the reply.

Dillinger threw his suitcase in the car and climbed in. He was bleeding from a leg wound. Billie drove out of the alley the same direction Van Meter had gone, away from the FBI and the police.

"What are we going to do?" Billie asked.

"Drive to Eddie Green's apartment." said Dillinger.

Paul Maccabee, in *John Dillinger Slept Here*, quotes a man who was a seventh grader and lived across the street at the time: "We had a quiet, well to do neighborhood, except for the Dillinger shootout and the kidnapping of [Edward] Bremer down the block."

At about 10:45 a.m., shortly after the shooting and Dillinger's escape, Beth Green received a phone call from Billie Frechette. Billie was speaking very excitedly, and Beth had difficulty in understanding what she was saying. Billie did communicate to

Beth that she and Johnny were ousted from their apartment and that Dillinger was shot in the leg. Although Dillinger had told Billie that the wound was not serious, she wanted Beth and Eddie's help to escape and Dillinger wanted Green to help him get to a doctor. Billie was apparently calling from very close to the Green's apartment on Fremont Avenue in Minneapolis, because a short time later she knocked at the door.

Beth and Eddie were out the previous night, and that Saturday morning Eddie was lying undressed in bed reading a newspaper. When Billie arrived, he still did not have his pants on. While Eddie was getting dressed, Billie told a hurried version of the story to Beth. She complained both about Dillinger's criticizing her driving and the fact that she had had to haul two heavy traveling bags down the back stairs because Dillinger was more interested in getting guns and ammo out of the apartment than clothes. Eddie came from the bedroom with his pants on then, and Beth and Eddie went out with Billie.

Dillinger was sitting in the car. He explained the situation a lot more calmly than Billie had. He told Eddie he needed a doctor. He told Eddie that he was earlier impressed with the quality of care provided by Dr. Mortensen. Eddie acted immediately, going to the pay phone in a drug store close by. From there he contacted Pat Reilly at *McCormick's* restaurant and asked whether Reilly would make arrangements again with Dr. Mortensen. Reilly refused, noting that Dillinger was too hot and Mortensen too legit. After this refusal, Eddie knew right away whom he had to call.

Eddie and Eddie's brothers were in trouble at various times since they were teenagers. Judge J.B. Sanborn, who sentenced Eddie to prison in 1922, had said, "From what I hear [the] mother is a good person but the rest of the family prefers to live outside the law." Margaret Green certainly tried to keep her sons in school, in the Church and in good health. For years, Eddie's mother had taken Eddie's older brother, Francis, to Dr.

Clayton E. May when he was sick, and Frank persuaded Eddie to go to Dr. May also.

It is obvious from the records of Eddie's trial in 1922 for 1st degree robbery, that Dr. May took an interest in Eddie. May, who had also worked with the fixer Danny Hogan, had tried to provide Eddie with an alibi and he testified that Eddie was sick and under his care during the time the robbery occurred. The jury didn't believe Dr. May, and Eddie had gone to prison. A year later, Dr. May repeated his testimony in the hope of getting Eddie released rather than being transferred to Minnesota's Stillwater prison, but May was not believed this time either.

When Eddie called on March 31, 1934, May agreed to see a patient at Eddie's urgent request. Eddie drove with Dillinger to May's office. Leaving Johnny and Billie in the car, Green went into May's office and outlined the problem for the doctor but did not name names; he mentioned a gunshot wound but swore the wounded man was not wanted by the police.

Dr. May was sympathetic. May's nurse, and former lover, Mrs. Augusta Salt, maintained a separate apartment that she and May used for performing abortions and providing other hard to obtain medical treatment. May told Eddie to drive his wounded friend there and he, May, would join them. Eddie begged the doctor to go with them there and then, and he promised May $500 extra if he would. With this incentive, May did go, leaving several patients waiting in his office.

When Dr. May got to the car, he discovered that a young dark-complexioned woman was sitting in the back with a wounded man, trying to comfort him but almost hysterical. Next to the wounded man in back was a sub-machine gun.

In his trial, Dr. May stated that he thought that, under the circumstances, Eddie's friend should go to a hospital. He told this to the wounded man. Johnny was impatient in this regard also. Speaking with force and a wave of the gun, Dillinger said to hell with that idea, he wanted to go someplace out of the public eye. May hurriedly agreed and told them that he knew where they should go.

May got his car and followed Eddie Green, Billie and Johnny. May said later that Johnny held a machine gun on him all the time, but the fact that the doctor and the patient went in two separate cars puts the lie to this contention. They went to the flat run by Mrs. Salt where Dillinger was placed on a bed and May gave Dillinger a local anesthetic and probed the wound for a bullet. When finished, May left and drove back to his office. A little later Green visited Dr. May again. Eddie said that Dillinger was demanding a tetanus shot. When Eddie promised Dr. May more money, he agreed to go back.

May was very unhappy about driving his car to the apartment in the first place, so this time Eddie called Beth, who drove over to May's office. She followed him and parked May's car someplace safe. She then followed May and the tetanus serum into May's apartment.

There were more people in that small place than had attended the party that Dillinger had thrown the previous night. And, according to Beth, all of the people were aware of who the guest of honor with the wounded leg was. Dillinger was to remain in this flat until he and Billie escaped from the Twin Cities.

Dealing with an important crook like Dillinger seems to have set the 46 year-old May's juices flowing. He contacted his 22 year-old current lover, Dolores Smart, and went over to see her. He acted particularly amorous in that encounter. And shortly thereafter, he asked Dolores whether she wanted to visit the real crooks. He took her to see Dillinger and proceeded to have sex with her in the sick room. Beth Green was there and was disgusted with May's behavior.

While Eddie and Beth were getting medical attention for Dillinger, and Dr. May was getting all sorts of other attention, the

FBI was searching the Lincoln Courts apartment. They found fingerprints, and they soon identified these as Dillinger's and John Hamilton's. They had had a good idea that these gangsters were in the upper Midwest, because of identification from Sioux Falls and Mason City, and they could figure out who Johnny was dealing with in St. Paul.

At the Lincoln Court apartments, the FBI found detailed maps and escape routes for the Mason City, Iowa job. These were in Eddie Green's handwriting. And they found a stash of arms. Beth later said these were Hamilton's guns, not Dillinger's. Dillinger had carried his away; small wonder Billie had complained to Beth about the bags being heavy. The FBI also found the picture of Dillinger as a youngster in a sailor suit and they found one of Beth and Eddie Green's telephone numbers.

After leaving Dillinger and Dr. May, Beth and Eddie went back home and tried to decide what to do. They discussed leaving town but Eddie's immediate family and best business connections were all in St. Paul. They also wanted to make sure that Dillinger was the one identified and that they really had to escape from the Twin Cities. So, they decided to hang around.

On the evening of March 31, Homer Van Meter came by the Greens' apartment while Beth was listening to *Marge and Myrt* and then *Amos and Andy* on the radio. Beth was not at all happy to see Van Meter. She was not aware that the FBI was close to locating Eddie, but she didn't like Homer and she thought Van Meter brought too much heat to the neighborhood just by himself. She told Van Meter to get out and stay away. Eddie calmed her down and talked to Homer for a while about what the various gang members might do or were doing to avoid the police. He also updated Van Meter on where Dillinger was and what his medical condition was.

During the next two days, Sunday and Monday, Eddie was busy trying to figure out where he and Beth should go until the heat was off, and Beth was busy trying to get a new car for Dillinger. The Ford, which Billie Frechette were driving when Dillinger escaped, was struck by bullets during the escape and they would have to abandon it if they could not find a safe way to sell it.

Beth's brother Almon was an auto salesman and he may have been of aid earlier in helping Beth find some cars for the gang members. Eddie and Beth had the new Terraplane, purchased on March 15, and Tommy Carroll had a Hudson, purchased at the same time. Since Dillinger was so hot, however, Beth did not want to use her family connections. She knew where to go under those circumstances.

The money launderer, the mid-management mob member who bought cars which might be identifiable, and provided the new clean titles was Tom Filben, the head of the Federal Acceptance Corporation. Over the phone with Beth, on Monday, Filben agreed to take Dillinger's Ford V-8 in trade for a new Hudson. He was unable to give Beth the black wire wheels that Dillinger requested; instead he agreed to supply a new black Hudson with cream-colored wheels to an unknown party for cash up front.

On Monday, Beth got cash for the car out of a safe deposit box registered to "Hester Hinds." Eddie had checked with Harry Sawyer who assured him Beth would be repaid if she fronted the money. She went next to the automobile dealer that Filben had specified, stopping first at *McCormick's* café to pick up the manager of the Federal Acceptance Corporation, a young man named Irving Gleeman, whose brothers Beth had known when they were associated with Danny Hogan and Leon Gleckman. Gleeman was to drive the Hudson, park it close to Mrs. Salt's apartment, deliver the keys to Dillinger, and pick up the Ford. This transaction occurred but Beth did not see Dillinger during the process.

Homer Van Meter came to Eddie and Beth's apartment again

on Monday night, April 2, to make arrangements for getting out of town. He was ready to leave at that point, and carried several heavy packages up to the apartment, telling Eddie to hang on to them for him. Van Meter also asked Eddie to make sure to close up the "safe" apartment on Marshall Avenue and get hold of whatever was left there. What was left there seemed to Beth and Eddie to be very possibly incriminatory and dangerous.

The previous September, apartment 207 at the *Charlou Apartments* in St. Paul on Marshall Avenue was rented by the Greens for the Barker-Karpis gang as a weapons' drop. The Greens continued to pay the rent and by March 1934 this apartment was being used by the Dillinger mob as a drop site for most of their weaponry. Homer Van Meter lived close to this depot in an apartment that had previously been occupied by Beth and Eddie as "Mr. and Mrs. D. A. Stevens." Homer asked that the "Stevens," i.e. Van Meter's, apartment be cleaned out as well.

While Beth and Eddie were not aware that a massive man hunt was going on and that they were close to falling into the FBI net, they had no intention of going into the weapon drop site and being trapped, if anyone was "talking." They determined to abandon whatever might be left there. They even questioned Van Meter closely about whether there was anything in the "Stevens" apartment that could cause them trouble. Van Meter said that there was nothing but clothing and some silver dollars and other silver money. No one would get harmed by getting this stuff, but Van Meter wanted it. Beth and Eddie agreed that they could arrange for a pick up and Van Meter left.

Fingerprints from the Lincoln Courts had informed the FBI that Dillinger was the hoodlum who was in the shootout, and might actually still be in St. Paul. St. Paul was a minor blip on J. Edgar Hoover's screen, but Dillinger was major. Hoover, was embarrassed both by Dillinger's escape from the Lincoln Court Apartments and by squabbles that were breaking out among his staff members in St. Paul as to who was to blame for John's escape. He therefore asked a senior inspector at his Chicago office, H.H. Clegg, to go to St. Paul and take over the search for Dillinger. Clegg was also supposed to enforce Hoover's instruction to shoot members of the Dillinger gang on sight.

Clegg rounded up as many agents as he could find to search for the Dillinger gang in the Twin Cities. About ten agents were brought back to their headquarters in St. Paul and another 20 were transferred in from Chicago and elsewhere. There were plenty of agents to stake out sites where Dillinger might be and information from the notebooks found at Lincoln Courts indicated what some of these sites were.

The next morning, April 3rd, Beth and Eddie got in their new Essex Terraplane and drove over to 778 Rondo Street in St. Paul, where Beth's friend, colleague, and occasional maid, Leonia Goodman lived. Leonia and her sister Lucy had worked for Beth in various capacities for many years, as had Lucy's husband. The sisters had also worked with Frank Nash, the Minnesota gunsel who was accidentally killed during the "Kansas City Massacre," the previous June.

When Beth and Eddie got to Leonia's house, they found that she was sick. Not caring much how she felt, and in a hurry to get potential evidence away, Eddie insisted that they wanted Leonia to go to their old apartment on Marshall Avenue and pick up what could be found. They told Leonia what to look for: dirty clothing, and perhaps some clean clothing, a topcoat, and some silver money that would be in a large soft suitcase with handles. They told Leonia to bring along anything else she could pick up there and to keep $10 of the silver as payment. As they were speaking, Lucy Jackson came in and Leonia suggested that perhaps Lucy might be sent if Leonia did not start to feel better.

Through the phone number found in Johnny and Billie's

apartment, the FBI had located the "Stevens" apartment and searched it. As Van Meter had promised Beth and Eddie, there was nothing of great monetary value there. The FBI found some shotgun shells, clips and a stock from an automatic rifle, and dirty clothes and an overcoat. With the influx of manpower, the FBI was able to leave agents at the "Stevens" apartment in case the occupants should return.

While the FBI agents were waiting at the Stevens apartment, Lucy Jackson showed up to clean it, and pack up the duffel bag. Leonia Goodman, still feeling ill, was waiting in a car downstairs. The FBI apprehended both women. They were threatened with being accessories to several crimes. The sisters told the FBI that "Mrs. Stevens" had sent them and the FBI immediately assumed that either Dillinger or John Hamilton could be "Mr. Stevens."

The sisters said that they had only met "Mr. Stevens" once, when they had gone in early March to clean "Mrs. Bessie Stevens's" apartment. But Leonia had had a good look at Mr. Stevens and described how Mrs. Bessie had sat on his lap, and whispered endearments to him and how they had acted like newlyweds while the maids were there. There is good reason to doubt that Leonia was telling the full truth here to the FBI. She was associated with Bessie as a maid and club employee for many years. Bessie had hired her and her sister to clean for various gang members. Bessie would hire her again. There was little doubt that Leonia would recognize the man who was called "Mr. Stevens."

As soon as the FBI agents heard that "Stevens" planned on stopping by the house at 778 Rondo Street later that day to pick up the bag from Leonia, they called Clegg and he planned a trap for "Stevens." Clegg listened to Leonia's descriptions of Eddie and Beth, and determined that he was probably not going to capture Dillinger, but, instead, was dealing with one of Dillinger's gang.

Agent E. N. Notesteen accompanied Leonia and Lucy back home. He agreed with Clegg and Hoover about how dangerous the gang was, both to citizens and the FBI image, and about the need to deal summarily with any gang member who might show up on Rondo Avenue. He arrived in mid-afternoon and posted sharp shooters in the kitchen and at the living room window. Another agent was stationed outside with a Tommy gun to cripple the car that the bandits would be driving.

Agent Notesteen had already told the sisters that their help would save them from Federal prosecution; he now told Leonia that if the man who came for the bag was "Mr. Stevens," she should say, "That's him." The FBI then waited.

At about 5:30 p.m. on April 3, 1934, a man and a woman drove across Rondo Street and down Avon in a new Essex Terraplane, and glided to a stop outside of Leonia Goodman's house. They sat and talked for a few minutes and then the man got out of the car.

※ ※ ※

The first reports on the shooting of Eddie Green appeared on April 4 in the St. Paul and Minneapolis press, and were both sensational and inaccurate. The headline (front page, three column, 36 point bold) in the *St. Paul Pioneer Press* read "Dillinger Clue Seen In Big Roundup of Desperadoes Here." The "big roundup" was in fact the shooting in the back of an unarmed man, and the capture of his "red-haired girl" lover when she went to staunch his wounds. Some desperadoes.

ST. PAUL PIONEER PRESS USED THIS PHOTO OF "FRED ROGGE" (EDDIE GREEN) IN THEIR STORY ON APRIL 4. IT IS OF A MUCH YOUNGER EDDIE.

On the evening of April 4, Dillinger read in the papers that Eugene "Eddie" Green had been wounded, and was captured along with a woman whom the press was speculating was Evelyn Frechette. John knew that he would have to leave Augusta Salt's flat and get out of town along with the actual Billie Frechette who was living there with him.

John Hamilton, on a tip from Harry Sawyer (who was tipped in turn by the St. Paul police that Hamilton was about to be arrested) had left St. Paul and was hiding hid out on Sawyer's farm in Shoreview, Minnesota not far from the Twin Cities. "Baby Face" Nelson was still in Nevada, Tommy Carroll was still in St. Paul about to drive the Hudson, purchased on March 15, to Mankato, Minnesota for repainting, and Homer Van Meter had taken his own advice to Eddie and Beth of two days before and was going back to Chicago. While the gang proceeded with their plans, Beth and Eddie, Leonia and Lucy, were left as the captives of the "big roundup" of the Dillinger gang.

The press was speculating that Dillinger was still in the Twin Cities, and in her early confessions (after April 6), Beth Green was telling the FBI where John might be hiding out. During the week after they left St. Paul, Dillinger and Frechette went first to Indiana to see John's father. Because all the newspaper reports had Dillinger remaining undercover in the Twin Cities, he may have felt safe going home this time. After seeing his family and taking Billie, John went by himself to Leipsic, Ohio to talk to Harry Pierpont's family and assure them that he was still trying to free Pierpont.

The Dillinger family held a reunion when John returned from Leipsic on April 8, and although the home farm was being watched by local authorities, Dillinger's presence at the party was not noticed and he left that evening for Chicago.

By the time he was in Chicago, the next day, the FBI had expanded its search for John. When Dillinger dropped Billie off, outside a downtown tavern that he was known to have frequented when in Chicago, the FBI had the place staked out and Melvin Purvis arrested Billie as she walked in. John saw this happen from the car, and he drove away.

Soon after this narrow escape and Billie's arrest, the reckless, restless John was back in touch with Homer Van Meter. On April 13, he and Homer drove to Warsaw, Indiana where they robbed a police station, getting revolvers and bulletproof vests. Over the next week, most of the new gang were reunited, Van Meter, Tommy Carroll, "Baby Face" Nelson and their "molls" all met at a Louie Cernocky's Crystal Ballroom, north of Chicago. Then, on advice of Harry Sawyer, transmitted by Pat Reilly, Sawyer's gofer, they went to join Dillinger, and hide out at Little Bohemia Lodge in Manitowash, Wisconsin.

After they were settled at the Lodge, Van Meter sent Reilly back to St. Paul to collect $4,000 that Sawyer owed him from earlier work. Reilly got drunk but did not get the money, and during the time he was in St. Paul, the resort owners, getting suspicious, tipped off the FBI where the gang could be found.

The FBI sent a small army to get the hoodlums, flying

reinforcements in. There was a raid and although Helen Gillis ("Baby Face" Nelson's wife), Marie Conforti (Van Meter's girlfriend) and Jean Delaney (Tommy Carroll's girlfriend) were captured, none of the male gang members were. Unfortunately, three innocent guests at the lodge were shot by the FBI when they were mistaken for Dillinger gang members. And during his escape, "Baby Face" Nelson killed one FBI agent and a policeman.

Beth was incarcerated during all this, but she was at Little Bohemia in one way: In their haste to flee their rooms there, the gang left behind a series of detailed get-away charts to be used in robbing banks in Wisconsin. The charts were in both Beth's and Eddie's handwriting and Beth's fingerprints were on them.

The fiasco at Little Bohemia again propelled Dillinger into the public's imagination. Will Rogers, in his radio show, commented, "Well, they had Dillinger surrounded and was all ready to shoot him when he came out. But another bunch of folks came out first, so they just shot them instead. Someday, Dillinger is going to accidentally get in with some innocent bystanders. Then he will get shot."

Recognized the next day in Hastings, Minnesota, while driving to St. Paul, Dillinger, Van Meter and Hamilton got in a moving gun fight with local police. Hamilton was wounded and died several days later.

Between the beginning of May and the end of June, Dillinger and Van Meter continued to pull jobs in the Midwest but Tommy Carroll was shot when identified by a policeman in Waterloo, Iowa. All the male gang members were dead soon. John Dillinger, betrayed by the infamous "woman in red," the prostitute Anna Sage, was shot and killed by the FBI as he left the *Biograph Theater* in Chicago on July 22, 1934. At the end of August, Homer Van Meter was betrayed by Harry Sawyer and was killed by St. Paul police. Finally on November 27, 1934,

Lester "Baby Face Nelson" "Big George" Gillis got in a shootout with police and the FBI in Barrington, Illinois and was mortally wounded, taking two FBI agents, one of them S.P. Cowley, with him.

Also, on November 27, Bessie Skinner, alias Beth Green, alias Hester Hinds, alias Bess Walsh, alias Bessie Moore, alias Bess Makeling, alias Mrs. D.A. Stevens, alias Mrs. T. J. Randall, had completed exactly one half of the time she was going to spend in Alderson Federal Women's Prison, West Virginia, for harboring the fugitive John Dillinger.

CHAPTER 14

The FBI Interrogates Beth Green

> "Taking no chances, the FBI [eventually] isolated Beth Green in Chicago for interrogation under the direction of Melvin Purvis. In a series of increasingly open confessions, Green provided many of the FBI's first tips on the Dillinger and Barker-Karpis gangs and the key roles played by local fixers Harry Sawyer and Jack Peifer."
>
> JOHN DILLINGER SLEPT HERE, PG.236

Within a year of Beth Green's arrest, not only were all the members of the last Dillinger gang dead, but all the members of the Barker-Karpis gang were either dead or in jail. Within two years of her confession, the St. Paul mobster Jack Peifer had committed suicide, his rival Harry Sawyer was serving a long prison sentence which because of the cancer that he developed became a life sentence, and the St. Paul police department was cleaned up. Beth's confessions played a considerable role in setting off all these events.

❋ ❋ ❋

The FBI had arrested Beth on a "Jane Doe "warrant, which was drawn up before a Federal judge. The warrant was covered under the new "National Motor Vehicle Theft" act. It was Dillinger's record of automotive theft and his obvious transport of the cars across state lines that gave the FBI an excuse for involvement.

Immediately after her arrest, Beth Green was brought to the FBI offices in a St. Paul police car and held for the first six hours in a locked room. She was questioned again and again by Agents Rorer and Clegg who were undertaking the initial interrogation. Rorer, who was normally assigned to FBI headquarters in Washington, was in St. Paul to investigate the kidnapping of Edward Bremer.

She talked, but only to deny everything. She denied that she had spoken to Leonia Goodman and Lucy Jackson that day. She admitted to being married to Green but claimed his name was Randall and claimed that she did not know what game he was in, she thought he was a salesman. She said that she had no idea of any shooting the Saturday before, and that she and her husband had spent the entire day inside their apartment except for going grocery shopping.

Late on April 3, Rorer advised his superior in Washington, S. P. Cowley, that the woman arrested refused to give her real name or give any other information.

Lucy Jackson and her sister Leonia Goodman were also held at the FBI office on a temporary basis. Beth had hired Lucy to clean for Dillinger at the Lincoln Court apartments; Eddie Green was shot from Leonia's house. Initially, the two sisters were not very forthcoming. They seem to have been genuinely fond of Beth and at first identified her only as "Mrs. D. A. Stevens," the name under which Beth and Eddie were renting the apartment used as a weapons' drop.

During her second questioning, Lucy Jackson identified Beth

as Bess Randall, and gave the location of the apartment where Beth and Eddie were living under the name of "T.J. Randall." The FBI immediately ordered a search of this location. When the FBI searched the Randall/Green's apartment, they found Van Meter's weapons, left there, and they also found well-organized notebooks in Eddie's handwriting with maps and escape routes from twelve different communities in the upper Midwest.

For at least the previous four years, Lucy Jackson was a servant to a number of mobsters as well as to Beth, and it appears likely that Beth arranged this work for Lucy. In addition to recently working for Dillinger, Lucy had also worked for Beth cleaning at a nightclub, where Beth was hostess and manager. Leonia Goodman was a cook and also worked for Beth in other establishments. Both Leonia and Lucy called Beth "Mrs. Bessie."

S.P. Cowley, in the first memo he sent to J. Edgar Hoover after Beth and Eddie's capture, called Beth "Mrs. Stevens" and gave her description as follows:

"Age - 36 years
Auburn bobbed hair
Height - 5' 8 1/2 "[sic]
Weight - 132 pounds
Dark complexion
Blue eyes
Wide mouth"

Cowley stated that Agent Rorer knew that the names Beth gave were aliases.

Either through questioning or based on fingerprints, Rorer also had discovered that Dillinger was the occupant of the Lincoln Court apartment and John Hamilton was one of the people who assisted Dillinger in making his escape. At this point the FBI knew the names of many past Dillinger associates, but it was unclear as to who was assisting him in St. Paul. Nevertheless, Harry Sawyer was close to the top on the FBI's list of suspects because they knew a great deal about Sawyer's past activities.

The federal authorities had no clue that Beth could tell them much more than they already knew about the extent of the involvement of the Barker-Karpis gang in St. Paul crime, or that she could give them the names of the current associates of that gang. Nor did they know that through Beth they could to get at the St. Paul fixers, police and mob bosses who protected the robbers.

Beth Green had $1,105 dollars tucked in her intimate apparel when she was arrested, and another $50 in her purse. She had registration cards for the Terraplane filled out with the name of R. Coulton, and a registration card for a new Hudson which gave the name Clarence Leo Coulton. She had two week-old invoices on the Terraplane and Hudson. Cowley told Hoover that the Hudson was a car to be used by "the Dillinger crowd."

After the FBI showed her that they had this information, she acknowledged her connection with the Greens and she gave her name as Beth Green. She demanded to know what had happened to her "husband" Eddie, and whether or not he was dead. She asked to be put in touch with Eddie Green's mother, Margaret, but otherwise she refused to cooperate. She did not ask for a lawyer. She did not want to talk to her own family.

Increasingly, however, Beth looked like a star witness to the FBI if they could just get a handle on her, and they decided to hold her incognito in their St. Paul offices. This was to be where she ate and slept from April 3 until April 10, when she was transferred to the Ramsey County jail.

During the first days that Beth was in custody, the FBI assigned Special Agent Thomas Dodd to find out as much about Eddie Green as he could and to find, through Green's associates, where John Dillinger was hiding out. Dodd's first job on the evening of April 3, prior to Beth talking at all, was to identify whom it was that the FBI had ambushed on Rondo Street.

In later years, Thomas Dodd joined the group of well-known, and sometimes infamous American crooks, politicians and officials with whom Beth Green had contact during her wild days in St. Paul. Dodd was a Yale graduate who became a U.S. senator from Connecticut. Much later as Senator Dodd, he too was to have troubles with federal agents over financial improprieties. But in these early years, he seems to have been a popular and intelligent agent who used his considerable presence to lend a feeling of *gravitas* to a situation. He also appears to have been a very good stage director, an actor along with other inventive agents at Eddie's bedside in Ancker Hospital.

Within a few hours of the shooting, Dodd was around the town trying to find out what the FBI had accomplished on Rondo Street. Eddie Green was unconscious and neither the St. Paul police nor Federal files could identify who the wounded man was. The local authorities had no information on the arrested woman or the Terraplane. Leonia Goodman had not given Beth and Eddie's real names when she was arrested on April 3. But Dodd and his superiors were convinced that the FBI had caught an underworld character and that the underworld would know who was shot.

To that end, Dodd began to open up contacts to the St. Paul mob. A St. Paul policeman, Frank Marzitelli, took Dodd to a party the evening of April 3 in either a brothel or speakeasy. As the two men questioned a young lady at the party, they discovered that she knew who was gunned down off Rondo Street. Dodd took out a notebook in preparation for taking a statement and the young lady unceremoniously threw them out. According to Paul Maccabee's interview with Marzitelli in 1991, the policeman then told Dodd "Tommy, you have a hell of an education, you went to Yale, but they should have taught you how to remember [without taking notes]." The policeman talked their way back in and the woman told them the person who was shot was Eddie Green and that he had worked in the local underworld for a long time. After Dodd reported his finding, he was assigned to Green's room at Ancker Hospital in shift with other agents.

Someone, probably with the St. Paul police, knew the wounded man's identity right away and relayed this information to Eddie's brothers and mother, and Harry Sawyer on April 3. On the morning of April 4, Eddie's mother and brothers along with Roman Catholic priests came to Eddie's room. By this time the FBI had decided that it was essential to get as much information from Green as possible even if they had to fool a man who was, in all likelihood, dying. The game that the agents played allowed them to stage manage those hours when Eddie was in and out of delirium as well as that later time when he was in and out of consciousness. Their goal was to keep Eddie talking whether or not his family was present.

Dodd and the other agents took notes about what Eddie said in his delirium. But Eddie's potentially incriminatory ramblings were interrupted on a regular basis by Eddie's mother and brother who were almost always at Eddie's side. Eddie's family encouraged him not to talk and when he did, they tried to drown out his words. In any event, none of what Eddie said was entirely coherent.

As a result of having identified a solid connection between the Greens and Dillinger, Hoover ordered H.H. Clegg to supervise Beth's interrogation. The first useful information that Beth Green supplied the FBI directly came late on April 4. The FBI told Beth that the delirious Eddie Green had confessed to being with Dillinger in the shootout at the Lincoln Court Apartments. Beth knew this was not true and told the FBI that Evelyn Frechette had driven Dillinger to the apartment that Beth shared with Eddie immediately after the shootout. Beth and Eddie had then taken Dillinger to a physician to be treated.

The FBI had found receipts and registration papers in Beth's purse, from the General Acceptance Corporation, a Minneapolis "finance and locating" company for cars. Faced with this evidence, Beth also provided information on Dillinger's car and the Terraplane, which linked the cars to Thomas Filben, the owner of General Acceptance Corporation, and a well-known underworld fixer and supplier. (The registration on these cars was to an R. Coulton and his brother, Clarence Coulton. A week later, these men, who appear to have been associates of the Barker-Karpis gang, were arrested and they began to fill in details of the story that Beth gave to the FBI.)

But on April 4, the FBI had only one sure name besides that of Eddie Green, and on April 5 they arrested Thomas Filben and brought him to their St. Paul office, where they held him for two days and questioned him. They also started looking for a crooked doctor named May.

Filben appears not to have helped very much, although he was known already to the FBI and, of course, the St. Paul police, as the owner of the Patrick Novelty Company as well as the General Acceptance Corporation. This 'novelty" company was a long-term front operation for the sale and installation of slot machines in the area. Filben was an associate of Harry Sawyer. Filben was also associated with Sam Taran, who was at a senior level in the Twin City mobocracy. (Taran, Bennie Haskells and others who were identified during this period as being mob chieftains continued to operate in the area legitimately and otherwise until the 1960s.)

Beth did not provide more information than this for a day and a half. It was clear that she knew a great deal, and with Eddie frequently incoherent, she was the FBI's main hope. Rorer wrote to Cowley, and Cowley passed on to Hoover that given her intelligence and poise, Beth Green might be the "brains" of the Dillinger gang.

The FBI still needed a handle on her. By April 6, the FBI had determined that Beth Green's real name was probably Bessie Skinner. This information came, inadvertently through Leonia Goodman who said that Beth had also hired a friend of Leonia's, Opal White, to cook and clean for Beth's son, Leonard Skinner. The FBI interrogated Opal White at length and found out that Leonard was a "senior in high school" (sic, actually he had graduated) and was boarding with a respectable family. He was later to marry the daughter of his landlord.

After Special Agent Peterson extracted this information, he then wrote to his superiors that Bessie Skinner had an eighteen-year-old son (sic) in the Twin Cities and that this was "an imposing lever to hold over her head as a means of obtaining information." Opal also told Peterson that Beth had a good friend named Grace Rosenthal (called "Aunt Grace") who could provide more information about Beth and Eddie. Opal mentioned "Consola" and "Blondie" among other working girls, and these two also remained Beth's friends throughout her long life.

The FBI began to expand its net as a result of the interview with Opal, the searches of Beth's purse and person, and questions Beth was now answering however misleadingly.

On the 6th of April agents interviewed Grace Rosenthal, who lived on Summit Avenue in the ritzy part of St. Paul. Grace told the agents that she knew neither Green nor anyone named "Colter" (sic) but had seen a man matching Eddie's description with "Bessie." She stated that she had known Bessie since 1929 when Bessie had owned a share of the *Alamo* restaurant and nightclub on White Bear Road and lived with "Roy" (actually Ray) Moore, "who was Bessie's man at that time." The *Alamo* was a notorious crooks' hangout, according to the FBI, and helped to link Beth to Harry Sawyer who was now its owner. Thomas Filben had also been an investor in the place. Later, in the federal women's reformatory, Bessie was to tell the prison authorities disingenuously that she had "kept the *Alamo* dry" during those days as manager.

"Aunt Grace" was, in reality, one of the more up-scale Mesdames in the Twin Cities, and her house was located close to the Mayor's mansion and the James J. Hill house, as well as to the St. Paul Cathedral. Beth had fled to Aunt Grace's house and hid out there when she had broken up with racketeer and gambler Moore in 1930. From Beth's old address books there is reason to believe that Beth and Grace Rosenthal's relationship went back much earlier than 1929.

Inspector Clegg ordered that Beth, or "Bessie," as the FBI was now calling her, continue to be questioned around the clock and he now took part in this questioning. He spent the night of April 6 and 7 interrogating her and by 6 a.m. on April 7, Beth had begun to crack. She asked about Eddie and his condition again and again, and she began to see that the FBI was so fixed on capturing Dillinger that if she cooperated, she might save something of her life. Clegg had noted that, "there seemed to be some friction between [Beth] and Dillinger." The FBI told her that they had not yet released anything about her identity to the press.

She told the FBI that Dillinger's gang was probably still in St. Paul. She identified Tommy Carroll and John Hamilton as members of the gang. She noted that she and Tommy Carroll's girl, Jean Delaney, had lived together briefly in early 1934. She described the meetings with Dillinger and Billie Frechette on March 29 and 30. She made a detailed statement on the shootout at the Lincoln Court apartments. She identified Homer Van Meter as the man who had shot at the policeman and FBI agent there. She mentioned a small young man called "Jimmy"; this was "Baby Face Nelson," who when socializing with the Greens called himself "Jimmy Wilson." She told the FBI that if they wished to catch Jimmy, they needed only to shadow his wife "a poor little thing" to whom "Jimmy" was devoted.

She described some of Eddie's association with the Barker-Karpis gang and she pointed to the *Alamo* night club as a place

Dillinger might be found. She gave an address where the FBI could look for Dillinger that was similar to Augusta Salt's as well. Immediate FBI raids at the *Alamo* and the apartment, which turned out to be the wrong address, yielded nothing.

She began to talk in considerable detail about the Barker-Karpis gang; she said that she had managed a night club in the fall of 1932 (the *Alamo*) frequented by the two Barker boys and Alvin Karpis; these men were sometimes accompanied by an older woman they called, "mother." She linked this gang to the kidnapping of Edward Bremer a few months earlier. In this connection, she mentioned the name "Sawyer." The FBI became increasingly convinced that they had a star informant, especially given their recently renewed investigation, because of the Bremer kidnapping, into how the St. Paul mob was organized.

She said that she knew about the "Kansas City Massacre," Verne Miller and Frank Nash. She also told Clegg that she knew nothing about Roger "Terrible" Touhy, who was then jailed for the Hamm kidnapping, or about the Lindbergh baby's kidnapping. She did imply that she thought that Touhy, a Capone rival, probably had not kidnapped Hamm.

At this point in time, the upper echelons of organized crime were in some disarray in St. Paul. The St. Paul mob boss, Leon Gleckman, was about to stand trial for tax evasion. The FBI was watching Harry Sawyer's home carefully, one of several times that they were to do so in the hopes of catching illegal visitors to the fixer. Beth now told the FBI, "Sawyer *was* the connection to the underworld" and because of Harry Sawyer's relations to the police, Saint Paul remained the safest place for mobsters. "Harry is always tipped off before raids are made." she said.

On April 8, Beth provided more information about the immediate occurrences in St. Paul, and included discussions of the "boat house" where Dillinger might be hiding, if he could not be found in an apartment. (The "boat house" was actually a pier/

club/houseboat combination on the Mississippi, which was a gang hangout. The FBI raided it that night with no results.)

On April 9, the FBI opened two safe deposit boxes with Beth's authorization. One contained about $4,500 and was held under the alias "Elizabeth Kline." The next day, the *St. Paul News* said that this box was held under the name of "R.Coulton," confusing details of the story.

The other safe deposit box had about $5,000 and was held under the name "Bessie Hester Hinds." This was Beth's maiden name. For the first time in the process, the FBI had found a name for her that could not be construed as an alias. They did not know that yet.

❋ ❋ ❋

At Ancker Hospital, in addition to Thomas Dodd, other FBI agents were always at Eddie Green's bedside. While Eddie's mother, brothers and priests (including the Archbishop of St. Paul) were also there trying to keep Eddie focused on his soul rather than his past, they could not be there all the time or stop Eddie's ramblings even while there.

As already mentioned, an elaborate piece of theater was organized by Thomas Dodd and other agents. Agents took the roles of doctors, nurses, priests, gangsters and Beth Green. In these roles, they tried to induce Eddie to provide information. After Beth had already given the doctor's name to the FBI, Eddie provided the name of Doctor Clayton May and also gave some locations where Eddie and Beth had lived.

By April 8, the newspapers in the Twin Cities were beginning to recognize that the towns had real image problems as a result of the Dillinger shoot-out. Editorials were being written all over the country deploring the corrupt atmosphere in St. Paul. For example, the *Baltimore Evening Sun* said in an editorial "Way back in February Attorney General Cummings made certain slighting remarks about the state of law enforcement in St. Paul. The honorable William Mahoney, mayor of St. Paul, replied with a good deal of heat to these charges. It cannot be said that Mr. Cummings has yet conclusively proved that St. Paul is a "poison spot of crime." But the developments of the last few days make pretty good supporting evidence."

The papers were also hanging on all the reports that the federal authorities were issuing from Ancker Hospital and the Pioneer Press called Green the "best hope for clues" about Dillinger. For a brief time on April 8, it looked like Eddie might survive and the morning newspapers were reporting that too. Then an infection set into his brain. The evening papers were reporting that he was near death on April 8. He became increasingly delirious before sinking into a coma on April 10.

The presence of family and priests, and Eddie's Irish Catholic guilt may have come through to him on his deathbed. Just before he became comatose, Eddie mentioned the names of Harry Sawyer, Leon Gleckman, the Ramsey County (i.e. St. Paul) Deputy Sheriff, and others as being in the mob. He also gave details on his, and others involvement in the Sioux Falls and Mason City bank robberies. He said that he got $7,100 for Mason City and $7,650 for Sioux Falls. He confessed to having planned the robbery of the Kenosha, Wisconsin bank with the Barker-Karpis gang; and said that they, rather than Roger Touhy, had kidnapped Hamm. He said that he was in on the robbery at Racine, Wisconsin with Dillinger and that his share was $3,000. All this information except the part about Racine was probably true.

But Eddie also told Dodd that the Dillinger gang had four automobiles, none either a Hudson or Terraplane; that he, Eddie, had married Beth on July 14 and Dillinger was present at the wedding; that Eddie had given Beth $35,000, and that Dillinger was now in Scranton, Indiana. Nope, you couldn't trust what Eddie said, even when he was dying.

At about this time during the interrogation process, the FBI told Beth that the press was eager for a story and there had been a lot of speculation about the "red-haired woman" who was with Eddie Green when he was shot. The FBI also told her that they had identified Beth's son as "Leonard Skinner" and knew that she was Bessie Skinner. They knew she had family in the Twin Cities and elsewhere in Minnesota. There was every reason for Beth to believe that if she did not cooperate the FBI would turn the press loose on her family.

Bessie Hester Hinds came from a family that was anything but overtly criminal. Her brother Adelbert, who had died the previous year, was a jockey, and liked to gamble. Her brother Almon, a car salesman, may have had some connections to Thomas Filben, slot machines, and illegal liquor, but he mostly stayed on the right side of the law.

(Mostly. Almon's daughter, Cleo, did recall, however, that one evening in the winter of 1931, her father parked his car on a Minneapolis street so that another car could use their garage for a few days. After several days, Almon moved his car back into the garage and Cleo's mother, Winnie, was the recipient of a new fur coat from the "renters." She speculated that her father was helping to hide a car that was used in criminal activities.)

Then there was another brother, Pharos Beatty, who lived in Northfield, Minnesota. By 1934, P.B. was one of the more prominent residents of that college town, helping to lead the local Boy Scout organization, head of the Community Chest drive, and a well-known businessman. While he did know, and taught his grandson, how you hold dice to increase your chances in craps, he was eminently respectable. Coincidentally, Eddie Green's mother Margaret Ryan Green, was also from Northfield.

Beth had her family and friends to protect and was not going to give all she knew to the FBI without getting some concrete benefits. She wanted to retain the Essex Terraplane; the money held in her accounts and found on her person was legally hers, and she needed protection.

More than anything else, she wanted to see Eddie, and she said that only if he died, would she give the FBI what they wanted in detail. She swore that if Eddie lived, she could not supply any more information. The FBI knew that Eddie was not going to live. They did not need to apply any more pressure to her. There is a brief statement in the FBI files that proves that the FBI did take Beth to Ancker Hospital as Eddie was dying, they cleared his room and let her be alone with her comatose lover, and she was the last person who cared about him to see him alive.

The FBI had acceded to Beth's terms. Now Beth filled in the gaps and corrected the errors in her previous statements; she made a full confession.

Interestingly, the FBI agreement was piecemeal and they thought the centerpiece of the deal was the protection of Beth from publicity. Rather it was to protect her family. The FBI record of the deal reads thus (April 13, 1934): "She has advised that she desires her real identity kept strictly confidential in view of the fact that she is the mother of LEONARD SKINNER, and she does not desire any publicity which would in any way reflect unfavorably upon him or which would enable her son to identify her." According to Beth's remembrances, only her brother Almon was aware what had happened and later that she was going to Alderson prison.

The deal which was struck held for almost fifty years: Beth's real name was not used openly or to the press; her family was to be kept out of the news, and she told everything she knew about Dillinger and the other mobsters associated with him. Beth gave increasingly accurate information as time went on, and her usefulness to the FBI ceased only when Dillinger was dead and the Barker-Karpis gang was broken up.

Many of the details of Beth's confession were immediately released to the papers. The story in the *St. Paul Pioneer Press* of 12

April, 1934, stated:

"The information [below] has been given to federal authorities and police in a series of confessions by <u>persons caught in a round up here</u> [emphasis added]. Eugene Green, who died on Wednesday at Ancker hospital, eight days after he was shot down by department of Justice agents contributed some of it.... His wife [sic], held by the federal authorities for harboring John Dillinger, a fugitive, is reported to have given more.

But <u>others</u> [emphasis added] whose identity has been held in the greatest secrecy by the authorities, for fear they will be killed by the murdering gang, have given even more."

There were no "others" at that point, at least according to all FBI and court records. Some, like Thomas Filben were questioned and later released, and there were weak links then and later in the St. Paul mob, e.g. the "Coulters." The FBI could piece together earlier informants' stories. There was some corroborative information. But the "persons" who "told," were Beth and Eddie Green, and only Beth was still alive. To continue with the *Press*'s story:

> "As a result, the members of the gang now sought are:
> Harry Campbell, Tulsa Oklahoma
> Alvin Karpis, Tulsa
> Fred Barker, Tulsa
> "Doc" Barker, his brother, Tulsa
> Tommy Carroll, Mankato [MN], St. Paul and Tulsa
> John Dillinger, Indiana and Chicago
> John Hamilton, Chicago
> Homer van Meter alias Wayne, Chicago
> George (Baby Face) Nelson, Chicago'

'Among the crimes for which the gang or its members are wanted are:
Murder near Webster, Wis., of George Anderson,
alias Cooper, father-in-law of Karpis, April 23, 1932.

Holdup of the Third Northwestern National Bank,
Minneapolis, December 16 ,1932, two Minneapolis policemen killed,
one St. Paul man, a passerby in Como park as the gang switched autos,
shot and killed; loot $20,000.

South St. Paul payroll holdup; August 25, 1933,
one policeman killed, one wounded; loot $30,000.

Robbery of the Union State bank, Amery, Wis., September 13, 1933,
loot $46,000.

Holdup of Federal Reserve messengers with mail sacks on Chicago street
September 22, 1933, one Chicago policeman killed, no loot.

Holdup in St. Paul of the Railway Express agency, September 11, 1933,
loot $5,000 in cash and $75,000 in non-negotiable securities.

Holdup of the First National Bank of Brainerd, Minn.,
October 23, 1933, loot $32,000.

Attempted holdup of the Marquette National Bank, Minneapolis, November 13, 1933, foiled by the escape of an official;
gang escaped when warned by a radio call to police squad cars.

Shooting in St. Paul of Roy McCord, 11 Alice court, January 13, 1934
on mistake of his airways uniform for that of a policeman.

Kidnapping in St. Paul, January 17, 1934, of Edward G. Bremer, who was held 22 days and released after payment of $200,000 ransom.

Murder of Theodore Kidder, St. Louis Park salesman, March 4,

after his auto
collided with that of the gang on Lake street in Minneapolis.

Holdup of the National Bank and Trust Co., Sioux Falls, S. D., March 6, 1934
one policeman shot and seriously wounded, loot, $50,000.

Holdup of the First National Bank of Mason City, Iowa, March 13, 1934,
two persons wounded, loot, $50,000."

This story, released by the FBI to the press, however was misleading as to its main source. Instead it accurately reflected information that the FBI got from Beth. Beth's knowledge, while helpful on the Dillinger case was extraordinarily detailed about the Barker-Karpis gang and the St. Paul mob.

From Beth, the FBI and police got the information that the current membership of the Dillinger gang varied at various times. In fact, there were two "Dillinger gangs" which occasionally 'hired out' personnel because of their specialties, or 'hired on' free-lancers. Beth also provided considerable information on each gang member, and she knew or had information on the members of "both" gangs, and their molls, often with acerbic comments.

Beth had another reason to need the FBI's protection beyond avoiding publicity for her family, keeping property or seeing Eddie.

That reason was named Harry Sawyer. That it was dangerous to be a moll who informed was obvious. One of the hallmarks of the Danny Hogan and Harry Sawyer system was the assurance that no one informed. There is no better example of this than the fate of Margaret "Indian Rose" Perry and her friend Sadie Carmacher. Margaret, in early 1932 had only <u>talked about</u> squealing on Barker-Karpis and Harry Sawyer. A month later both were found shot dead, disfigured with acid and in a burning car.

If you compare Beth's confession to the FBI of April 11 to the press reports, it is clear that the information released by the FBI to the press came from Beth.

Had Harry Sawyer been aware that Beth was giving information, he would have had her killed. In the event, he did not know whether she was talking at all and he tried to find out by "helping" her and the Greens, sending his lawyers to represent her and Eddie's family.

In addition to providing misleading information to cover Beth's aid as a witness, the FBI did not tell the press all the information it had received from Beth. This served both to protect on-going investigations and also was cover for Beth. For example, there is no mention of the information that Beth had already provided on the Hamm kidnapping in 1933. She knew Sawyer was involved and that his rival, Jack Peifer, had helped to plan the snatch. She said this to the FBI. That information was to prove an embarrassment to the federal officials, when it was discovered to be accurate. It showed that the government had arrested the wrong man by hanging the charge on Roger "Terrible" Touhy.

The FBI kept the information that Beth was adding to the FBI files on the corruption in the St. Paul police department, city hall, and judiciary very secret. Hoover did fulminate on crooked officials in St. Paul, as did Attorney General Homer Cummings both before and after Beth's confession.

A small piece of information that Beth repeated to the FBI, only adding to what they already knew, was ultimately fatal to Dillinger. She confirmed to the agents how much he loved motion pictures. The FBI did not report this to the press, although it had appeared in magazine stories. In July, the authorities used this knowledge when it set Dillinger up at the *Biograph* movie house in Chicago.

As the Dillinger angle faded from the front pages in St. Paul, Beth's and Eddie's story grew in the local press, perhaps owing to local sympathies. Although Beth's true identity remained secret, the public image of Eddie and his "red-haired wife" went through a sympathetic change.

Sympathy from the Twin Cities press toward Beth and Eddie can be seen undergoing this gradual evolution. The initial reports in the St. Paul and Minneapolis newspapers after the ambush on Rondo Street appeared with three and four column headlines on the front page. They all describe the dangerous "gangsters" at the ambush and the brave federal and local "gangbusters." These stories are not accurate about, or sympathetic to either Eddie Green or "the red-haired woman."

Two points will indicate their inaccuracy. First, the St. Paul Pioneer Press on April 4 has Beth sitting in the car, saying "Don't shoot, there are no criminals here!" And a few paragraphs later, it has her jumping out of the car saying approximately the same thing before kneeling beside Eddie.

Second, the paper also has the FBI speeding up behind Eddie Green's auto and spraying the back with machine gun bullets while Beth was inside. It is doubtful that Beth said anything at the time, and there was no speeding car of Feds. Shortly after the shooting, St. Paul police and more G-men, including H.H. Clegg, arrived on the scene, as did a police ambulance; but it appears that the earlier dramatic stories relied on civilian witnesses at the scene and creative journalism.

In their next reports, the Minneapolis Star and the follow-up Pioneer Press stories concentrate on Eddie's relationship to Dillinger and paint him as a well-known criminal and associate of criminals with a long police record. This is the story provided by the FBI and St. Paul police in press releases and interviews immediately after the shooting. The press accepted it without question and was not at all sympathetic.

For the record, these first stories in the press were also inaccurate. The underworld knew Eddie to be a criminal, but in the public record Eddie had not served any prison time since he got out of Stillwater Prison in 1930.

The FBI and St. Paul police made a larger mistake in their version of the story. Against what several witnesses said, they tried to blame Eddie Green for the shooting on Rondo Street.

The information provided by the FBI said variously that Eddie had a gun, and then when no gun turned up, that Eddie had made a "suspicious move." The coroner and the eyewitnesses agreed that Eddie was shot in the back. He had no weapons. Most of the people who knew him were not crooks, or at least not in the Dillinger league. But he was also popular and well known in the underworld in St. Paul. He had not been arrested since 1922.

In fact, Eddie's value to the mob, especially as a "jug marker" was that he could easily pass as ordinary, 30 something, well off citizen, with a pretty wife, a nice car and money to deposit at the bank.

The next thing that seems to have started the press being more sympathetic to Eddie was Bessie. She was initially described as attractive and well dressed. She obviously loved Eddie. Eddie's mother, Margaret, believed that Beth and Eddie were married, and the FBI, the press and the courts all acted as if the marriage was real. It is hard to see "Beth Green" who was cooperating with the FBI as an under-aged and tough-girl gun moll. The FBI needed Beth's help and had no other Federal criminal interest in her. Thus, after the initial stories they did not blacken her name.

Then there was Eddie Green's mother and brothers, always at his side in the hospital, where the St. Paul Roman Catholic establishment also visited Eddie. Eddie's desperate struggle against dying was reported and also made him into a more sympathetic figure.

The public also doubted the veracity and ability of the government and the police. Immediately after Eddie Green's capture and Hoover's self-aggrandizing comments on it, Attorney-General Cummings sent a note to the Director asking sardonically whether the FBI was capable of guarding the wounded Dillinger gang member (Eddie) in the hospital. This was meant to remind the Director that the FBI had let Dillinger escape from the Lincoln Court apartment.

Just as this mistake was fading in the public's eye, on April 23 and 24, before Beth's trial, there was the fiasco when Dillinger and his gang escaped again, this time from the resort in Little Bohemia. This event caused the FBI's competence to be questioned again by many newspapers around the country.

There was also fear expressed by both conservative and liberal newspapers and magazines in the country that giving a "national police force" more responsibility might lead the FBI to become like the secret police in the fascist nations then forming in Italy and Germany. This fear led to criticism of the FBI as an institution.

At a local level some of these concerns also surfaced. Shortly before Eddie Green's death the St. Paul press began to question whether the FBI had acted correctly in Eddie and Beth's capture. It was reported that the Ramsey County attorney's office had announced, on April 12, that it was beginning an investigation into Green's shooting. After the coroner's report, the St. Paul Pioneer Press raised the question of whether the FBI had shot too soon and killed an unarmed man. The paper reported that the County planned on bringing its evidence before a grand jury inquest on April 25.

The FBI had a response to both national and local criticism. The national criticism was answered in interviews and articles and, in time, in such books as *Ten Thousand Public Enemies*. On a local level, Hoover gave instructions to his agents in St. Paul to speak to the rival papers in Minneapolis in order to contradict the growing public impression that the FBI was dispensing "frontier justice." He also wanted to squelch local investigations into the FBI's handling of the Dillinger matter. He did not entirely succeed in this.

Doubts about the FBI did not go away. Similar accusations surfaced again after John Dillinger was shot down in the summer of 1934. In 1936, it was reported in the national press that Secret Service agents were investigating the Dillinger and Green shootings. These stories appear to have originated in an attempt from within FDR's administration to stem Hoover's growing power. In Congress there was an effort to combine the various national investigative agencies in a single agency.

Both the President and Attorney General supported Hoover, however, and the Secretary of the Treasury was forced to apologize for "the irresponsible actions taken by [Secret Service] men." Nonetheless, the FBI released a self-serving story from its "secret files" which was picked up and printed on August 11, 1936 by the Minneapolis Tribune. The story is a web of innuendo and inaccuracies, and repeats many of the earlier untrue stories about Eddie Green's shooting.

CHAPTER 15

The Trials, and Beth Green Goes to Prison: "A Mistake in Identity"

While Eddie was in the hospital and Beth was incarcerated, Eddie's brother, Jimmy, contacted Harry Sawyer and Harry seems to have arranged for a senior criminal lawyer who was beholden to him, named Edward K. Delaney, to help Beth. The FBI investigated Delaney at Hoover's request and found hearsay links to Sawyer, Danny Hogan and others in the area's rackets.

Delaney was joined by two young lawyers who were just starting careers in criminal defense. These three lawyers, in their petitions to gain access to Beth, claimed to be acting on behalf of Beth Green's relatives and family. They tried to get Beth sprung as soon as it was known she was being held. She refused their assistance. She knew that none of her family was even aware that she had been arrested although she could assume that Eddie's mother and brothers, her "in-laws," did.

Beth appeared in court on April 7 to be charged, and bond was set in the amount of $25,000. Although Beth had not asked for a lawyer when she was first arrested, the lawyer Delaney who was described by FBI agent Peterson as a "shyster" was there, and he sought her release. His petition was denied.

On April 10th, Beth had to appear in court again. Delaney and his colleagues had continued to press for a lowering of the amount of the bond and Beth's release. The lawyers moved the court to issue an order permitting them to interview Beth. The United States attorney acting on behalf of the federal jurisdiction stated that he had reason to believe that Beth did not want to be talked to by the lawyers. The three lawyers wishing to see Beth seemed to doubt this representation, so the judge ordered Beth brought before the bar. He had her stand next to the three attorneys and asked her to look at them. He then asked her whether she had ever seen them before. She said "No." The judge next asked her whether she had engaged them to represent her. She said "No."

Then the judge asked her when she had sought any legal representation. Again, Beth said "No."

The male members of the Green family were actively hostile to the FBI at this point, small wonder: Frank Green, Eddie's brother was arrested the night Eddie was shot and brother Jimmy Green had also been questioned by the FBI. Both Frank and Jimmy were associated with the St. Paul mob. Frank was a numbers runner and had sold bootleg whiskey and Jimmy was a gofer for Harry Sawyer. Frank and his mother had been in the hospital room with Eddie as he lay dying. Whenever Eddie appeared not to be delirious, Frank had urged him not to talk to the FBI. Eddie's mother, Margaret, was another story. She was honest and loving and devoted to her family.

In addition to any questions of self-interest, the Green family was fond of Beth and they probably thought that the lawyers would help her. Beth and Eddie had lived with Eddie's mother for several months the previous year after having returned from Chicago, and Mrs. Green thought that they were married, and treated Beth like a daughter. About this time, April 10, Margaret contacted Beth's brother, Almon, who she knew, and told him that Beth had been arrested. (There is a very sweet letter to Beth in prison from Beth's sister-in-law, Almon's wife Winnie, telling her the news of Mrs. Green, who sent her love and describing Eddie's grave and monument.)

Beth wanted to keep her blood relatives in the dark about her problems, and she knew that her family, excepting Almon who was talking to Beth regularly, would be horrified by her notoriety. The family may have been semi-tolerant of wrongdoing, but if so, their tolerance took the nature of "We don't care what you do, as long as you don't do it in the street and frighten the horses." Beth had done it in the street.

Harry Sawyer (and his lawyers) and the Green family were not the only people interested in seeing and talking to the "redheaded" woman, Beth Green. So was the public, or so the press claimed. The story of the Green shooting had run regularly in the St. Paul papers during April.

In mid-April, reporters from the St. Paul papers, particularly the reporter "Mr. Thompson" from the St. Paul Dispatch, pursued the story of a supposedly scheduled public inquest into the death of Eddie Green. The inquest was held, in part, to see if Eddie really was "shot in the back." When the inquest did not occur immediately, the press asked that it be initiated.

Hoover stated to the U.S. Attorney General on April 20 that the inquest was proposed by the reporter for the purpose of obtaining a newspaper story and photographs of Bessie Skinner (Beth), and learning her aliases. Hoover stated that he had squelched the inquest at Beth's request, and because she was furnishing valuable information concerning Dillinger and his gang, and the activities of other notorious criminals.

On April 15, the Federal courts received a Teletype from the three lawyers seeking Beth's release on a writ of habeas corpus. A few days later the FBI obtained Beth's formal written statement that she did not wish to have a defense attorney, that she was willing to plead guilty to harboring John Dillinger. The information on her guilty plea was kept secret until May 4. Shortly thereafter she agreed to being represented for civil matters by a lawyer recommended by the FBI.

The memo from Agent Cowley to Hoover stated in full: "In talking with Mr. Clegg at St. Paul he advised that they had obtained a lawyer today for the Green woman; that he is a young man of high standing; that he prefaced his talk with her by advising her that he was not going to take any part in the concealing of any crime or evidence of a crime; that he is representing her civilly. Mr. Clegg stated that they could not overhear the entire conversation but that the lawyer is a close personal friend of Agent Hall and that Agent Hall is having lunch with the lawyer today." The lawyer's name was Harold Stassen and Hall had worked with him on investigations of the Barker-Karpis gang.

Like Thomas Dodd, Stassen was to make a peculiar mark upon politics, becoming the youngest Governor of Minnesota, the man who, with the aid of Hubert Humphrey, really cleaned up the corrupt Twin Cities, and who, along with his friend Alger Hiss, was a United States representative at the founding of the United Nations in San Francisco in 1945. In 1956, Stassen was instrumental in seeking Richard Nixon's replacement on the Republican ticket and was the man who many speculated would replace Nixon as Eisenhower's Vice-President during Ike's second term. Stassen was also a many time independent candidate for President of the United States--the last time in 1988.

Stassen, who in the mid-thirties was also Dakota County (South St. Paul) Attorney, seems to have done a very good job representing Beth in her civil law needs. She retained the Essex Terraplane and all the money that the FBI found in her brassiere and safe deposit boxes, and the car and money were waiting for her after her return from prison.

During the time Beth was being interrogated by the FBI, the

federal prosecutors in the district were beginning to use the information she provided to build a wider case. After Eddie and Beth had identified the doctor who treated Dillinger's wounds, the FBI was very eager to find Dr. May. They had hopes that he could provide them with material evidence as to Dillinger's condition and whereabouts. On April 5, Thomas Dodd had managed to track down May through another piece of theater He posed as a man who sought an abortion for his girlfriend and was directed to May's back street "office." Dodd caught May red-handed. May was in the the "operating room." Dodd also arrested Augusta Salt, the nurse. Close by, he also found Mrs. Salt's eleven-year-old son who later testified in the trial.

✷ ✷ ✷

Dillinger came back to Chicago from his family reunion in Indiana on April 8. On April 9, he dropped Billie Frechette off in front of the State and Austin Tavern on State Street. There, Melvin Purvis arrested Billie and came close to getting Dillinger. Billie was not cooperative after she was arrested, but she was questioned for several days by the FBI.

Her statement came three days after her arrest. It confirmed most of what Beth had just told the FBI about events in St. Paul surrounding the shoot-out at the Lincoln Court apartments. Billie, however, provided no information that the FBI could use to advance the hunt for John Dillinger.

At this point, the FBI speculated that, by holding Billie, the gangster's inamorata, Johnny like Gary Cooper in *Beau Geste*, would do the honorable thing and would ride in to her rescue (and his capture). This was not a totally vain hope. In fact, Dillinger's attorney, Louis Piquett, later stated that Dillinger appeared in a car in front of the court house in St. Paul during Billie's trial in late May. Johnny called Piquett over and asked how the trial was going and how long Billie was likely to be in jail.

A FULL CONFESSION

The government operatives were, however, also realists. The federal attorneys had the recent events in St. Paul cold, they had Beth's agreement to appear as a witness for the prosecution and their best case against Frechette was for harboring Dillinger in the Twin Cities. When questioned by agents about other criminal activities there, she had nothing to contribute about any doings of the Barker-Karpis gang or the St. Paul mob.

Because the case in Minnesota was sure, the federal attorneys originally planned that Billie appear at the trials to be held soon in St. Paul as a defendant and witness against Beth, Dr. May and Augusta Salt. She was transferred to the Twin Cities on April 25. Beth, Billie Frechette, Clayton May and Augusta Salt were all formally indicted on April 28 for harboring Dillinger.

Dillinger was once more front-page news during late April. Again, the press releases from the government indicated that the FBI had a great need to look competent. The context of the need was that Dillinger was continuing to make fools of his pursuers and the Twin Cities press; the press across the nation was reporting a bloody farce in Wisconsin.

As noted earlier, on the evening of April 24, the FBI had raided the Little Bohemia Lodge in Manitowash, Wisconsin. Dillinger, Baby Face Nelson, John Hamilton and Homer Van Meter all escaped again. Commentators, humorists and local officials were laughing out of one side of their mouths and criticizing Hoover out of the other. But Nelson had shot and killed law enforcement officials and the lawmen had shot innocent locals. In response to the whole fiasco, the federal authorities need to prove they were able to accomplish <u>something</u>. At this point, Hoover ordered that Beth Green be taken to Chicago to be interviewed by Melvin Purvis; Hoover seems to have been hoping that Beth could provide even more information than she already had given. (There is no record that Beth went to Chicago then.)

201

The Trials

When she was arrested, Beth's naturally auburn hair was made even more red by the use of henna. J. Edgar Hoover's had frequently expressed his distrust of women with red hair. According to Anthony Summers, in his 1993 expose of Hoover, "Official And Confidential," Hoover had even told the New York Round Table that a female criminal "always has red hair... She either adopts a red wig or has her hair dyed red."

For whatever reasons, Hoover seems to have been less judgmental when it came to Bessie Skinner. Perhaps this was because Beth was as close to a star witness as the FBI and federal prosecutors could find in the upcoming trials in St. Paul. Beth was cooperating completely by this time and she appeared less self-serving and much more reliable and presentable a witness than Dr. May. She was more knowledgeable and considerably more intelligent than Billie Frechette. May was an abortionist and Billie had trouble putting a sentence together.

On April 27, Dr. May's attorney had arranged for him to talk to the press. May provided a story of having been forced by Dillinger at gunpoint to provide medical care. He was more that happy to incriminate Billie Frechette and Beth Green. This remained his position throughout the trial. May's attorney, who also represented Augusta Salt, arranged for the press to know that the FBI had interviewed Mrs. Salt's eleven-year-old son who was described in the press in sympathetic terms. (Mrs. Salt was not convicted.) In addition, the papers were reporting that the FBI was questioning associates of Harry Sawyer concerning Dillinger's whereabouts, and was actively searching for Albert "Pat" Riley, Sawyer's chief hanger on.

At about the time of Eddie Green's death, Beth had been transferred to the Ramsey County jail, and she was officially held there up until her indictment. She was in consultation with the prosecutors and FBI at that time, and was providing information on her co-defendants in the upcoming arraignments and trial. If she did go to Chicago to talk to Melvin Purvis and discuss the St. Paul mob, it was between April 28 and May 2.

On May 2, Beth Green, Dr. Clayton May, Augusta Salt and Evelyn Frechette all appeared in federal court and all pleaded "not guilty" to harboring Dillinger, and in Dr. May and Nurse Salt's case "not guilty" to treating his wounds and not reporting the fact.

Because Beth had already agreed to plead guilty and had agreed to appear as a witness against the others, in private she had told the judge that she would plead guilty, so that now her "not guilty" plea was a ruse, engineered by the prosecution to keep the other defendants thinking that she, like them, was only concerned with the consequences of the Dillinger shootout at the Lincoln Court Apartments.

Although the government was continuing its part in the cover-up to protect Beth, the press began to pick up on considerable indirect evidence that Beth was cooperating, and that she was giving additional information, at least on the Dillinger gang. On May 4, the St. Paul Dispatch was speculating that she was to be the principle witness against Dr. May and Augusta Salt. In similar stories, other Twin Cities' papers also have May and Salt contending that it was Beth and Eddie Green who brought Dillinger to them, and that Eddie held them at gunpoint, making them treat Johnny. The press reports strongly suggest that Beth had talked to Melvin Purvis by this time and given copious information about Johnny's gang.

In the press, it also was reported that her life had been threatened by Dillinger gang members, and that was why she was turning against him and his gang. Realistically, Dillinger was on the run after Little Bohemia and his gang was not much threat to her. The press, as it had earlier, was creating more Dillinger drama.

Even the Attorney General of the United States chimed in on Dillinger in St. Paul during the first week of May. AG Cummings had already indicated his intention to prosecute Dr. Nels Mortenson for treating Dillinger, after the Mason City robbery. The U.S. attorney was unable to find a federal case against Mortensen, however, so Cummings was excoriating him in the press. Cummings also said that the May/Salt case showed how terrible it was that Minnesota had no law that would require physicians to make immediate notification of treatment of a gunshot wound. Dillinger's escape was hot news.

Beth had little to fear from the gangs of bank robbers: She had embarked on an even more dangerous path. She was continuing to provide, in greater and greater detail, information on the whole mob structure in Minneapolis and St. Paul. Her history since 1924 guaranteed that she knew a great deal about the way St. Paul worked. She did not need protecting from Dillinger, she needed protecting from Harry Sawyer.

When Beth was called before the federal judge again on May 5, she pleaded guilty to the charge of harboring a federal fugitive and it was reported in the papers that she was planning to turn states evidence. Immediately after her plea in the courtroom, surrounded by federal agents and marshals, she was hurried out, through a side door and through several other courtroom halls and doors to evade observation and danger. Leaving the court, she was first taken by FBI agents to Ramsey County jail where it was reported that officers were placed on special guard duty around her cell. It may be that these efforts were designed as well to keep her away from the press as part of the cover up agreement - despite all the front-page articles on the trial, her picture never appeared in the paper.

The information that Beth provided on the St. Paul mob between early May and the time of her trial, was comprehensive. She talked about the mid-level mobsters detailed knowledge of how the mob was organized in St. Paul, as well as further information to impart on the Barker-Karpis gang. During this period, she began to discuss in detail the names and agendas of the corrupt officers in the St. Paul police department. She fingered in particular Officer Bill McMullen. Thus, when shortly thereafter, Officer McMullen was directed to lead the investigation into St. Paul based gangsters by his supervisor, the FBI knew where to set up surveillance.

Newspapers throughout the period of the arraignments and trial refer to the "the red-haired woman" and almost always identified her as "Beth Green" or Eddie Green's wife. Nowhere was she called Bessie Hinds or Bessie Skinner. In 1936, an enterprising reporter found her real name in a follow up story but that story did not seem to "have legs" so late in the game.

J. Edgar Hoover preferred to call her "Bessie Skinner" and while the FBI might have been leaking some information related to Beth's cooperation, the FBI was not releasing any personal data on Bessie.

Beth's sentencing was deferred by the judge until after the trials of the other defendants. The deferral was intended to ensure her testimony against Billie, Dr. May and Augusta Salt. If she balked in her testimony, the judge would give her a harsher sentence. The FBI was also preparing to try to ensure that whatever sentence was given by the judge would work to their advantage in having Beth available to provide further information for a period of time.

During the trial of Doctor May, the St. Paul Dispatch disclosed that there was a secret witness against him. This was Dolores Smart, for whom Beth had already expressed her disdain after she had witnessed Smart and May's sexual antics in front of

Dillinger at the "clinic." The Pioneer Press described Smart as "the 22-year-old blond and attractive girlfriend" of the doctor." However, the paper also disclosed that the star witness at the trial against the other three defendants was to be "Mrs. Beth Green, widow of Eugene Green... [who] has pleaded guilty to the charge of conspiracy to harbor Dillinger and is expected to take the witness stand against the three...."

Beth could not have been pleased to have her name linked with Smart's or to have even this information about her possible cooperation available to Harry Sawyer. But it was better than it might have been. Dr. May, Mrs. Salt and Billie Frechette were not in Harry's circle and could go down without causing him worry.

During his testimony Dr. May tried his best to blacken Beth and show Eddie Green as a gun toting and threatening gangster. But May's early association with the Green family, which was a matter of criminal record, and which Beth also had discussed, was significant in persuading the judge that Dr. May was grasping at straws in his defense. At May's trial, Beth helped the court understand what Clayton May's role was in caring for Dillinger. She indicated that May knew who his client was and demanded more money because of Dillinger's notoriety.

Beth was less forthcoming about Augusta Salt; Mrs Salt was there but operating under May's direction, according to Beth. Mrs. Salt appears to have had both a good lawyer and a loyal son on her side as well. In any event, the court found Salt not guilty but sent Dr. May to prison for two years. His medical license was subsequently revoked.

During mid-May 1934, while the government was preparing its case against Beth, Billie Frechette, Dr. May and Mrs. Salt, there were other, more private actions being taken to curtail criminal activity in the capital city. At this time, a gentleman named Wallace Ness Jamie arrived in St. Paul. He was not with the FBI. In fact, he was working for the *St. Paul Daily News*, and a group of concerned citizens, who had hired him to head a team of investigators, and look into police and other municipal, mob-related, corruption.

Jamie's credentials were impeccable: his father was Alexander Jamie who had busted Al Capone; his uncle was Eliot Ness of the Untouchables. Beth Green was not involved in the civic effort responsible for Jamie's hiring. Wallace Jamie deserves the credit for getting the goods on Harry Sawyer and company, and the fall of the St. Paul mob consequent to his work, and he shares this credit with the *St. Paul Daily News* and the committee of concerned citizens. But Beth did provide information to the FBI that eventually went to the investigators and that helped the reformers to direct their search.

It is easy to understand why St. Paul citizens might be interested in a clean-up. As a major and continuing irritant to civility the police department was corrupted almost throughout, and the "O'Connor layover system" was no longer even protecting businesses in St. Paul. Although many officials claimed to be reformers, and a new "reform minded" chief was installed in the spring of 1934, there was no discernible change in the levels of criminal activity.

In fact, steps were afoot to broaden the influence of the Harry Sawyer owned cops. For example, shortly before Beth was sent to prison, she gave some interesting information on the political scene in St. Paul. Tom Brown, who had been demoted from his position as city Chief of Police was made Chief of Detectives. He was then assigned to a job that took him around to all precincts in town. Perhaps disgruntled with this role, he planned to better his lot, with Harry Sawyers connivance. He had, therefore, in February, started a campaign to be elected sheriff of Ramsey County (St. Paul). During March, Beth had been responsible for collecting and delivering campaign contributions to him. Beth stated that these contributions came from

Eddie Green, John Dillinger, Homer Van Meter, John Hamilton, and "Baby Face" Nelson, among others.

Until the time of the trial, Beth Green proved valuable to Hoover in his search for Dillinger as well as because of the other information she provided. On about May 20, Hoover set in motion a plan to ensure that Beth remained available to give information to the FBI for at least a year, and that she remained safe.

The FBI spoke to the Director of the Bureau of Prisons, in order to ascertain whether Beth might be sent to the Alderson, West Virginia federal reformatory, where the FBI would have easy access to her. The answer was that if she received a sentence of less than a year she would be sent to the prison in Milan, Michigan and could be paroled within six months. In St. Paul, the FBI spoke to the U.S. Attorney, and the U.S. Attorney spoke to the judge. As a result, Beth, who was more than cooperative, received a longer sentence than she might have. (Although less cooperative defendants received even longer terms, e.g., Billie Frechette was sentenced to prison for two years, which she served.)

On May 23, Federal Judge Gunnar Nordbye sentenced Beth to a 15-month term in the federal women's industrial reformatory at Alderson, West Virginia. A few hours earlier, a jury had returned a verdict of guilty in the cases of Dr. Clayton May and Billie Frechette. Billie was sentenced to a two-year term, and Dr. May was sentenced to two years in the Leavenworth, Kansas penitentiary.

Before sentence was passed at Beth's trial, her lawyer, Harold Stassen, urged leniency. He argued that Beth had a 19-year-old son and family in the area. He also recalled that the FBI had received considerable information on the Dillinger gang from Beth. The report in the St. Paul Dispatch describes her at sentencing: "Mrs. Green is 36 years old. She wore a dark brown fur trimmed coat and a dark brown felt hat that she wore down over her head in an effort to conceal her face. As she approached the courtroom, she hid her face behind a brown pocketbook apparently on guard against reporters."

Although Nordbye and the Bureau of Prisons were responsive to his request, Hoover was still not satisfied with the sentencing arrangements. Again, an FBI agent approached the U.S. Attorney, and the attorney went to Judge Nordbye. At the government's request, on May 24, Nordbye ordered that U.S. Attorney General Cummings select the place of imprisonment for Billie Frechette. (She went to the prison in Milan, Michigan; a much harsher sentence than Beth's both in terms of time and in terms of place.) While no reason for this disparity was reported in the press, Beth had been far more cooperative than Billie, and did not not have the arrest records that Billie did.

Two days after her sentencing, Beth was placed aboard the Milwaukee Line "400" for Chicago and ultimately West Virginia. She was to make at least two stops en route to prison. The first stop was brief and was at Alma, Wisconsin. There, Beth met her niece, Cleo, who was 18 years old and a brand-new bride. Cleo's mother Winnie was also there.

Cleo had been married two weeks earlier, and it was only just before the time of her wedding that she learned that her favorite aunt, Aunt Bess, could not attend because Bess was under arrest. Cleo was married in a Depression wedding, a small affair with family and two witnesses. She was doubly disturbed that her aunt could not make the wedding, and determined to see her. As Cleo asked what had happened she was told that Bess was in custody because of "a mistake in identity."

It was a few weeks later when her mother, Winnie, called to tell her that Aunt Bess would be coming through Alma on the train that she also learned that Bessie was going away to prison. At that point Cleo continued to think that the authorities had the wrong person.

During the brief visit at Alma, Beth made final the arrangements for communicating with her family: She arranged that Almon's wife, Winnie, would pretend that she was Beth's sister, and Beth would address her brother as "A.R." in letters. Only Winnie, Cleo and, if he would, her son Leonard were to know where she was and write directly to her. Beth's mother was not to be told anything, and if the other brothers or outsiders were to find out that she was incarcerated, they were to be told that she was imprisoned wrongly as the result of the "mistake in identity." Beth's motives in this charade have been enumerated, but to Cleo she emphasized that she wished to keep the press confused if information should leak to them.

The other important stop that Beth made on her way to prison was in Chicago. The FBI had arranged with the U.S. Marshal's office in St. Paul to bring Beth to Chicago where she was to be turned over to a U.S. Marshal operating there. She was to be held at Cook County jail for forty-eight hours while Melvin Purvis and H.H. Clegg questioned her. Then the Marshal Service was to transport her on to Alderson. The FBI's purpose in arranging this stopover was their interest in getting an identification of locations in and around Chicago where gangsters, especially Dillinger, might go for help or to hide. They also had a list for her of crooks, ne'er-do-wells, and gangsters who may have been guilty of general mopery. The FBI wanted Beth's input and Beth was questioned once again in detail. The FBI had hopes that a little additional information could be squeezed out of her.

Beth arrived in Chicago on Saturday May 26. On that day and on Sunday, Beth Green, Marshal Newby, Special Agent McIntyre, and H.H. Clegg toured Chicago and environs. They asked Beth to point out places where Dillinger and members of the Barker-Karpis gang might be found. She pointed and she started by showing where she and Eddie had lived in Chicago in the spring of 1933 when they were there doing business for Harry Sawyer with the Chicago mob.

The apartment that she pointed out was also a place where the two Barker boys and their Ma had lived in December, 1932. She said that Doc Stecci, who was helping to run the empire for Al Capone while Al was in prison, had directed Eddie and Beth to this apartment.

While in Chicago in early 1933, Beth and Eddie had bought a 1933 Essex Terraplane from the same dealer that handled cars for the Barker-Karpis gang. She pointed out this dealer's showroom, and discussed who the fixer was for these deals. She provided guidance to four other locations in Chicago where the Barker-Karpis gang members had lived.

By 1933, Beth had become well acquainted with many famous bank robbers and thugs, and she saw (or met) some of them in the Windy City. She told the FBI about her contacts there with Earl Christman, Volney Davis, and Verne Miller whose wife Vi, Beth said, was a good friend. She showed the FBI the locations where some of these people had lived. She stated that at this point Eddie was involved with the Barker-Karpis gang when they robbed the bank in Fairbury, Nebraska. (In his memoir, Alvin Karpis does not mention Eddie as being in on this job, although other crooks said he was there; it is probable that Eddie's role there was as "jug-marker," that he did not go into the bank with a gun.)

When Beth was taken back to the Cook County hoosegow on the evening of May 26, she found that her accommodations there did not meet her standards. The next morning, before setting off on tour again, she complained to Melvin Purvis. She told him that her bed was very bad and uncomfortable. In order to keep her in as good spirits as possible, Purvis called the jail and requested that better accommodations be afforded her. The jail obliged. Beth, after all, was providing him with valuable information on the mob structure in St. Paul in addition to her information on gang venues in Chicago.

On the 27th, Beth and her entourage roamed outside Chicago. Beth pointed out *Buckley's Eating Place* a favorite outdoor barbecue for the gang. *Buckley's* was of outside town on a rural highway. She pointed out a bar by the Veteran's Hospital that was a gang hang out and she talked about the haberdashery habits of the gang members. The Barker-Karpis and Dillinger gangs seemed to have a particular fondness for clothing from *Maurice L. Rothschild's*, patronizing both the Chicago and St. Paul stores.

She told how crooked car dealers would fix license plates by means of a device that would stamp a line in the proper location so that by application of paint it was possible to make a naught look like an eight. Then she took the agents to the garage where this was done. She identified a garage that Fred Barker owned in St. Paul, where this service was also performed.

Either Beth was beginning to be exhausted or she was running out of useful information. According to the FBI files, the last piece of information she gave in Chicago concerned Ida Gold, a letter from whom was found addressed to "Myrtle" when a raid in Des Moines on May 26 had just missed discovering the Barker-Karpis gang. Beth said that both Ida and Myrtle Eaton worked with the mob. Ida's husband was a small-time fixer in St. Paul and Myrtle was the moll of William Weaver, a sometime member of the Barker-Karpis gang. Beth said that Ida and Myrtle had a taste for fur coats and together from time to time would use the "old poor girl- rich girl trick" in stealing them. This was weak stuff in comparison to earlier facts that Beth had provided.

A day after Beth's departure from Chicago en route to prison, a wire service reported that she had been brought to the FBI offices there and questioned; various papers picked up this story and speculated that Beth was asked about the whereabouts of Dillinger.

J. Edgar Hoover was livid that this information was leaked to the press. He wrote a very cold letter to Melvin Purvis, who up until that time was a favorite of his, and demanded an explanation. Purvis was unable to provide any explanation but tended to place the blame on the Cook County jail personnel; Purvis told Hoover about the special treatment Beth had received in improved accommodations. He theorized that this better than ordinary treatment might have led jailers to know that they had an important guest and to contact the press.

Beth transferred trains in Pittsburgh in order to go to Alderson, West Virginia. In Pittsburgh, the FBI's Special Agent in Charge was J.J. Waters, and he was to be Beth's last FBI handler.

(Alderson is not an elite prison. At the time of Beth's incarceration, inmates were expected to work while they were there. It does have some notoriety for having later housed many well-known prisoners such as Billie Holiday and Martha Stewart.)

When Beth arrived at prison (she was "received" on May 30), the prison authorities, had given themselves to the latest in sociological and "penological" theories and their expression. But they still did not trust all these new-fangled things completely. So, they measured everything they could from her intelligence on the Binet-Simon scale to the depth and condition of her vagina. They found that she was intelligent and that she had had tubal ligature several years earlier. They also attempted to judge her criminal physiognomy from the older scale. The results here were that she was not outwardly criminal.

A small mystery arose around Beth soon after her arrival in Alderson: Naturally enough, all the mail addressed to her was opened by prison officials and communicated to Agent Waters, who in turn passed the information on to Washington. On June 4, a letter was sent from St. Paul to Beth from a Margaret Harveaux.

This letter said that the writer was glad to get Beth's letter, and said how much Beth was missed "around here," but was glad Beth "enjoyed her trip" to prison.

It went on to say "The boy-friend was up and had dinner with me today and I let him read your letter, and he said tell her hello for me and a lot of luck. He is staying at the St. Paul Hotel since you left but thinks he will leave any time now." Waters was particularly interested in establishing "the boy-friend's" identity, "inasmuch as it appears that he may be closely related to Beth Green."

The FBI hopped right to the investigation, and did not have to look too far. About a week later, Agent Waters was informed that Ms. Harveaux was the matron who had watched over Beth when she was incarcerated at the Ramsey County jail in St. Paul awaiting trial. The "boyfriend" was FBI Special Agent George Costello, who was assigned to guard Beth at the jail. The three had struck up a friendship during the weeks that Beth was there.

During her entire stay at the Federal Industrial Institution for Women in Alderson, West Virginia, Beth was judged fit and cooperative, in the prison reports, as well as intelligent. She not only cooperated with the authorities there, but, during the first few months continued to work with the FBI as Waters and other agents questioned her about her connection to the mob in St. Paul.

Shortly after her arrival, an FBI agent from Pittsburgh, told her that Jean Delaney was also coming to Alderson. Delaney's sentencing arrangements were manipulated by the FBI just as Beth's and Billie Frechette's had been. Jean Delaney was sent to West Virginia rather than Michigan, so that Beth could talk to Jean, who perhaps would provide some more nuggets on the gangs. Dillinger had not yet been caught and Hoover felt that Beth could help draw some information out of Jean that could help in the search for Johnny.

In prison Beth had regular contact with Jean Delaney who was assigned to live in the same cottage as Beth. This was not the first time that the two women had shared quarters. Jean Delaney had lived with Beth for a brief period in January 1934 and they were in regular contact until Dillinger came to town in March.

Beth was a dozen years older than Jean, and Jean felt that she could confide in Beth. In prison, Beth seems to have acted a bit as a protector for Jean. Nonetheless, everything that Jean reported to her friend Beth, Beth reported to the FBI. One of the things that Beth knew about Jean, and told the FBI at this point, was that two of Jean's sisters also had lovers who were involved with gangsters: one sister was Alvin Karpis's lover and the other was married to Pat Reilly.

She first lied to the FBI, and then to the prison authorities and continued to obfuscate and mislead them about her background and family. Perhaps her public crimes were such that the FBI took little interest in pursuing her personally. There are strong indications in books written about this era, with Hoover's approval, that Hoover was less harsh in his judgments of "Bessie Skinner" than he was of other molls.

In any event, she was smart enough to mislead in the details. The basic outline of her life, the outline that she gave to the FBI and for the prison records, was relatively accurate. But she did not seem at all compelled to provide accurate details about her life, and she was evasive with both her interpretations and omissions. This is what she said for the record:

She gave different accounts about where she was born, eventually specifying only North Dakota. She told her life to age 18. Beth recounted her move with Nelson back to Canada in July, 1917, and the bare bones of her leaving him early in 1918 and going from Canada, eventually moving to Minneapolis in late

1918 (sic, actually in the Spring of 1919). There she worked as a waitress and selling movie tickets.

In her autobiography written for the prison authorities, she skips a lot of history from 1919 to 1933, implying that she worked her way up in the restaurant business, stating that she worked at places that did not sell liquor, and implying that she lived without men friends. She stated that she met Eddie Green in August 1933 (she meant 1932) and cohabited with him from November 1932 to April 1934.

In her prison autobiography, in the FBI files and statements, and in various police and court reports, Beth Green tries her level best to paint herself as something other than a typical gangster's moll. With all her experience with Billie Frechette, and the girl-friends of the gangsters, and Aunt Grace, and now with Jean Delany in the same prison "cabin" as Beth, Beth had a good idea of the parallels and discrepancies between her life, and that of a "real moll."

Thus, both Beth Green and Jean Delaney had taken up with home grown, Irish Minnesota crooks and free lancers bank robbers. Their lovers both were signed on to the two premier bank robbing gangs of the thirties, and they worked together. Both Beth and Jean had their lovers shot down in front of them. (Another parallel was that these two gangsters were the only members of the gangs to be buried in Minnesota

Beth also seems to have felt compassion for the younger woman, and in a letter home, Jean Delaney said, "There are some pretty descent (sic) girls here and then there are the others of course. The majority are (sic) in for narcotics. There's a girl from St. Paul here Bess Green, I don't think you know her. She is very nice; we work together in the dining room."

Tommy Carroll, the gangster boy-friend of Jean, was a freelancer and a home-grown Minnesota associate of Harry Sawyer like Eddie. Tommy, again like Eddie, worked on several jobs for the Barker-Karpis gang, and was an early confederate of "Babyface" Nelson. Carroll moved from gang to gang, and from woman to woman, and did pick up work such as robbing the First National Bank of Brainerd, Minnesota, of $32,000 in October 1933.

(Carroll had several girlfriends, sometimes at the same time. The most famous of these was "Radio Sally" Bennett, a popular vocalist in the Twin Cities area. But his connection with the Barker-Karpis gang was in part owing to the fact that one of his girls, Jean Delaney, was the sister of Delores Delaney who was stuck on Alvin Karpis.)

From 1933 to late spring 1934, Tommy lived a very dangerous life and barely escaped the FBI raid on the Little Bohemia lodge. Tommy was shot to death as he and Jean sat in his car in a gas station in Waterloo, Iowa on June 7, 1934. The station attendant saw a bunch of different license plates piled in the back of Carroll's car and called the Waterloo cops who recognized him and his companion, Jean Delaney. Here too, was an echo of Beth and Eddie.

. Tommy Carroll, like Eddie, a good Irish Catholic and a Minnesota boy, was buried from the Church of the Assumption in St. Paul.) Unlike Beth Green, however, whose siblings were married substantial citizens, both Jean Delaney's sisters were "molls" Moreover, Beth would have been offended if these parallels were drawn in any way that implied that she was <u>like</u> Jean Delaney. Her efforts in prison and afterwards were to paint herself as a person of breeding and taste, a mature member of the community who has had some adventures, but is basically solid.

Because of her deal with the FBI, and in spite of "some backsliding" toward criminality in her life after prison, Beth Green mostly succeeded in this endeavor. Perhaps she succeeded because the truth was that she was both a criminal and an intelligent and empathetic person.

The prison evaluations of Beth's character are filled with

praise and kind words from officials throughout her stay. Phrases used included: "Splendid house member, quiet, courteous, does work well." "Sensible, always quiet, fine worker." "Attends class regularly, is a good pupil [with a] splendid attitude." "Attends strictly to her business, helpful, cooperative." "First to grasp instructions in class, has good brain and uses it." "Very refined and courteous." , "Very rapid worker, accurate and efficient." "Reads, member of Cottage book club."

❋ ❋ ❋

One of the things that the "good" Beth worried about in prison was what was happening with her son Leonard Skinner. Leonard was turning nineteen when she went to jail and just a year out of high school. He had two first cousins his age with whom he was close. One of his first cousins, Cleo, was already married, and another, Ray, was a freshman at St. Olaf College. Beth hoped that Leonard would follow the latter's example; but Leonard, instead of enrolling in the University of Minnesota when he finished high school, got a job at a refrigerator factory, ostensibly to earn money for his further education. (Ostensibly, because Beth had more than enough money to finance Leonard's higher education, although her access to it was limited from prison.)

In 1934, Leonard was dating the younger Kernkamp girl, Harriet, the daughter in the family in whose house he lived. He seems to have been quite smitten with her. He shared with her the little that he knew at that point of his mother's problems and answered a letter that Bessie sent to him on the occasion of his 19th birthday. The letter is full of discussion of what he and Harriet had been doing, and stories about friends whom he had known at high school and also details about Bessie's poodle, called "Smartie," who was left with Leonard and adopted by the Kernkamps when Bessie was jailed in a "mistake in identity."

The letters from Beth to her family, "Sister" (Winnie) and "A.R." (brother Almon), however, indicate that she was concerned that Leonard was on a path better taken by a more mature young man. She did not like the fact that he was only writing to her very occasionally. She was worried that the reason that he did not write her was because he hated her for being what she was and having done as she did. She was even more worried that he would get married to Harriet soon, when the Depression would make their life together difficult.

She could not do anything about these worries except express them. In a letter from prison to her sister-in-law Winnie, Bessie said," Hope Leonard doesn't get serious for a least two years. I think Harriet a very nice girl but the way things are with jobs so scarce and money so uncertain ...I hope he doesn't get serious until he is capable of making a dime and a decent living."

Remembering that Bessie Skinner was married at 15 and divorced at not much older than Leonard's, and that she had really tried to provided him with the material things, and given that Leonard was educated beyond her eighth-grade level and that the Kernkamps were very solidly middle class, she had real hopes that he would make something of himself.

Leonard was in love and HE didn't like the wild life, the life that he saw his mother lead from 1926 to 1934. He loved his mother. Later in his life he was to make this obvious.

But he wanted to make his own way and, as he approached age 20, he thought that included a home and family of his own. He did do his mother a favor and waited to get married until she got out of jail. Then on June 26,1935, a month after Beth was released from Alderson prison, 20-year-old Leonard married Harriet Gwendolyn Kernkamp at the Holman M.E. Church in St. Paul.

※ ※ ※

The Depression worried many more people than Beth. It changed the nature of crime in St. Paul and elsewhere as it changed the nature of most aspects of most American lives. But the Depression also carried with it a new political spirit, both nationally and locally. That spirit helped to end the police and gangster cooperation in St. Paul known as the "O'Connor layover system."

With the Committee of Concerned Citizens providing the political clout, with Leon Gleckman on his way to jail, with crimes of all sorts being committed within the St. Paul city limits, and with the town gaining a national reputation as the place for a crime spree, public attitudes began to demand a cleanup. Violence and violent crimes appeared too wide spread. The fall of the St. Paul mob, or at least a good portion of it, was inevitable.

CHAPTER 16

A Diversion: P.B. Moves to Northfield

In the mid1-850s, the very productive farmland of southern Minnesota, especially that part that was on the tributaries flowing into the Mississippi, was being developed both for planting wheat and for mixed farming. In 1854, a settlement had grown up on the Cannon River downstream from the prosperous milling town of Faribault. John Wesley North, a graduate of Wesleyan College, in Middletown, Connecticut, and one of the founders of the University of Minnesota, arrived at this location in 1856, in the hope of establishing a shrine to his industry and the virtues of New England.

The settlement that he found there, he wrote in a letter, was called "by the euphonious cognomen" of Northfield. North established a sawmill at Northfield, and also a grain mill and had a bridge built across the river. Shortly thereafter he supported the founding of a lyceum and encouraged settlement of the community by abolitionist and prohibitionist Congregationalists from New England.

In the Depression of 1857, investments that North had elsewhere in Minnesota failed and he left the Cannon valley, but he left a town, not just a settlement, behind him.

In 1858, Minnesota became a state. More mills came into

being along the Cannon. In 1866, Union General and carpet bagging Governor of Re-construction Mississippi, Adelbert Ames persuaded his father to manage a flourmill that General Ames had purchased on the Cannon at Northfield. The Ames wheat mills in Northfield and nearby Dundas, and a milk condensing plant sent Northfield flour and condensed milk across the nation and indeed around the world. Also, in 1866 the Minnesota Valley Railroad was established with Northfield as a main stop, and other railroads and highways began to make Northfield into a rich city. More settlers, many of them from Scandinavia, followed the rails and came to this area from the 1870s on.

Spiritual and intellectual life also grew as John North would have wished. In 1866, the Congregational Church Conference and citizens of Northfield established an academy for students who were going to go on to college or university; it was called Northfield College, and by 1870 a college program was adopted at the academy. In 1878, a philanthropist named William Carleton, from Charleston, Massachusetts, gave a large sum to the school on the understanding that it would be named after him.

The Baptists came and built a church in 1859. The Methodists came to Northfield in 1859 and built a church. The ubiquitous and sainted (at least in Minnesota) Rt. Rev. Henry J. Whipple established *All Saints Episcopal Church* in the town in 1867. (The Ames family in Northfield was Episcopalian, as were the Nuttings whose family manufactured hand trucks.) The Irish and Bohemian Catholics consecrated *St. Dominic's* that same year.

In 1872 the First National Bank of Northfield was founded by the Nutting and Ames families. That same year the *Lockwood Opera House* was established downtown on a nicely laid out square on the river. The Lockwoods were also Episcopalian. In 1875, the *Society for the Protection Against Horse Thieves* was formed and citizens were trained to respond to outlawry. That year Joseph Lee Heywood became Treasurer of the First National Bank, Treasurer of the city of Northfield and Treasurer of Northfield (Carleton) College.

In 1880, there were 2,300 people in Northfield including college students; the Norwegian Lutherans had arrived in numbers at this time and established their own college, named after the patron saint of Norway, St. Olaf. *Ware Auditorium* replaced the *Lockwood Opera House* in the mid-1880s, and Northfield continued to grow and prosper. Rich farmers and education allowed Northfield to revel in clean small town and country living and its proximity to the capital city of St. Paul, provided sin just a short distance away.

By 1926, when Bessie's oldest brother P.B. (Pharos Beatty, named for both his grandfathers) moved to Northfield from the failing Dakotas, the town was thriving on both sides of the Cannon River. The Scandinavian Lutherans controlled the west bank of the community, where P.B. moved. The program at St. John's Lutheran Church, the Lutheran establishment church, featured the estimable F. Melius Christiansen as organist and church choir director, and services were held in Norwegian on Sunday afternoon at 3:00 o'clock. Just off St. Olaf Avenue, lived O.E. Rolvaag who was teaching at St. Olaf College and still busy writing his prize-winning fiction about the settlers in the Dakotas.

Northfield did not have a Main Street, more tellingly its main street was called "Division Street." And it divided the east side of town from the west. As was true for Sinclair Lewis's Sauk Center, Minnesota in 1926, Northfield had its boosters and its booster clubs, and it also had a strict social hierarchy. Or rather, it had three strict social hierarchies: the New Englander and richest class lived on the East side of the Cannon. Norwegian Lutheran and rich, and "Bohemian" (Czech) Catholic, still rich, lived on the West. Each set had its own doctors, lawyers and leading businessmen. And in contrast to many towns, each hierarchy had a sterling intellectual institution located on site.

The Congregationalists were still tied to Carleton College. The quasi-New Englander "East-siders" also controlled local politics: the mayors of town from 1876 to 1944 were all WASPs, with an emphasis on the Anglo-Saxon.

The Norwegians had St. Olaf College, an institution with extreme rectitude, and some humor, founded in 1874, which prepared young men for the Lutheran ministry and young women for teaching music. In 1920, the St. Olaf College Choir, celebrating the College's 45th anniversary and led by the ubiquitous F. Melius Christiansen, made a world tour that included singing at Carnegie Hall.

The Norwegian Lutherans had intellectual heroes as well, not only Rolvaag, but Soren Kierkegaard's translators. Edna and Howard Hong, the great American authorities on Kierkegaard, were at St. Olaf. They were of Norwegian settler descent and they wrote a book for children called *Muskego Boy*, about an immigrant Norwegian youth in the 1880s. The transplanted New Englanders made do with the multimillionaire Nutting family, the professors at elite Carleton and the defection of the Scandinavian Thorstein Veblen who was a graduate of Carleton.

The Czech Catholics had the wealthy St. Dominic's Church and Rosary parochial school (1926) and the Northfield Foundry and Machine company (founded in 1920). Around the fringes of these three groups hovered the German Lutherans and the Irish Catholics. Outside of the town were wealthy dairy, pig and turkey farms and Northfield was pleased with itself: "Cows, Colleges and Contentment" went the town motto.

By the time P.B. arrived, there was one great common public institution, built in prime space and occupying a lookout's position over downtown Northfield. This was the Northfield Public Library, which was first organized in 1898, with a new building constructed with the help of Andrew Carnegie in 1910.

Also, by the time P.B. arrived, Col. Marion Savage of Minneapolis, owner of the most famous pacing horse of all time, *Dan Patch*, had finished his *Minneapolis, Northfield and Southern* railroad, and commuters were using the *Dan Patch* line daily to go from Northfield to work in Minneapolis, about 35 miles away.

Northfield had a criminal past, or at least a brief criminal episode, in which it took enormous civic pride; its great myth of the wild west. For it was in Northfield, on September 7, 1876, that the Younger brothers' gang, along with Jesse and Frank James, attempted to rob the *First National Bank*.

The robbery did not go well for the outlaws, and Northfield offered up a martyr to commerce: Joseph L. Heywood, the bank's treasurer and bookkeeper, was killed when he refused to open the vault for the gang members. Also killed, but with less fame attaching to the event, was Nicholas Gustafson, a Scandinavian farm helper who lost his life when he failed to understand the Missouri accents of the gang and did not get off the street in time to avoid being shot.

Those were the casualties on the civil side. The casualties among the robbers broke the gang. A. R. Manning, who owned the hardware store next to the bank, and who was a member of the Northfield *Society for the Protection Against Horse Thieves* shot one of the outlaws, the robber fell and died. H. M. Wheeler, a medical student home from the University of Michigan, shot another from the *Lockwood Opera House*. The gangs were driven away. Posses chased them southwest from Northfield, and most members of the Younger gang were killed or captured shortly thereafter.

The *Northfield News* was first published in 1876 and the great hold-up took place shortly thereafter but enough later that the *News* could provide front-page coverage to the story.

P.B. and Grayce seem to have been pleased by Northfield, especially the Protestant part of the town. The Norwegian Protestant sub-set, in contrast to the more staid New Englanders, seemed to show some humor and considerable inventiveness.

For example, the unofficial motto of St. Olaf College, which rose on a hill above the town, was "Built on a Bluff, and Maintained on the Same Principle." One of its football cheers in the mid-thirties was: "Football, baseball, swimming in a tank. We got money but we keep it in the bank. St. Olaf…St. Olaf. It's a college." Carleton was more snooty than that. WCAL the first listener supported public radio station in the country was founded at St. Olaf College in 1922. Grayce and P.B. subscribed to WCAL, bought books written by Howard and Edna Hong and other local luminaries, and sent their son to St. Olaf. They joined St. John's Lutheran Church where P.B. became chief usher.

Now, all of this local history and education might seem a bit daunting to an Orangeman from the Dakotas, married to a girl who was the maid in his grandparents' hotel. But Northfield, in the great scheme of things, would not prove a particularly tough nut for P.B. and Grayce to crack. After all, over his mother Minnie's clearly stated and remaining objections, he had married the "Norwegan," and here, in Northfield there were Protestant secret passages for climbing two of the hierarchies, the Scandinavian and the WASP: Odd Fellows and Masonic Lodges; P.B. and Grayce Peterson Hinds found their own. They were allowed to try to invent themselves, just as their parents had. Their children and grandchildren would try the same thing.

GRAYCE AND PHAROS HINDS WITH OFFICERS OF THE REBEKAHS IN FRONT OF ODD FELLOWS HOME, 1941 (PRIVATE COLLECTION-MHO)

And invent themselves they did. In contrast to his parents, David and Minnie, to his grandparents Pharos and Rebecca Pierce, and to his siblings, P.B. was successful in his self-invention. In 1926, P.B. was hired in Northfield as manager of the Gipson lumberyard. He was working his way up through the ladder as a regional manager in all the Thompson yards in the Dakotas. But in 1926, he was ready to go East again, and both his brother Almon, and his sister Bessie Skinner Walsh, lived a short train ride or drive away from Northfield.

Northfield was a good place to come to. Its real wealth was based in agriculture and education and while it had its moments as a boom community, there was solid and continuing base of expansion and building. P.B. made a very good career move, securing a place that was to hold him steady. The population of Northfield in the mid-twenties was about 4,000 people. It was growing steadily, but many of the downtown buildings and institutions already were in place. So new housing and commercial buildings were springing up around the town. It was frontpage news in *The Northfield News* when the Gipson Lumber

Company decided to build a new outlet in Northfield to sell building supplies, coal, and hardware; they brought in P.B. to manage it.

A fact of Northfield's history at this time, however, kept it somewhat hidden. It was a place that was contrarian. It wanted the highways that were being developed in the twenties and thirties to pass by. So, it became a place that lay on none of the major highways linking Chicago, Des Moines, or other cities to Minneapolis. And Northfield seemed just as happy when highway map-makers had a penchant for forgetting about the town's existence. The community was left off major road maps twice in the 1930s; ironic considering P.B.'s sister's profession and her use of highway maps in the same period.

Northfield, as a strict Prohibitionist burg and as a "Gopher Prairie," had its failings; in 1933 the town voted to allow 3.2 beer served in taverns, causing John Wesley North to spin in his grave. It kept up with all the liberal life agendas, and school busing for farmer's children was introduced early to the community. Later Northfield became an early proponent of water fluoridation. After World War Two it welcomed and helped to educate the largest settlement of "displaced persons" in the state. It may have been staid and content but it was a decidedly liberal place too.

The families in Northfield were happy to be away from the problems that beset American cities in the late 1920s and the 1930s. It almost seemed to Northfielders that all criminality, social unrest, and even the Depression were happening elsewhere. The dream of a better life, a life that included increasing educational opportunities, wealth, recreation and stability, was alive and active in Northfield in the thirties.

Pharos and Grayce and, perhaps, part of their progeny, grew, in Northfield, in the essential glory of America. This is not to say that P.B. really took chances or bet on much. He was obviously the smart one <u>and</u> the careful one in the family. He was truly known to wear belt, suspenders, sleeve garters and ink guards at the same time. (Much later, Bessie would say:" He only had two jobs in his life...." She meant he had one with the Thompson Yards and one with the Gipson company. This was intended both as sarcasm and as praise).

PART IV

FAMILY LIFE ON THE FRINGE:
Aunt Bess--Her Life After Beth
Green (died September 17, 1983)

ILLUSION: THE LUMBERMAN'S SHOW

One Easter Morning in the late fifties there was much rejoicing in the house where P.B. and Grayce's grandkids lived in Northfield, not because He Was Risen, even if He was, for that was celebrated with a hymn in a Lutheran home. Rather the kids were overjoyed because they had just heard that while their parents and grandparents went to Minneapolis for the annual lumberman's trade show for several days, they would be watched by Aunt Bess.

Aunt Bess arrived after the Easter service was over. She didn't go to church. She brought in wine and whiskey although a dry Easter was very Lutheran. She was wearing a gray sheared lamb coat, a cute black hat and driving a flashy new Pontiac. Her hair was very auburn for a woman who was in her late fifties. She was heavenly, and the opposite of the morning's sermon.

The grandkids thought they knew Aunt Bess well. She was cool, she was competent and funny, she never swore except when she was sewing, but she had a fast and edged tongue and a raunchy sense of humor. Their mom trusted her implicitly, and left the older girl and boy, and the considerably younger brother in her care, and even before, when they were babies.

She dressed well and drove fast cars. She sold liquor and had boyfriends, but no husband. From the late 1940s to the early eighties she was close to her Northfield family, especially the kids. Although she lived in Minneapolis and they lived some forty miles south, they saw her often, and she showed up for many family holidays, birthdays, and parties.

CHAPTER 17

Crime Continues to Pay, but Not So Well: The Clean-up of the St. Paul Police; the Fall--but Not the Demise--of the St. Paul Mobs

In 1936, when he was suffering intense public and political scrutiny, J. Edgar Hoover hired professional public relations experts to help set in motion a "spin" operation. One of the stories that Hoover had his writers tell, and they told it well, was the myth that the Barker-Karpis gang followed a coherent master plan. It was put about that the gang was a nest of brilliant criminal minds and none was so brilliant as "Ma" Barker, sexually voracious, dominating and a genius at planning crimes.

Hoover's instrument for perpetrating this hoax was FBI Information Circular #7-576. The circular is filled with misinformation and misjudgments from top to bottom. If there was such gang planning and brilliant efforts concerning the crimes that the gang committed while in St. Paul, Harry Sawyer was the planner. Even Harry, in reality, had very loose control. It was the on-going protection system and Harry's inherited contacts that made him central to the criminal web. Ma Barker, whom Hoover described, was a laugh; Ma Barker, according to Alvin Karpis did not even know what was going on.

In order for Hoover to tell his story in the way that he wanted to tell it, the FBI exhaustively researched their 1925-1936 files on the members of the gang, and related criminals. Then they changed the facts to come to the conclusions that they wished. This was the point when the Director began to refer to one of his chief informants, publicly, as "Bessie Skinner." In these papers, Hoover treated Bessie more respectfully than most "gun molls" and certainly better than Ma Barker.

Nonetheless, the extent and usefulness of the information Bessie Skinner provided to the FBI was never publicly acknowledged, nor did Bessie want it to be. Neither does the FBI talk about those criminals that Bessie fingered but who were corralled in the civic cleanup by authorities in Minnesota, not by the FBI. Hoover never gave much importance to those who the FBI did not arrest.

Names were mentioned in passing, Tom Brown, Sam Taran, Bill McMullen, Tom Filben, and Isadore "Kid Cann" Blumenfeld, but the FBI seems to have considered them only a local problem, even when they stole much more money and corrupted many more lives than Karpis or Dillinger. The Twin Cities mobs continued to operate well into the 1960s and the same names in the FBI files of 1925-1936, show up as the people who controlled the mobs for 25 or more additional years.

Hoover wanted a story that showed G-Men facing outlaw gangsters, even as Harry Sawyer or other capos directly involved with Barker-Karpis and Dillinger are not given much prominence in official FBI reports. In Harry Sawyer's case this is more than benign neglect, because the information that the FBI gained on the overall structure of the St. Paul mob in 1935 came indirectly from Harry and directly from his wife, Gladys, when she decided to spill everything to the FBI. Gladys's information led to the final demise of the Barker-Karpis gang. But it was not the FBI who took down the mob in St. Paul and honest history is not to be expected from Hoover.

Propaganda is, and Hoover portrays Hoover as the greatest crime fighter of a generation. To do this he gives the immediate members of the Barker-Karpis gang a prominence that he would never give the Mafia, or even organized crime in St. Paul.

Hoover also returned to similar self-praise in the book *Ten Thousand Public Enemies* that was written with FBI assistance, and glorified Hoover's battle against gangsters. Hoover provided the preface to this 1936 tome.

Arguably, the lack of acknowledgement by the FBI and Hoover of Bessie Skinner/Beth Green's role in the demise of the gangs and the mob was part of the FBI's promise to her to keep her out of the limelight. Hoover, however, is selective everywhere as to whom he gives credit. He does not care to give it to underworld informants even when the information they provided was what allowed Hoover to praise the skill and professionalism of "his G-men."

Not all people who could approach the public were so willing to place the blame on the gangsters and underplay the corruption of police and politicians that went along with "the O'Connor layover system." There were journalists in Minneapolis and St. Paul, and politicians, and concerned citizens who believed that the social contract was violated from top to bottom in the Twin Cities and that a new order was needed.

On the same day, March 31, 1934, that John Dillinger and Billy Frechette were making their escape amid Tommy gun fire from the Lincoln Court Apartments, and then seeking help and succor from Beth and Eddie Green, the St. Paul press was reporting that a grand jury in Ramsey County was about to issue a report that, in effect, called the city no more of a refuge for hoodlums than any other city of the same size in America. The grand jury's report, for many local authorities, was a happy whitewash. The grand jury refused to send up indictments, and instead praised the bravery of city cops.

As much as the grand jury report was to please the likes of Tom Brown and the Mayor of St. Paul, this public and journalistic exercise in self-deception was to be a final straw to reformers. The white wash was especially appalling to one newspaperman, Howard Kahn, the crusading anti-crime editor of the *St. Paul Daily News*.

Kahn had, for many years, been urging the city to act on corruption within the St. Paul police department in his editorials and implying that certain cops, whom he named publicly, were less than straight. In his media role, Kahn was a leader but not unique. Other newspapermen, including Walter Liggett in the Mill City, had increasingly expressed their anger and frustration over the criminal control exercised over civil life in the Twin Cities.

Well before Dillinger stopped in the Twin Cities in March, this reform movement was afoot, aimed at fixing the many things wrong with the St. Paul police and ending the "O'Connor layover system." Throughout the twenties and thirties there were regular efforts at reform; most citizens supported such efforts. However, one of the problems that civic reformers faced was that the moment a new chief of police was in place, he proved himself either incompetent or corrupt.

There had long been a progressive tradition in Minnesota, and citizen advocates of "good government" had long formed a strong movement in the establishment in both municipalities. Many prominent citizens, in addition to Kahn, were embarrassed by the national publicity the city was getting. St. Paul was becoming a laughing stock for its corruption and was named by U.S. Senators and Roosevelt administration officials as being one of the main crime capitals of America.

The mayor of St. Paul, William Mahoney, had decried Kahn's efforts and railed against the Senators and federal officials who were, in his view, unfairly blackening the city's name. He tried to point out to the good government advocates that his moderate administration could accomplish what they wanted without upsetting social order. The conservative newspapers agreed with him.

At the same time, reformers and good government advocates pointed to a bigger threat than that of marauding gangsters. This was the threat to civility and democracy that was a consequence of corrupt centralized control of law enforcement.

Shortly before the Dillinger escapade, for example, Tom Dahill was named Chief of Police. He was introduced as an honest cop, but soon appeared to be one of the long line of "reformers" who promised to bring in a clean department, but failed to act on that promise.

Although editorial opinion was split on whether Dahill could succeed, the new chief moved quickly to satisfy civic demands by getting rid of the police officers that were most obviously corrupt. He made several changes in the operation of the department. For example, he removed Tom Brown from a position of influence at headquarters and sent him out to inspect precinct stations. But, a year later, when there was unimpeachable evidence of police corruption, Dahill was proven to have acted much more timidly than his knowledge of the corruption would have allowed.

By April 1934, crime was not the only threat to civility and democracy in the Twin Cities. Violent crimes, kidnappings, and robberies where innocent by-standers were killed were frequently explained, by sociologists, as symptoms of the Depression. Outlaws were not revolutionaries, and few observers saw them as such. But "class" violence and discontent were also rising.

A FULL CONFESSION

The headlines on the front page of the establishment *St. Paul Pioneer Press* on April 7, 1934 are fascinating as a window to the relative importance that the local press appears to have given to crime, on the one hand, and possible revolution, on the other. This front page reveals the multitude of uncertainties facing the Twin Cities public at this point in the Depression.

Leading off the front page, top right, is a report under a banner headline stating that an "Arsenal [was] Found in Old Green Lantern Café (sic)... Dynamite and Guns seized in Dillinger Hunt....[Red haired] Woman's Identity Hinted."

The arsenal was a not particularly impressive weapons cache. The "red-haired woman" was Beth Green. Next to this article, to the left is a barely disguised pro-Republican Party boxed "story" which is actually an editorial, and which excoriates Minnesota's *Farmer-Labor Party*. (Minnesota had never really had a Democratic party at this point. The Republicans were divided into Progressives, still loyal to Teddy Roosevelt's principles, and the increasingly pro-business and anti-FDR Republicans.)

In 1934, the two political parties that counted for anything in Minnesota were the *Farmer-Labor Party* and the Republicans. The Farmer-Laborites were the home-grown populists who controlled Minnesota's state house. They were hated by the businessmen who controlled the *Pioneer Press,* and thought to be communistic, radical and dangerous. The Governor of the State, Floyd B. Olson was the creator of this populist consortium, a movement that combined some progressives, poor farmers, miners, union members, agrarian populists, socialists and self-described Marxists under a single banner. The *F-LP*, was likely to win big again in the next Minnesota elections in November 1934. The *F-LP*, however, was not itself a political party that crusaded against crime.

Next to the story about the *Farmer-Labor Party* is a two-column headline that says "Mill City Riot Quelled as 3,000 Jobless Quit Scene of Battle." A four-column picture below shows a mob storming the Minneapolis city hall as the police fire tear gas into their midst to quell the riots.

Tucked in between is a plea by the *Pioneer Press*'s management for contributions to a fund started by the paper and the police to provide weapons and bullet-proof vests to the police at least equal to those carried by the gangsters whom the police were theoretically hunting down. Gangsters, reds, and rioting workers all threatened Minnesota's capital. A corrupt and foolish looking police department only added immediate insult to potential injury.

During mid-May 1934, when Wallace Ness Jamie arrived in St. Paul, he was not with the FBI, in fact he was working for the *St. Paul Daily News*, Howard Kahn's paper which supported reform and the F-LP, and also for a group of concerned citizens formed to combat the image that St. Paul was suffering from nationally. He was reporting to the recently appointed St. Paul Commissioner of Public Safety, H.E. "Ned" Warren.

Warren was a real reformer and had ties to all the people and parties who really wished to clean up the Metropolitan area. A group of concerned and active citizens of St. Paul had asked Warren to hire Jamie to head a team of investigators, and look into police and other municipal, mob-related, corruption.

At about this time the police themselves, under Chief Dahill, set up a new flying squad to combat gangsters and move quickly against them before they could escape. This squad was set up under the direction of Officer Bill McMullen. This was the same Bill McMullen that Beth Green had talked about to the FBI in April. She had told them that he was "a friend to Harry Sawyer and a contact man between the police department and the underworld." In other words, Bill McMullen was an officer, probably the main officer, who told the hoodlums when raids were about to take place. No doubt the FBI agents were laughing sometime in June, when they shared this information with the reformers.

Beth Green was present and talking at a propitious moment for the reformers and the FBI was willing to share, quietly, information on the structure of the relationships between the police and mob that she provided. This in turn helped the reformers to direct their search. It would be foolish to claim that Beth's confession led to the clean up attempt and the fall of the St. Paul police-mob axis consequent to Jamie's work. She was not interested in reform. She was interested in keeping her role and name secret

Her confession was not essential, it only provided details, but it helped. As previously said, the decision to bring in Wallace Jamie from Chicago, taken at high levels among the best citizens of St. Paul deserves the credit for getting the most corrupt members of the St. Paul department either fired or imprisoned. The initial effort took several months, and Jamie was also thorough in his approach to recording and transcribing information. He gathered massive amounts of information which when published could only lead to one conclusion; that the St. Paul Police department was riddled with corruption. It is obvious that the St. Paul officials and citizens wanted to build a case that would break the back of the O'Connor system, as operated in 1934.

The investigation into police corruption in St. Paul took a full year. It was to change the criminal structure in the town to which Beth Green returned after her time in Alderson. Beth Green got out of prison just as the revelations in the *St. Paul Daily News* were at their climax. When the investigation and trials was over, even the "true reformer," now ex-Chief Thomas Dahill was shown to be tainted. The Chief that replaced Dahill, another self-proclaimed reformer Michael J. Culligan, was forced to resign.

The criminal system within which Beth operated was falling apart while she was in prison. Over that year indictments were handed down and trials were held. They involved some twenty police officers, detectives, and officials in St. Paul.

The most resilient of these officials seems to have been Tom Brown, yes that Tom Brown. While he was named publicly as a contact between Harry Sawyer and the police department, and while he was charged with having received a portion of the ransom money from the Bremer kidnapping, he was named but never tried. As a result of an assignment from the "reformer" Cahill, Brown was on outside detail during most of Jamie's recording time and little direct evidence could be found against him. Eventually Brown resigned, still proclaiming his innocence, and moved to northern Minnesota where he ran a liquor store.

Throughout this investigation and the subsequent arrests and deaths of the major gangsters in St. Paul, it was obvious to interested observers, such as Alvin Karpis, that there was a peculiar code of honor which still operated among the bosses in the capital city. When offered the opportunity by the FBI, Karpis refused to inform on Jack Peifer in connection with the Bremer kidnapping; his refusal, he says, was based on Peifer's earlier loyalty to Karpis.

As the heat turned up and the police corruption charges mounted, the local gangsters either scattered or hunkered down. Few of these men informed on their fellows for easier sentences, however, or provided much information about their connections with the police.

Therefore, Beth Green's confession may have been more than just useful; the collapse of the St. Paul mob itself began in earnest at the same time that the police were being investigated, that is in April and May 1934, after Beth Green gave information to the FBI that linked Harry Sawyer to Dillinger and to the Barker-Karpis gang. Beth Green's information was obviously helpful in the collapse. Beth's finger pointed directly at Harry Sawyer.

Beth had two straightforward reasons for hoping that Harry would be removed from the St. Paul scene. The first, and most obvious, was that Harry represented a great threat to her life. She could remember "Indian Rose" Perry. The second was that Harry had cheated the participants in the Fairbury, Nebraska, bank job, including Eddie, out of their "earnings"; when they gave part of the money and bonds to Harry to launder, he kept it all.

In part her confession was venal and retributive. When she talked about Sawyer's retreat not so far from St. Paul, a farm, where many criminals called on Sawyer and in early April John Hamilton had hidden out, Beth had a certain satisfaction. She said that this place was a possible hideout for Dillinger as well. She supplied the thought that Harry Sawyer might be harboring Dillinger on his farm. The farm was purchased with money owed to Eddie Green.

Harry was not unaware that he was hated by colleagues in St. Paul. As the heat turned up during the investigation, Harry started to try to mend fences with the gangsters he had cheated. He gave money to some and did favors for others. He indicated that he was wiling to sell his interests in the mob.

Harry stood by some of his partners but was willing to see the cops murder others, e.g. Homer Van Meter. Although, Harry's wife Gladys was later to complain that Harry should have turned over his criminal companions, and not have been sent to Alcatraz, he was not totally a "stand-up" guy. It seems more than likely that Harry did a favor for his police contacts and gave up Homer Van Meter to the cops. Van Meter was shot dead in an alley in August 1934, in what has been described as a "police ambush" in Paul Maccabee's book. JDSH.

After the events in St. Paul in April, and up until mid-1934, Harry was more circumspect than usual. He and his wife Gladys attempted, in the summer of 1934, to adopt a little girl who was five years old. He not only began to act as if he were a normal husband and father, and a legitimate businessman, he also sought out certain gangsters to help them with their money problems.

In mid-summer, after Beth gave information on Harry's farm and Harry's police connections (e.g., Officer Bill McMullen) to the FBI, and the FBI had collected enough further information confirming what Beth had said to want to question Harry about the Bremer kidnapping case, Harry Sawyer went on the lam.

Harry took off for two reasons. He was likely to be arrested if he stayed in St. Paul and he needed money. Not only was the FBI seeking him for questioning, Harry had unfulfilled business to take care of. That business could gain Harry considerable cash. When he left St. Paul in July 1934, he was going to get the Bremer kidnapping loot from Alvin Karpis so that he could launder it. Although Jack Peifer had planned this kidnapping, Harry was in on it too, and was to handle the ransom. Harry also had stored away bonds from the Dillinger gang jobs in Sioux Falls and Mason City, but he could not use these. They also had to be cleaned. For these economic reasons Harry had to get out of town.

Harry also had to absent himself for legal reasons. The Bremer kidnapping plot was unwinding. Doc Barker and nine other alleged participants were arrested for the Bremer kidnapping between late 1934 and the end of January 1935. They went on trial in April 1935 and five kidnappers, including Doc Barker were convicted. Harry Sawyer was named as a defendant, and as a fugitive, he moved about the country visiting five states in seven months.

When the FBI caught up with Harry it was through luck and

family: Harry's wife Gladys was hiding out in Cleveland with the little girl whom the couple had expected to adopt. Gladys got drunk and disorderly at her hotel, and was hauled in by the police. The child inadvertently told the police who her mother was and after the FBI was called in, Gladys agreed to testify against Harry and gave the FBI information on where Harry could be found. He was finally captured in Mississippi in May 1935. The revelations about corruption in the St. Paul police department were then at their height and Harry Sawyer's name and connections were all over the place in the press.

Harry was tried in January 1936 and sentenced to life in prison. Gladys divorced him. Harry remained imprisoned until 1955, and was paroled that year when he was found to be dying from cancer.

Two other gangsters with whom Beth Green had dealings in her wildest times died sooner and more spectacularly than Harry Sawyer. Leon Gleckman, the boss both of Danny Hogan, and later of Harry Sawyer, was convicted of tax evasion in 1934, just as Beth Green was going to trial. This trial ended Gleckman's powerful hold on the syndicate in St. Paul.

Although the repeal of prohibition in December 1933 would probably eventually have had the same effect, in the event, Gleckman came back from prison and when he went back into the rackets in 1936, he was convicted again of tax evasion. After his second release, he was under investigation once more in July 1941, when he got drunk and drove his car into a bridge abutment in what his friends believed to be a suicide.

Jack Peifer, the owner of the Hollyhock's Club, was arrested at his club in April 1936. He was named in the Hamm kidnapping, as well as a principal in the Bremer job, and he was placed in the Ramsey County jail. He was tried and convicted in early May, and given a thirty-year sentence. Before he could be sent to Leavenworth Prison to begin serving his sentence, however, he swallowed a capsule of cyanide that someone had smuggled in to him in the Ramsey County jail, and he died.

Gleckman's jailing, Jack Peifer's suicide and Harry "Dutch" Sawyer going to prison were clearly signs of the demise of the St. Paul mob. But the O'Connor system had more resilience than that. So, it is not necessary to worry too long about the collapse of the mob in the Twin Cities, because, although badly damaged it never completely went away in 1936. The three chieftains, Peifer, Sawyer, and Gleckman, and all the bank robbers with some mild exception being made for Alvin Karpis, were only unlucky. They did not continue to profit from their crimes. They died in prison, poor or by suicide.

Others, whom Beth knew, survived, profited, and went on to live comfortable lives. From the ranks, Bob Walsh married, had children, continued to work for the *Schmidt* brewing company. He retired and bought an RV just as they were coming into fashion.

The Gleeman brothers stayed in the liquor trade, stayed honest, and made money at it.

Tom Filben, according to his *St. Paul Pioneer Press* obituary, was from a "well known pioneer St. Paul family" in addition to being a receiver of stolen goods. He survived, and prospered until he died in Palm Springs, California on September 6, 1973, rich, and with a wife who was a fine art and antiques dealer.

Filben had continued to make money from his various enterprises during all the years between 1935 and the 1960s. He made much more money on the slot machine rackets when slots became totally illegal in Minnesota under the crusading Governor, young Harold Stassen in the early forties. He remained well advised by police departments and advising the resorts in northern Minnesota, which sold illegal liquor and had illegal slots well into the early 1950s.

His customers would be warned by Filben's minions (including Beth's brother, Almon) when another Minnesota crusader, the Reverend Henry J. Soltau, would set out with federal and state troops to close down the dens of iniquity.

Interestingly enough, Tom Filben was questioned in, and had knowledge of, the murders of "Indian Rose" Perry and Sally Carmacher arranged by Jack Peifer back in 1932. Filben was also associated with Robert Perry, who was "Indian Rose's" estranged husband and a colleague of the bank robber "Shotgun George" Ziegler. Filben and his wife adopted and raised "Indian Rose's" and Ziegler's daughter.

The greatest survivor, however, appears to be Isadore "Kid Cann" Blumenfeld, the head of the Minneapolis mob. "Kid Cann" was born, like Harry Sawyer, in Rumania at the turn of the 20th Century. Blumenfeld was a young man during the time he ran the Minneapolis mob, younger than Beth Green and Eddie Green, younger than Harry Sawyer. He was the same age as the members of the Gleeman-Gleckman syndicate who were in their early twenties when they, and Blumenfeld, took over bootlegging in the Twin Cities. When he had installed his mistress to replace St. Paul's most famous madam Nina Clifford, he was 28 years old. When he attended Harry Sawyer's criminal ball on New Year's Eve at the *Green Lantern* in 1932, he was 31.

He continued to control rackets in Minneapolis up until the 1960s. He and his brothers, Yiddy and Harry Bloom, started out very early as tough guys, and made fortunes during prohibition They remained "the usual suspects" up until the Kennedy administration. His hold on the Minneapolis rackets lasted even beyond a late arrest when for the first time in many years Isadore saw the inside of a prison: in 1960 he was convicted of running a ring of prostitutes and sent to state penitentiary in Stillwater. He had last been arrested and sent away much earlier: he was convicted four times from 1920 to 1934 on bootlegging charges.

The *Minneapolis Sunday Tribune* in January 1952 published a brief history of Kid Cann's life up to that point, including an interview. Kid Cann had told the press that he was going to leave the Mill City for sunnier climates, perhaps Miami Beach, perhaps Palm Springs, mostly because he could not get any respect as a legitimate businessman in a town where everyone thought he was a crook.

Blumenfeld did not leave, but much earlier he had begun to winter over in Florida where he owned shares in several famous hotels in Palm Beach including the *"Fontainebleau."* (Like Kid Cann, the hotel has more letters than it needs in its name.)

"Kid Cann" did not much like his nickname, and the Tribune reported that his enemies gave out that it arose from his "old street fighting days when he would lock himself into a [public] latrine until peace was restored." Isadore himself disputed this and said that his nickname arose from his early days as a boxer with Sam "The Tailor" Taran.

The Tribune reported that Blumenfeld had two favorite hangouts in his middle age. One was the *Flame Bar and Grill* in downtown Minneapolis and the other was the *Artistic Barber Shop*. His fondness for the *Artistic* may have arisen because of a singular episode there in 1935. Anti-crime reporter and St. Paul newspaper editor, Walter Liggett was having his hair cut in the *Artistic* when a man came in and shot him to death. Liggett's wife who was waiting outside in their car swore in court that the man who walked in with a gun was Isadore Blumenfeld. Nonetheless, "Kid Cann" was found "not guilty.

CHAPTER 18

*Crime Continues to Pay, but Even Less Well:
Penny-ante Prohibition*

Beth Green was released from the Federal Industrial Institution for Women in Alderson, West Virginia, exactly one year to the day after she entered the facility in 1934. She had previously served seven weeks and three days in the Ramsey County jail (St. Paul), the Cook County jail (Chicago), and the FBI offices in St. Paul. The FBI had sucked her dry but on general principal it retained its interest in her information after she was released. Because most of the big crooks that Beth had information about, and in whom the FBI was also interested, were under arrest, in jail or dead in June 1935, the FBI dismissed her personally.

By June 1935, the FBI, and local authorities, were successful in tracking down Dillinger and like gangsters, eliminating threats to domestic tranquility, and had caught or killed a large number of the members of the Midwest bank robbing gangs and their freelance associates.

Local police, "valuable sources" such as Beth Green, and the very active involvement of the FBI in hunting down the gangsters who had killed fellow agents, had resulted, in the period between April 1934 and June 1935, in the elimination of most of the "romantic" gangsters. Among the dead were the freelancers such as Tommy Carroll, the psychopaths such as "Baby Face Nelson," and most of the Barker-Karpis and Dillinger gang members.

Beth's interest to the FBI was only because of the hunt for Dillinger and whatever information she provided on the Barker-Karpis gang and the agency was no longer of interest. Records indicate that they sought her help only once after she got out of prison in the summer of 1935.

After Bessie's parole to Hennepin County (Minneapolis), despite very minor checks by local parole officers, Bessie's niece Cleo says that the federal agents came to her father's home on 32nd Avenue only once, in July 1935. When they did not find her at her brother's home, they did not look any more to find her.

If Beth's status as a star witness had changed so had her personal life. This was symbolized by the fact that at her release on parole she was no longer Beth Green. She had resumed her legal name of Bessie Skinner and it was under that name that parole officers were to check up on her. Her conviction carried a three-month period of parole and the authorities in Hennepin County occasionally checked her whereabouts and employment status.

After her three-month parole, Bessie slipped out of the public criminal records. If personal reports on her post-prison history are to be credited, however, she continued to be active in the criminal life for at least ten years after her release. In her future, she managed to keep the sort of low profile that she had kept when she was a protégée of Dapper Danny Hogan.

As a condition of her parole, Bessie had committed to stay with her brother Almon, who lived in Minneapolis. It was at Almon's apartment, that the local and federal officials called on her, but in fact she never lived at his place; she only stayed there a few days when she first got back. Because the authorities were not interested in her for anything serious, her brother and sister-in-law were more than willing to cover for her in the minor parole violation of lying about her whereabouts. In any event her time on parole ended soon.

Her desire for personal comfort and a need for independence gave her immediate reason not to live with Almon. While she had a very good relationship with her brother, and an even better relationship with Almon's wife, Winnie, this couple lived in a small house.

Bessie, after jail was financially better off than her brother. She had disposable cash at hand, and, she thought that she had good contacts in the local criminal world to help her re-launch her career. Almon could not help much in this regard either. At this point he owned part of a car dealership, a small Nash agency, but this was the Depression and no one was buying cars. He did not have much money; his wife Winnie was working.

Bessie, on the other hand, had left prison with plenty of money in the bank and although she had enough to buy the sort of resort on a northern lake that she and Eddie Green had wanted, she did not have a man. She knew that men were needed for some things but she decided to try without at first. Bessie's past work led her to judge how she could succeed best with her present work.

The money she had, about $11,000 less lawyer's fees, was indisputably hers: Her attorney, Harold Stassen, had successfully argued that Bessie should keep the money found by the FBI on her person and in her safe deposit boxes when she was arrested, as well as keeping the car that she and Eddie had owned. Almon stored the car and had it ready for her on her return. (Although efforts were made earlier by the Justice Department to claim Bessie's money and possessions, her money and car could not be proved to be bank loot, ransom or otherwise illegally obtained. In this regard, Harry Sawyer had done his job well, and Bessie's cash was clean.)

Bessie was relatively well off when she was released and she went back to Minneapolis determined to make good. She did not owe anything to anyone. Bessie had few family obligations when she came back to Minneapolis. She did not even have a son to care for.

Her son, Leonard, against Bessie's wishes and advice, determined to marry his girl, Harriet Kerncamp, and did so about a month after Bessie arrived home. The wedding was small. There may have been something of the general opprobrium in this. Whatever tales Bessie might have told around, it was clear that she had stayed in prison. Her family in Minnesota knew this and her general denials and the willingness of her own family to forgive her was not enough for the future; Harriet's family intervened.

Bessie attended the wedding as did her brothers, Almon and P.B., and their families It was a study in contrasts: Almon's wife Winnie, from Minneapolis, and Grayce, the "Norwegan" risen to success in the small Minnesota town, Northfield. The more proper Kernkamps, there in small number.

But at the wedding, Bessie's family reformed a bond. There was a moment when they discovered that there would be people who looked down on them, because they were related to criminals, because they were small town, because they had problems in their pasts.

They formed this bond mostly, not knowing the whole truth about Beth Green. All her immediate family knew that Bessie was gone for a year. Those who knew for sure that she had been in prison (except for Almon and Winnie) thought that this had resulted from "a mistake in identity." But the wedding made a difference, and from that point Bessie's immediate family would support her no matter what.

One expected guest was unable to be there. Bessie's favorite niece, the still teen-age Cleo had a baby, her first daughter, on the same night that Leonard was married. Curley and Cleo called this baby "Winnie Bess" after Cleo's mother and her beloved aunt.

Because of the circumstances surrounding her illegal activities and incarceration, and her long-standing independence from her mother and brothers, at this point Bessie was largely released from familial obligations. Even so, Bessie continued to be in regular contact with her family and soon voluntarily undertook a family obligation that was to turn around and bite her.

Soon after she got home from West Virginia, she told Almon and Winnie that she would be willing to take Winnie's daughter, "niece" Maxine, under her wing. Maxine was Cleo's older sister. The deal that Bessie proposed to Maxine, and Almon, was that Bessie would provide housing and employment for Maxine. Maxine, in turn, would provide something that Bessie needed very badly: an unblemished criminal record.

In 1935, in Minnesota, if you were a convicted felon you could not get a liquor license. You could, perhaps, depending on the locality, get a temporary permit to sell 3.2 beer in a tavern.

The work that Bessie knew was managing nightclubs and restaurants. If, in 1935, Bessie Skinner's reasons for living alone had little to do with antipathy towards her relatives in the Twin Cities, she nonetheless wanted to make her own way, and she felt that she eventually would need a liquor license to do it.

Bessie, upon her release, seems to have a business plan to accomplish her goal of having a place: she first needed a place, a "roost," a bar or something similar where she could look around for a while and work back up to once more to running a successful night club, and she needed to be "legal" there.

Bessie does not appear to have figured the new improved

Twin Cities into her business plan. The Twin Cities, and indeed the country, had changed while Bessie was in prison. Prohibition was over, as was the "O'Connor layover plan." Bessie had not, under these circumstances kept up on what was going on in the real world. She seems, just as an example, not to have been too aware that, with the Depression still on, and Prohibition over, Minnesota was dealing in its own, very complex way with statewide, and local, liquor licensing laws.

Bessie would have had a problem with such licensing in any event because she was a convicted felon. She already knew that. But another problem that she faced was that Minnesota had strange arrangements for selling liquor as a result of the repeal of Prohibition in December 1933, and Repeal's gradual implementation over the next year. Localities in Minnesota had locally particular opening, closing, license fee and serving laws. What Bessie could do legally in one place she might not be able to do right up the highway.

Minnesota was unique in its arrangements but liquor laws in all the states had a tendency to be particular to the state in the wake of licensing laws passed in 1935 as Prohibition ended. One of the deals that the opponents of Prohibition had made with states was that if the state legislatures complied by ratifying the repeal of the 18th Amendment, then the state legislatures could decide about whether that state would become "wet" or remain "dry." Thirty-six states ratified but all states were freed to make their own laws.

Different states had different traditions of state control of social issues, such as selling alcohol, and had stronger and weaker legislatures, which might bend variously, to liquor industry interests or to the Women's Christian Temperance Union. The most Saudi Arabia-like States, where liquor remained anathema, Kansas being a good example, kept prohibition in force. The older, more tolerant, states, New York being a good example, opted to pass laws regulating the liquor industry on a statewide basis. In some states, citizens could drink at 18, in some, like Wisconsin, they could drink beer at 18, in some they could not drink at all, no matter how old they were.

States that came from a more "populist" or progressive tradition, Minnesota being a good example, opted to pass general Statewide licensing laws, but to leave the decisions on whether to keep prohibition, and how to sell liquor, up to local communities. Merely a city or county line then, in Minnesota, could result in changed arrangements as to how, or whether, liquor was served. In Minnesota, the system resulted in what was called "penny-ante prohibition." The arrangement lent itself easily to minor corruption and violation of the liquor laws.

Thus, Bessie had to learn complex legal and licensing arrangements to set up her business. She also had to find new suppliers, or at least legal suppliers, and she had to protect the money that she had left from her pre-jail enterprises. But she knew her trade and she was smart enough to begin small with the hopes to remake contacts and build her knowledge up. After all, she had a very substantial nest egg.

She knew how to run a "roost," and she was able to renew her business with suppliers of the product. Her earlier lover, Bob Walsh at *Schmidt's Brewing* was listed in her address book and probably helped.

Either statewide, or more locally there was money to be made in bars and liquor stores, even in Minnesota, with its local pockets of Prohibition and its liquor stores owned by municipalities.

However, since Bessie Skinner could not hold a liquor license in her own name, she need help. There was a loophole in the law, and Bessie could own or manage a place that only sold 3.2 beer and get a year's permit for this as long as she did not serve the beer herself. At the end of a year a license would be granted if nothing untoward happened at the place.

She also needed help in the actual operation of a place. She sought help first from Maxine, Winnie's daughter. In the midsummer of 1935, just out of prison, Bessie rented one-half of a commercially zoned bungalow on Minnehaha Avenue by the Veterans Hospital in Minneapolis, and set up a small place called unimaginatively enough "The Bungalow." The bar was in the "living room" and Bessie and Maxine slept in the back bedroom.

Bessie was particularly fond of Winnie, her sister-in-law, Maxine's mother, and as the thirties gave way to the forties, they became much closer. In 1935, both women were in their late thirties and both liked to have a good time. Bessie, had shown herself generous to Winnie's daughters from the time the girls were small. She provided clothes, housing, and help buying cars to Maxine and Cleo over the years. She even bought a gravesite for Maxine.

In 1935, both of these nieces were grown and living independently of Almon and Winnie. Maxine had her own apartment, but she had trouble holding a job, and seemed to be living hand to mouth. Cleo, now 20, was married to Curley Litz, and her young husband, who had practical expertise both with boats and engineering, had good jobs in marine construction along the river between Minnesota and Wisconsin where locks on the Mississippi were being built. Cleo had a baby daughter "Winnie Bess," who became a favorite of her great aunt Bessie.

Maxine was another story. Maxine was 22 years old in 1935, having been born 1913 in Pennant Canada. She started running wild at age 14. Her sister, Cleo, later said "nobody could stop her." But Maxine admired her "Aunt Bess" a great deal, indeed sucked up to her, and by 1935, Maxine was old enough to serve 3.2 beer.

At this point, Maxine was an attractive and voluptuous young woman. She was dark haired and dark eyed and had a quick tongue and a generous body. Maxine, in later years would become grossly intemperate, increasingly foul mouthed and obese. In the 1930s, however, she was in her prime.

Maxine was trouble to her parents and a conundrum to her friends when Bessie first took charge of her; she was to remain one. Bessie criticized her to her parents and to her face, but never abandoned her and Maxine was to remain Bessie's thorn and dependent through the rest of her life.

Their close lifelong relationship is all the more interesting because Maxine was not a blood relation to Bessie. Maxine was not Almon's daughter, rather she was Winnie's, adopted by Almon when he married the very young Winnie in Canada in 1914. This was not something that was talked about in the family, but as Maxine became more and more egregious in her old age she was acknowledged in an underhanded fashion as "not one of us."

Bessie's nephew Raymond, Maxine's slightly younger cousin who knew her well, was later to describe Maxine as a "Bessie Skinner Green wannabe." In any event, Maxine was known early by the family in Minnesota by a nickname, "the wild child," and she was in scrapes and was partying and trying to hang out with gangsters since her early teens.

But everything we know about Bessie indicates that she was both tolerant and loyal to friends and the family that was around her. She certainly overlooked major faults in the personalities or preferences of her many close friends and companions until those faults affected her.

So it was that Bessie paid for a 3.2 beer permit for *The Bungalow* and hired Maxine, placing Maxine several steps up the ladder economically.

This eleemosynary endeavor was not to last long. Although the location of the tavern by the Veteran's Hospital and Fort

Snelling could have provided a steady clientele, conflicts immediately arose between "Aunt Bess" and Maxine. Maxine did not want to be under anyone's wing. In fact, once the liquor license was in Maxine's name, according to Maxine's sister Cleo, Maxine began to act as if she were "queen of the roost." She forgot that she owed her good fortune to her aunt.

Whether or not Maxine tried to play the enterprising lady, another part of "Aunt Bess's" problems with her niece was that Maxine "loved to run at the mouth." Maxine talked about her aunt's immediate past, and implied to men who hung around the bar that she, Maxine, was also well up in the mob. This did not sit well with the more mature woman, Bessie, whose years of living the life that Maxine was aspiring to, had taught her the cost of being wild.

Bessie had also learned to keep her eyes open and her mouth shut out of loyalty to her family. Although her mother in Canada, and her brother, P. B., in Northfield were to have a general idea of what happened to Bessie in 1934, they never knew any details.

Bessie was not completely forgotten by one of her "admirers' at this time, however, one person who did know details of Bessie's involvement with the gangs. The Director of the FBI was publishing what were in effect "white papers" justifying the FBI's role in shooting down the various criminals. In these papers, and in *10,000 Public Enemies*, a book that was published for Hoover in 1936, "Bessie Skinner" was treated as different from the average "gun moll," almost with grudging respect.

Bessie could not control what Hoover said about her. In any event, it appears unlikely that Bessie's relatives read any of the material coming from the FBI. On the other hand, Maxine's behavior was unacceptable just because Maxine could jeopardize Bessie with the family.

It appears, also, that Bessie was just as afraid of what Maxine might say as that what Maxine might do to her just established business. Maxine's strong-minded aunt had words with her niece. Within two months Bessie no longer ran *The Bungalow* with Maxine. She had sold the place and effectively silenced her niece's public voice. Although they were to work together again, and Bessie was to take care of Maxine as Max became more and more dissolute, their relationship was to be strained by this incident.

Bessie, with an eye to the main chance, had continued to look around for a more mature partner to invest in more upscale establishments. Bessie was not only used to being the boss in a place, she was used to having a man around. Her next man, a partner to be, was a veteran of the First World War, whom she probably met at *The Bungalow*. His name was Jack Garrett, he had served in the Minnesota Third Infantry Battalion, and at this point he was stationed at Fort Snelling. Garrett was born in Bismarck, North Dakota, and said that he was of Irish descent. He was 37 years old in 1935.

The details that Bessie had about Garrett were probably burned in the barrel in 1973. It is difficult to find any more description of the man than what is given above, although Bessie's niece Cleo said that he was very handsome. He carried a swagger stick, and had not previously been married. On his marriage license he listed his occupation as a salesman but Cleo's nickname for him was "the thug." Bessie's niece Cleo said that Garrett's real occupation was "servicing slot machines."

Given Bessie's past and her initial discussion of Eddie Green with the FBI, i.e. "she thought he was a salesman," the thug description is probably accurate, and certainly warranted by his later treatment of Bessie, but Garrett had no criminal record. Bessie married John (Jack) Garrett in Hudson, Wisconsin, on November 21, 1935, less than five months after she had returned from prison.

Using Bessie's money, the couple first bought a building that housed both a café and a bar and grill on a main road into Minneapolis from the South, the Lyndale Highway: they called the café "*Garrett's*" and retained the name "*The Meadows*" for the bar and grill. Bessie managed both establishments.

It was at this time that Bessie's mother, Minnie, made one of her few trips to visit her three children in Minnesota. She stayed with son Almon and his wife at their small apartment and made life difficult for all. Winnie, Almon's wife, was working in the evenings, and Minnie resented the fact that Winnie would sleep late. It is said that she would sit around in her housecoat until Winnie would rise and fix breakfast, and that she would not even turn on the radiator when she was cold, but rather order her son to do so. When she went to visit her son and daughter-in-law in Northfield, she played the same sort of tricks, and the family was happy when, after three weeks, she went back to Canada.

Many of Bessie's personal records that pertain to this entire time, 1935 to 1941, were among those burned by her in 1973, and most of the people who knew Bessie in the thirties and forties are dead. However, two things may be surmised from later history: Bessie and Jack Garrett never got along very well, and Bessie, with Garrett as her "front," was a successful businesswoman from 1935 to 1937. Thereafter, her fortunes begin to fade.

Whatever Jack Garrett's initial attraction was to Bessie, it seems to have also faded soon. By late 1937, Bessie had begun to spend considerable time away from Jack with her sister-in-law Winnie. Winnie had a strong opinion about Jack; she thought Garrett was a phony and she told Bessie this. Jack was running around with other women, or so Winnie said.

Bessie and Winnie were particularly close at this point, and they could be found in the evening at their favorite hangout,

"The Streamline Bar." In 1938, mutual friends of Winnie and Bessie, Pete and Faye Faber bought *The Streamline*. Winnie had known Pete since he had been a bootlegger in the twenties.

During this period, and from this point on, Bessie was a regular guest in her Minnesota brothers' homes. When she visited she was alone. Because no one in Bessie's family ever really spent any time with Jack Garrett, and the wedding was very "private," the family assumed even in the late thirties that Bessie's relationship with Jack was rocky. The family later speculated that Jack was a husband only to provide Bessie with legitimate cover for liquor licenses.

All the time Bessie was married to Jack, she continued to work very hard. As in her earliest days in St. Paul, and during her time in the late twenties, she spread herself fairly thin, owning, managing, and working at different establishments.

After late 1937, Bessie again took up criminal enterprises. In the late thirties, Bessie became a "hostess" again at a dive on Rockford Road that was owned by a minor figure in the Minneapolis mob, Joe Schara. Bessie and Jack Garrett rented this place in northwest Minneapolis and it catered to union members and then to soldiers. It was named *"The Red Hen."* Niece Maxine was again unemployed when *The Red Hen* became Bessie's chief source of income, and Bessie hired her as a waitress there. (At least the family hoped that it was as a waitress.)

Sometime in late 1938, Jack and Bessie bought and operated a nightclub called *"The Gables,"* close to *Garrett's Cafe*. She was hired to manage other joints, as well as owning them with Garrett, and that may indicate that her finances were shakier than they were when she returned from prison. One of Bessie's less reputable occupations at this time was "marking dice" in bars. As 3.2 beer was to liquor, so "marking dice" was to gambling. It was not illegal in the late thirties and forties. In effect, Bessie's chore was to count the points rolled by the drinkers and keeping score for a bar game, called "Fourteen." The drinkers could win free drinks or prizes.

The Red Hen, however, was the most clearly illegitimate of Bessie's enterprises. The place had some pretensions of being a nightclub. While it served 3.2 beer and food, it also served set-ups to men who had brought their own bottles. In all likelihood it had slot machines and it certainly had other ways of earning money on its premises. Bessie's favorite niece Cleo, who visited her Aunt there, described it as "beer in front, fun in back."

In 1954, brother Almon's adoptive daughter from his second marriage, Shirley, was riding with her "half-sister" Maxine up to Cleo and Curley's resort, the *Seguchie Lodge* on Mille Lacs, to stay with her Aunt. Shirley, as a 14 year old would, complained about her "Aunt Bess" as being too strict and proper. Maxine guffawed and said, "'Proper,' girlie, is no way to describe a *Madame*." Maxine went on to describe the nature of a particular one of Bessie's businesses. For *The Red Hen* also had a brothel in the back and it was at this establishment that Bessie was to make contact again with many of her friends from the good old days; women she knew from her St. Peter Street days and perhaps at "Aunt Grace's" establishment in St. Paul.

Bessie was only associated with *The Red Hen* for about a year. When she left the place, she was replaced as manager there by a woman who was an earlier acquaintance, and was a life-long friend, Pearl Heineman Olson Riley Yerxa (about whom more later). Pearl first worked at *The Red Hen* with Bessie on weekends. It appears that Maxine may have been technically incorrect when she was referring to Bessie's role at *The Red Hen*. Bessie was the general manager, very possibly Pearl was the Madame, at least on weekends, before she replaced Bessie as manager.

In addition to the stories about T*he Red Hen* and Jack Garrett's job and reputation, there is at least one other indirect indication that Bessie remained involved in criminal activities in the forties: Among her possessions at her death was an almost full, and forged, gasoline ration book from the Second World War.

During this time and also during the next few years, Bessie was to work as a waitress at various bars. Bessie was falling on increasingly harder times as the thirties gave way to the forties. In addition to her other enterprises, Bessie and Jack, by 1940, had bought a liquor store in Minneapolis on the intersection of Lyndale and Franklin Avenues. Shortly afterwards it was owned solely by Jack.

At this point Jack Garrett listed his home address at the location of *The Red Hen,* and Bessie listed hers elsewhere. Given the description of the place's layout and nature, it seems unlikely that he or Bessie lived there. According to Cleo, Bessie's niece, Bessie and Jack lived apart much of the time after 1938. Certainly, the Twin Cities directories do not show them as cohabiting after 1939.

Bessie appeared to have shed one responsibility for a while when she left *The Red Hen*. It was a responsibility that was to come back to her, however: Her niece Maxine married Pat Griffin. He was 20 years older than she was and about half her size. Although he was steadily employed, he never earned much money. What little Max and Pat had, they would spend on liquor and dining out. As the passage of time would show, the marriage only added another problem for Bessie, it did not free her from Maxine. Max and Pat would come back into Bessie's life, as dependents, many times again.

Jack and Bessie jointly owned several places until mid-1942. Their partnership in business must have done well some of the time because from 1937 to 1942 they owned or operated as many as three businesses at one time. But they did not do well as a married couple and Bessie seems to have been strapped for cash.

According to Pearl's daughter, Marlys Heineman, who lived

off and on with Bessie during the Second World War, Bessie and Jack were apart well before 1942, and when they finally did break up it was because Jack was skimming money from their businesses and using it to support a girlfriend. Again, according to Marlys, when Bessie found this out, she went to confront Jack and the woman at Jack's apartment. A physical fight ensued, which resulted in injuries to both women.

In 1943, Bessie and Jack were divorced. This divorce was a financial disaster for Bessie, because all the liquor licenses and half of the property were in Jack's name. Bessie's money from the "Dillinger days" was now gone. Her status fell abruptly and the Minneapolis city directory for 1944 listed her employment as a "grinder" at *North Side Motors*. The family has speculated that Jack Garrett was able to walk away with the money because Bessie was a convicted felon and could not afford another arrest, e.g., for running a brothel. This was the point at which she registered her birth in Linton North Dakota, in order to ensure that she could contribute to Social Security and collect from it when she was 65 years old.

Immediately after Bess divorced Jack Garrett she worked for her sister-in law Winnie's good friends, the Fabers who owned *The Streamline Bar*. During the mid-forties to the mid-fifties, Bessie worked at a series of bars, restaurants and liquor stores. She was a waitress, nothing more, or a "clerk," this time for real, and many of the places where she worked such as *Pino Canables, The Cozy,* and *The Mills End* by the Milwaukee Depot, were owned by people that she knew from the Dillinger days. She also worked at liquor stores owned by friends, for example Ed Stow, who owned the *Brooklyn Park Liquor Store*.

She did seem to have some money left, however, because in 1944, she used savings to buy the small *58 Club*. There are some indications that Bessie also employed Maxine at that club. In any event, she turned the ownership over to her brother Almon in early 1945. He and Winnie ran it until July 1945, when they bought *The Seguchie Lodge* on Lake Mille Lacs. But there are other indications that she was in financial trouble. In late 1947 she lived with the Fabers for a while and then with Pearl and Pearl's husband at that point, Bill Riley, (whose own history is of some interest in Minnesota.)

Despite what only can be described as a disastrous history with male companions, Bess Garrett, as she now preferred to call herself, did not give up on men in 1943 after she divorced Jack Garrett, and she certainly did not give up on her friendships with women. In 1947, according to Pearl Heineman's daughter, Bess was dating Lyle, a bartender at the *Broadway Bar,* "a sharp guy with wavy hair." Lyle was sufficiently smitten with Bess that he gave her a valuable sapphire and diamond ring and she wore it to the end of her life.

She did not give up on trying to improve her lot either or at least to appear as she had in the early photographs, In the late forties, she worked for *Likkerman's Furs* where she got a gray shearling coat at a great discount. This coat and the ring seemed to suit her. Her nieces and nephews saw her flash and dazzle then, and viewed her as a visitor from a classier and more exciting place.

Bessie and Winnie, her brother's wife, continued to party together, she continued to visit Danny Hogan's widow Leila, and she saw Consola, Heloise and Blondie, friends from the "Aunt Grace" era, as well as being a good friend to Maxine in her troubled times, all the time from the late thirties until at least the fifties. But her dearest friend at this time, and for the rest of her life, was, Pearl Heineman Olson Riley Yerxa.

Pearl had lived an even more chaotic (wild) life than Bess. At the end in 1975, when Pearl died of the complications of syphilis, she had been married five times, each one but the first an unsuitable marriage. Pearl had started out, however, as very middle class. She was married to a very respectable businessman named Heinemann in Minneapolis. Marlys, their daughter was born in 1932.

Pearl left her small daughter and husband in 1936 for Bill Riley. Riley was the son of a very prominent man in the Twin Cities, a Baptist minister who was instrumental in setting up a well-known Baptist college in the area. But Bill Riley was what would have been described 100 years earlier as a "wastrel." In 1936, Marlys went to live with her mother and Bill. The now married couple partied all the time. Eventually, Pearl left him because he refused to stop drinking and running around.

In the late thirties, Pearl had to support herself; and it was at this time she and Bessie became acquainted. Pearl's daughter, Marlys said that Bess lived with Pearl and Bill in 1942. When Bill and Pearl split up in 1947, and Pearl took off, Marlys lived with Bessie (whom she called "Aunt Bess") for a brief time while Marlys was attending high school.

CHAPTER 19

Minnesota Reforms and So Does Bessie

The sort of gangster crime that Bessie was involved with did not last into the late forties and fifties. Larger issues were afoot--war, communism, the reconstruction of Europe, the founding of an international order. Some crime stayed local, however.

Up in the resort communities of northern Minnesota in 1948, people continued to fear that they would be caught supplying services that other people wanted. According to Cleo, Bessie's niece, people believed that criminalizing gambling and various forms of consuming liquor "was dumb." They laughed at particular reformers and representatives of the morals squads who would be searching for illicit sex, booze and gambling.

One of the suppliers of the means to violate the law and have fun was Tom Filben, still a force in the Minnesota underworld. Because he controlled the slot machines in place in many resorts in Minnesota's lake district, he also made sure the proprietors of the places where the slots were used were warned, by phone or more safely by messengers in cars who drove up State Highway 169, when "the Reverend" was on the warpath.

"The Reverend" was a Methodist minister who was without parish, but not without a mission, and his name was Henry J.

Soltau. Soltau, who was born in 1888 and died in 1974, was a crusader from 1920 until his death. According to his obituary in the Minneapolis Tribune on April 14, 1974, Soltau was "Minneapolis's leading crusader against drinking, prostitution, dirty movies, and professional wrestling." When he died, in 1974 he had already prepared testimony to be given to the Minneapolis City Council and was leading a campaign against the proposed laws in Minneapolis which would grant certain rights to homosexuals.

Even back in 1935, Minnesota was a peculiar place. Unless you lived in a heavily ethnic community up on the Iron Range, or in a really tiny town, of which there were quite a few, people were just about as tolerant of differences as could be found anywhere in the country. Soltau always fought a lonely battle.

In Minneapolis and St. Paul there was no '400' (except for the train line to Chicago) and the Blue Books had a tough time keeping up among the various families who were more or less socially prominent; the field of families to choose from shifted too often. Many prominent people had made their money selling beer or were involved with dubious activities. Therefore, while Soltau waged his lonely campaign Bessie, and many others, made fun of him. But he was sometimes successful and one of his victories was in getting the bar dice games such as *Fourteen,* and the slot machines which were legal until the mid-forties in some counties, outlawed on a statewide basis.

In addition to campaigns against gambling, there was official repression at this time of selling hard liquor in places that were only permitted to sell 3.2 beer. Soltau was active in this endeavor. Usually, the "family" resorts in Northern and Central Minnesota were not given liquor licenses. This was a county by county or town by town decision. Nonetheless, state law could be enforced out of St. Paul.

The slot machine magnates, the liquor distributors and the

resort owners developed systems to warn of impending raids. When Soltau would be on one of his campaigns and demand the attention of the state authorities in St. Paul, the State Police would move up the highways, and the early warning system would go into effect. Bessie's family believes that her brother Almon was a member of Tom Filben's group who carried warnings up the line.

At this time, in the late forties, Bessie was working part time for her brother at the lodge that he had purchased on Lake Mille Lacs. In neighboring Milaca County, to the south and where most big resorts were located, the county sheriff was on Filben's payroll. Not so in Crow Wing County, where *Seguchie Lodge* was located. There it was up to private enterprise. During this early period of statewide investigation into organized crime, the telephone could not be trusted. It might be tapped. The messengers carrying the suggestions to hide the slots and the hard liquor came by car.

The crimes that Soltau and the State investigators were pursuing were not as profitable for the perpetrators or as violent, as those pursued by the Barker-Karpis gang. These was all small violations of "penny ante prohibition." Soltau, did not even spend most of his time chasing the gamblers and illegal licensees. He was more interested in actively campaigning against the liberals and moral relativists at the time. He railed against those people, Humphrey, Naftalin (Mayor of Minneapolis), and others, who were actually making Minnesota politics clean.

Minnesota in the Truman and Eisenhower years was a much more placid place than it had been just a little earlier. Moral righteousness began to seem like a general virtue. As the Twin Cities entered this period, however, and even midway through it, they still retained, underneath the righteousness, some of the old reputation for the other sort of tolerance. In a muckraking book, *U.S.A. Confidential*, published by Crown in 1952, its two authors surveyed the "capitals of crime" across the U.S.

Their discoveries in Minnesota were revelations to them, but can be seen now as only small and left-over signs of the glory days of the "O'Connor Layover System."

"Minnesota has long been thought of as the habitation of peaceful, home-loving Svenskas whose only vices were Saturday night binges on 100 proof aquavit and a yen for their neighbor's wives, mostly gaunt Anna Christies. To picture this as a commonwealth where organized hoodlumism thrives under the protection of a bi-partisan political alliance takes imagination- or deep digging." (In the case of these researchers, it is mostly imagination and reading the local newspapers.)

In the Dillinger days, you did not have to dig even to the hoarfrost level. You could find "hoodlumism" by asking, for example, the editor of the St. Paul Daily News to point out the hoodlums. They were sitting, plotting crimes and drinking coffee in a local sandwich shop. Bessie was waiting on them.

And you cannot imagine what a "gaunt Anna Christie" would look like. No, the confidential exposé of sin in the Twin Cities in the early fifties rings pathetic and the authors seem to have to strain to find anything very corrupt. What they describe was commonly printed in the *St. Paul Dispatch* and *Minneapolis Tribune*. Deprived of real expose, mostly the authors lambasted liberal Minnesota politicians such as Hubert Humphrey.

Nonetheless, the authors did turn up one interesting fact. In 1950, some of the criminal "bosses" in Minneapolis and St. Paul that they identified were names one could recognize from the bootlegging rackets in the twenties. In Minneapolis, they named Isadore "Kidd Cann" Blumenfeld, and in St. Paul, Tommy Banks, Thomas Filben, Alex Glickman, Maurice Roisner, and Sam "the Tailor" Taran.

Most of these names appear on the list compiled by the Justice Department in 1926 of the members of the Gleeman/Gleckman syndicate. Some of them also figure on the guest list compiled by Alvin Karpis when he discusses Harry Sawyer's blowout at the infamous *Green Lantern* saloon New Year's Eve in 1932. All of the men had a rich criminal history in the area. All were still active in the underworld.

CHAPTER 20

At the End

In 1946, an event occurred which reminded Bessie of her own mortality and affected her both emotionally and materially. Her closest friend, her loved sister-in law, Winnie, died of a heart attack. While Bess still had flash, beyond 1946 her jobs were increasingly less dazzling and the bars where she waited table were seedier.

She went to work, at least part-time for her brother, Almon, who, shortly before Winnie's death had bought *Seguchie Lodge* in a joint investment with their daughter and son-in-law, Curley and Cleo. While he owned the lodge, Almon continued to run the small bar that he owned in Minneapolis. He married a woman who was a waitress in the bar in 1948. (She had an 8-year-old daughter named Shirley. By 1950, Almon had a son, named after his father, David. When David was born, Almon was 60 years old. Bess became very close to both Shirley and David, perhaps closer than she was to her own grandchildren.)

It was at this time, probably for Almon's wedding, when Bessie's mother visited her son Almon in northern Minnesota. Bessie went to see her. There was a family picnic, and Bessie's mother and her sister, who was also visiting, fell asleep on the picnic blanket. Bessie carefully arranged beer bottles close to the hands of the teetotalling and sleeping old ladies and took a picture. She would later show this photo to friends and Minnesota relatives and always break out in raucous laughter. As far as can be determined, this was the only "revenge" that she took on a mother who, even in 1948, barely spoke to her.

Money was tight for Bess throughout the fifties. She found it difficult to get work in bars and restaurants, and frequently found herself working for old friends, their favor to her, or clerking at liquor stores. But when she would show up at the homes of P.B. or Almon or their families she would invariably put on the dog. She would drive up in her Pontiac, or Nash Sportster or later her Renault Dauphine, and act as if she had just stepped out of a movie.

While her family that was her brothers and their children, remained close to her, Bess was increasingly isolated from her son and his family. She spent more and more time with her brothers and their children and grandchildren, but was not so welcome at her son's home. In part this was because her son was increasingly marginalized in his own home. Leonard's in-laws considered Bess disreputable, as indeed she was.

In early Spring, 1953, her mother Minnie died in Webb, Saskatchewan. The brothers, P.B. and Almon, were up to see Minnie when she was ill, and Bess was chosen to represent the Minnesota family at the funeral. Shortly after this she began to make more frequent contact with friends from the Dillinger days. She still wandered up to the lake country to visit Danny Hogan's widow. She brought her good friends Blondie and Consola to visit her brother in Northfield.

In the spring of 1954, she was hit by a car and broke her back. She was unable to work and was laid up for months in a hospital. She continued to recuperate at a nephew's home. Her brothers and their families visited her as did her son. His family did not.

Bessie was not an old woman in the late 1950s, far from it, but Bessie's family was aging. Her older brothers were considerably older than she was. Her oldest brother, Pharos, died in 1963, Her mother Minnie had died in 1953, 29 years after Bessie's father died. By 1960, Bessie had both grandchildren and great-grandchildren. But from 1940 on great nieces and nephews had been coming into being; in fact, there was a baby boom.

Now, babies were born all along. In 1935, Bessie's favorite niece, Cleo had a baby, Winnie Bess, on the same night that Bessie's son, Leonard Skinner married Harriet Kernkamp. Both Cleo and Leonard were 20 years old at this time. Cleo had another daughter in 1937, and Raymond, Bessie's nephew to whom she was very close had a daughter in 1941 and a son in 1943. These were the folks that she visited constantly.

After their marriage in 1935, Leonard and Harriet wasted little time in starting their own family. Bessie's granddaughter, Valerie was born on July 4, 1936. Harriet and Leonard soon had another daughter, Jacqueline Rae was born on November 2, 1937. A third daughter, Marvel, was born on January 12, 1940.

Despite having small children, Leonard served in the Navy during World War II. Harriet and the children moved back home to her parents while Leonard was in service. In February 1942, their son Neil was born. The Skinners bought a big old house for their growing family and when Leonard was done with his military service their lives settled into a routine with children's activities, and a growing involvement by Harriet and Leonard in Eastern Star and the girl's in Job's Daughters.

As already noted, Bessie was increasingly excluded from this household. Harriet, as she matured, got more priggish. Bessie, involved with illegal activities at least until the late forties was not perceived as a good example as a grandmother. Nonetheless, several times a year Bessie's brother in Minneapolis, her brother in Northfield and Leonard and Harriet, and their families, got together for a pot luck supper in the Twin Cities or a picnic in Northfield.

By 1956, Bessie's two oldest granddaughters, Valerie and Jackie, were in college and they were ready to be on their own.

At this point, Leonard who was 41 years old, was offered a job with an insurance company in Savannah, Ga. This appeared to him to be an opportunity for better pay and a warmer climate and he took the job. He persuaded Harriet to go to Savannah with him but she went, leaving her parents, only reluctantly.

The move agreed with Leonard but Harriet, Marvel and Neal had a hard time adjusting to southern life away from the Kernkamps, relatives, and friends. Harriet missed her own family in Minnesota and was no longer beholden to or in love with Leonard. Eventually, Harriet issued an ultimatum: return to Minnesota or she and the children would return without Leonard. They agreed to get divorced.

Leonard did not like being alone. Within a year, he married a local woman, Joyce Owens, then 35, who had a 12-year-old daughter, Rose Ella. They bought a house and Joyce got pregnant. Timothy (Timmy) was born November 3, 1959. Rose adored her little brother. Leonard and Joyce and the children made trips back to Minnesota to see the older children and Leonard's grandchildren who had started arriving. Bessie made several road trips to Savannah to visit Leonard and his new family. The cross-country road trips of the Dillinger years may have made her brave enough to set out on her own; in any event, she drove from Minneapolis to Savannah until she was almost 70 years of age.

Until 1973, when Leila died, Bessie remained friends with Danny Hogan's widow. And indeed, one of the reasons that Bessie did not mind so much living far away from the city lights in the resort area of Garrison was that many of her friends from her more notorious times lived in the area, as did her favorite niece, Cleo.

Living close to her, and in and out of the hospital because of the results of syphilis, was Pearl. Pearl was both a link to Bessie's past and a person in need of a friend. While Pearl's daughter,

Marlys Krussow was frequently able to see her mother; it was Bessie who helped Pearl and Marlys make arrangements for a grave site and burial when it became obvious Pearl was going to die. This was in the small cemetery in Garrison where her niece Maxine's husband, Pat, was buried.

Maxine provided another reason that Bessie felt that she had to live where she did. Even before Pat's death, she had become obese and a public nuisance. She lived in a small house with at least a dozen cats, but no real means of support. It was clear that Maxine was likely to drink herself to death, and Bessie bought a gravesite for her, and also for herself.

In late 1977, a series of incidents began which combined to make Bessie's last years miserable. Her son Leonard, now in his sixties, lost his job in Savannah and was unable to find equivalent work. He took a job as a clerk at a chain photo shop. His wife Joyce who had had drinking problems before buried herself in alcohol.

In late 1978, Leonard and Joyce's son, Timmy, then 18, was involved in an automobile accident and was hospitalized in a coma for six weeks until he died. Two weeks after Timmy was hospitalized, on July 19, 1978, Leonard died of a heart attack. Joyce died of grief on the same day that Timmy died. Bessie was to continue to live for five more years. She visited and was visited by her brother, Almon, who was still alive, and also went to see her youngest brother Marvin, and her nieces and nephews including Cleo and Raymond. But it appeared that the accident that killed Timmy also killed Bessie's spirit.

CODA

In 1995, when Raymond and Cleo, Bessie's nephew and niece--born on the same day in the same year, 1915, both still very mentally sound--were facing difficult challenges because of their age, a book was published by the Minnesota Historical Society Press. This book was Paul Maccabee's *John Dillinger Slept Here*.

Raymond, who read the book shortly before he died, was greatly amused by the references to his Aunt Bess. As a child, he had known Danny Hogan, and he particularly remembered Bob Walsh with great fondness. Cleo also had many kind things to say about Bob Walsh; she seems to have been a favorite of his and she was aware that her aunt kept in touch with Bob until the time he died.

By 1934, both Raymond and Cleo had met other St. Paul gangsters through their aunt. Cleo was better acquainted than Raymond was with the somewhat shady women with whom Bessie associated. She was later to know the less glamorous crooks who practiced "penny ante" prohibition when she and her husband, Curley, ran Seguchie Lodge, and she and Curley had employed Bessie.

Raymond, visiting his aunt on his own when he went to college during the Dillinger days, kept up with the night spots where his aunt worked, or which she owned. He was a great jazz fan and as a college student frequented many of the nightclubs that Paul Maccabee mentions as gangster hangouts.

When his children were growing up, Raymond had told stories of these days to them, and of their Aunt Bess, and they had said "Sure Dad." When the reality turned out to be even more lurid than he had depicted, he pointed out to them that he had not even exaggerated enough to tell the whole truth. Only one of his stories was inaccurate; he had claimed that Aunt Bess was the "lady in red" in the Dillinger case. Rather, her sobriquet in the papers in April 1934 was "the red-headed woman."

Cleo Litz was less enamored of her aunt's past and while not forgetting it, was more inclined to speak of Bessie's humor and her many kindnesses over the years than about Bessie's misdeeds. She talked a great deal about Bessie's life from 1936 until her death, but was careful in her discussion of the Dillinger days. Neither Raymond nor Cleo had ever heard of Beth Green before Maccabee's book was published.

Now distance and time lend a romantic tinge to the story. But the life of Beth Green was really not romantic, it was hard. It included bankruptcy and bank robbery, divorce, desertion, and turning in her "friends" to the FBI. She endured Eddie Green's and Danny Hogan's deaths on the streets, and bad booze deaths and friends dying from syphilis. She survived her only child and she dared the rejection by many she loved. She lived.

BESSIE H. GARRETT
JUNE 28, 1898
SEPT. 17, 1958

ACKNOWLEDGMENTS

Books, Authors, and People

First, and most important by far for this book, the *sine qua causa non*, is Paul Maccabee's book, **John Dillinger Slept Here**, Minnesota Historical Society Press, 1995. To quote Bryan Burrough, author of **Public Enemies**, "Paul Maccabee's *John Dillinger Slept Here* is not just one of the best books about Minneapolis-St. Paul, it is one of the best books of local history I have ever read-about any city anywhere on earth." Amen. When Raymond Hinds, Bessie Hinds's nephew, was dying of cancer, his daughter read about this book's publication, went to a reading and signing and bought several copies. She also talked to Paul Maccabee. Upon hearing about her Aunt Bess, Maccabee said, "Oh yes! Beth Green! Your aunt! You are going to enjoy this book!" Amen.

The other main book you need, if you want to study this period, is John Tolland's **Dillinger Days**. Readable, very well researched, and absolutely necessary if you are a student of this history.

Two other books stand out for the authors: These are Ellen Poulsen's **Don't Call Us Molls** and Rupert Christiansen and Beth Brophy, et al.'s, **The Complete Book of Aunts**. Both were being written during the initial research and writing phase for this book, 1999-2005. The authors of these two books, Ellen Poulsen and Beth Brophy, were extremely generous and helpful in our writing about Beth Green/Aunt Bess. Ellen Poulsen read the manuscript and provided many good suggestions. A chapter highlighting some of the authors' experiences with and knowledge of Aunt Bess appears in *The Complete Book of Aunts*.

Main Travelled Roads

Raymond Hinds read Maccabee's book and told stories of the times that he remembered, of the jazz clubs and bars of St. Paul, and his Aunt Bess. His cousin, Cleo Hinds Litz, and the woman with whom he shared a birth date and a birth year as well as friendship, also read Maccabee's book and also shared many, many stories with the authors. These people were eyewitnesses to the thirties and forties. They knew Bessie Walsh and Bess Garrett but they did not know Beth Green. Their stories were true and foundational to this book.

Professional ball teams have "closers," pitchers whose skills allow the team to finish the game successfully. Our master closer was **Ginge Anderson** who read the manuscript, told us more stories, kept us correct and steady, and added quite a few strikeouts. The authors also wish to thank John Palmer, who read the manuscript closely and didn't like a lot of the structure and writing. (He liked the story.) His suggestions have certainly helped

The authors also spent many days and miles on the road visiting the locations in North and South Dakota, in Saskatchewan, Canada and in Ireland where Bessie's Hinds family originated. They talked to friends and relations of the family from County Cavan to the three-person town of Burnstad, N.D. Of these, there were several forthcoming about the family, and they wish particularly to thank Dale Pierce, whose remembrances and whose gift of Wilbert Pierce's self-published book was very useful about the frontier days of the family. Also, the Irish relations of the family, especially Maura Newman of Counties Cavan and Longford help paint pictures of the Protestant Irish emigration. The Peterson Family, Pollock, South Dakota gave generously of their time and remembrances as well.

The authors spent many days in newspaper morgues, in historical societies, in graveyards, and in County offices. They visited little museums, such as the birthplace of Lawrence Welk, and much bigger institutions. Of these, the three of the most helpful were the Minnesota Historical Society*, which gets five stars in the author's ratings, and the FBI and the National Archives offices in Washington, D.C. and Gaithersburg, MD. There were many helpful people in these institutions as well who acted like researchers for the authors, not like bureaucrats. The authors also visited and researched in many of the sites where Beth and Eddie Green marked jugs and Dillinger and the Barker-Karpis gang robbed those banks. They heartily recommend a trip to Mason City, Iowa. Many of the sites and buildings where Bessie/Beth's life played out in Minneapolis and St. Paul still exist.

And **thanks for support along the way** to Anne Sinnott, Gloria van Demmeltraat, Allene Mosler, Jo Nysteun-Kies, and Shari Olson Kahl.

---

*Especially valuable from the MHS were Paul Maccabee's files and research materials used for *John Dillinger Slept Here*. The authors not only used the fruits of his thorough research, but used his research as a jumping off place for more research into Beth Green in her various guises.

BIBLIOGRAPHY AND RESEARCH

The authors apologize for the sloppiness of their research methods. We did not set out to write an academic book, so we are not displeased that we didn't succeed. That being said, we now wish we had paid a bit more attention to writing down the pages and by-lines for journals and newspapers as well as book's pages used. This bibliography represents our best information from our records.

NON- FICTION BOOKS:

1. Anderson, Jack and Mortimer, Lee, **USA Confidential**, (1952) New York, NY, Crown
2. Burrough, Brian, **Public Enemies**, (2004) New York, NY, Penguin Group
3. Christiansen, Rupert and Beth Brophy, **The Complete Book of Aunts (2007),** New York, NY, Twelve,
4. Cooper, Courtney Ryley, **Ten Thousand Public Enemies**, (1935) New York City, NY, Printed and Bound Cornwall Press, Inc. for Blue Ribbon
Books, Inc.
5. Cromie, Robert and Pinkston, Joseph, **Dillinger: A Short and Violent Life**, (1962) (1990)
McGraw Hill Book Company, Republished: Chicago Historical Bookworks, Evanston, IL.
6. George, Henry, **Our Land and Land Policy**, (1999) Michigan State University Press, East Lansing, MI
7. _____ , **Progress and Poverty**, (1939) (1879)   George Schalken Foundation Press, New York, NY
8. Girardin, G. Russell with Helmer, William. **John Dillinger: The Untold Story**, (1994)
Bloomington and Indianapolis, IN Indiana University Press,

9. Karpis, Alvin, **The Alvin Karpis Story**, (1971) New York, NY, Coward, McCann and Geoghegan, Inc.

10. Lee, Maggie, **Northfield Ink:** *Community and Stories along Division Street*, (2005), Northfield, MN. Loomis House Press

11. Maccabee, Paul, **John Dillinger Slept Here**, (1995) St. Paul, MN Minnesota Historical Press,

12. Mahoney, Tim, **Secret Partners: Big Tom Brown and the Barker Gang,** (2013)

St. Paul, MN, Minnesota Historical Press,

13. Neuhaus, Marjorie, *History of Northfield for the Rice County Bicentennial Book*, privately published and written, March 3, 1976, (Northfield, MN, Public Library]

14. Pierce, Wilbert, **Grandfather's Tales I Saw and Heard**, (1984), Finlay, ND,

Steel County Press

15. Poulsen, Ellen, **Don't Call Us Molls: Women of the John Dillinger Gang,** (2002)

Little Neck, NY, Clinton Cook Publishing Corp.

16. Purvis, Alston, **The Vendetta** *Special Agent Melvin Purvis, John Dillinger, and Hoover's FBI in the Age of Gangsters*, (2005) New York, NY, Public Affairs Books

17. Quimby, Myron J, **The Devil's Emissaries**, (1969) Cranbury, N.J., A. Barnes and Company, Inc. Publishing

18. Summers, Anthony, **Official and Confidential-** *The Secret Life of J. Edgar Hoover* (1993), New York, G.P. Putnam and Sons,

19. Turner, Frederick Jackson, **The Significance of The Frontier in American History**, (1894) (2014 Reprint), Eastfield, CT., Martino Fine Books

20. Toland, John, **The Dillinger Days**, (1963) New York, NY, Published by DaCapo Press Inc., Subsidiary of Plenum Publishing Corp.

21. Webb, Walter Prescott, **The Great Plains,** *A Study in Institutions and Environments (1932)* (1959) Lincoln, Nebraska, University of Nebraska Pres

BOOKS OF FICTION, MEMOIR, POETRY, AND LITERATURE

1. Fitzgerald, F. Scott, **The Great Gatsby,** (2000), New York, NY, Scribner Paperback, 75th Anniversary Edition

2. Garland, Hamlin, **Main-travelled Roads**, (1891), New York, NY, Harper Bros.

3. _____, **A Son of the Middle Border** (1917), New York, NY,

Harper Bros.

4. Hammett, Dashiell, **Red Harvest**, (1929) (2003) NY, Orion

5. Longfellow, Henry Wadsworth, **The Song of Hiawatha**, (2006) Mineola, NY, Dover Publications

6. Norris Frank, **McTeague**, (1899) (1994), New York, NY, Penguin Classics

7. _____, **The Octopus: A Story of California**, (1901) (1994), New York, NY, Penguin Classics

8. _____, **The Pit: A Story of Chicago**, (1903) (1994), New York, NY, Penguin Classics

9. _____, "**Oceans of Wheat**," (partial ms.) "A Deal in Wheat, 'posthumously, 1903, Doubleday, New York, NY, Page and Company

10. Rolvaag, O.E., **Giants In The Earth**, (1927) Harper Bros. New York, NY

11. _____, **Peder Victorius**, (1929), Harper Bros., New York, NY

12. Stegner, Wallace., **Wolf Willow**, (1962) New York, NY, Viking Press,

13. Wilder, Laura Ingalls, **The Little House on the Prairie**, (1935) (1994), New York, NY, Harper Trophy

DIRECTORIES, NEWSPAPERS, AND MAGAZINES:

Directories

1. Minneapolis, Minnesota **City Directories**, 1922-1940
2. St. Paul, Minnesota **Blue Books**, 1924-1954
3. St. Paul, **Minnesota City Directories**, 1922-1954

Newspapers

1. Pollock, SD, **Campbell County News**, 1904
2. Linton, ND, **Emmons County Record**. (Williamsport, D.T. [i.e. N.D.]) 1884-Current 2001
3. Minneapolis, MN, **Star; Tribune; Journal; Spokesman**, 1910-1940
4. Moosejaw, Saskatchewan, **The Times-Herald**, 1905-1920
5. Northfield, MN, **Northfield News**, 1876-1966.
6. St. Paul, MN, **Dispatch; Pioneer Press; Recorder, The Daily News**, 1910-1945
7. Swift Current, Saskatchewan, **The Swift Current Sun**, 1899-1930

Magazines

I. **Liberty Magazine,** *Death Comes for Eddie Green- Postmaster of Gangdom,* by Frederick Lewis, Nov.26, 1939

2. **MASTER DETECTIVE Magazine,** *Follow the Big Shot, The Crime File of Eddie Green* by Richard Hirsch

3. **The TRUE DETECTIVES MYSTERIES Magazine,** *With the Dillinger Gang- The Fatso Negri Story,* by Fatso Negri, February 1941

ORGANIZATIONS USED FOR RESEARCH

1. **Brown County Registrar of Deeds,** Brown County Court House, 25 Market St., Aberdeen, SD.
2. **Emmons County Records,** Emmons County Court House, 100 NW 4th St. Linton N.D.
3. **Federal Bureau of Investigations,** FBI Records Research
J. Edgar Hoover Building, Washington, DC
4. **Federal Prison Camp,** Public Records, Alderson, WV
5. **First National Bank, Mason City,** 5 North Federal Ave., Mason City, Iowa 3/2020
6. **Hanson County Registrar of Deeds,** Mitchell, S.D.
7. **Hennepin County District Court,** Records, 300 S. 6th St., Minneapolis MN.
8. **Jackson County Assessor of Land Records,** Jackson County Court House, 405 4th St., Aberdeen, S.D.
9. **Minneapolis Central Library,** 300 Nicollet Ave., Minneapolis, MN
10. **Minnesota Historical Society,** 345 Kellogg Blvd., St. Paul, MN
11. **Minnesota Liquor Licensing,** Records, 444 Cedar Street, St. Paul, MN
12. **Minnesota Secretary of State,** 180 State Office Building, St. Paul, MN
13. **National Archives and Records Service,** 700 Pennsylvania Ave., Washington, DC and Records Center, 4205 Suitland Rd, Suitland, MD
14. **Northfield Public Library,** 210 Washington St. Northfield, MN
15. **Pierre Historical Society,** Research Desk, Pierre, S.D.
16. **Ramsey County Court House,** 15 W. Kellogg Blvd, St. Paul, MN
17. **Sonoma County Recorder,** P.O. Box 1709, Santa Rosa, CA.
18. **Saint Cloud Reformatory,** File: Minnesota Reformatory, Minnesota Historical Society, Eddie Green #5774
19. **St. Paul Gangster Tour and Wabasha St. Caves,** 215 Wabasha St. St. Paul, MN
20. **St. Paul Public Library,** George Latimer Center, 900 W. 4th Street, St. Paul, MN

21. **South Dakota Health and Vital Statistics**, 600 East Capitol, Pierre, S.D.

22. Webb, Swift Current and Moose Jaw Saskatchewan: all at **Saskatchewan Public Archives,** 2440 Broad St. Regina, SK, Ca

PERSONAL LETTERS

ALL THE LETTERS used in the research for this book in copy or original form are in the private collection of Myrna Hinds Otte. These letters contain numerous letters written and received by Bessie Hinds Garrett, Mrs. Almon (Winnie) Hinds, Mrs. A.R. Hinds, Raymond Hinds, Cleo Hinds Litz, Myrna Hinds Otte and Leonard Skinner.

PRISON LETTERS USED IN BOOK (Author, Year, Receiving Person, Place)

1. **J.J. Waters,** 8/1/34, Dr. Mary B. Harris, Alderson , WV. 2. **Winnie Hinds**, 7/10/34, Beth Green, St. Paul, MN. 3. B**eth Green**, 7/15/34, Mrs. A. R. Hinds, Minneapolis, MN . 4. L**eonard Skinner**, 7/16/34, Beth Green, St. Paul, MN. 5. **Beth Green**, 5/28/34, Mr. Clegg, Chicago, IL. 6. **Beth Green**, 7/13/34, Mrs. M. Green, St. Paul, MN. 7. **Beth Green,** 7/22/34, Mrs. M. Green, St. Paul, MN. 8. **Cleo Hinds Litz,** 7/27/34, Beth Green, Alderson, West VA

INTERVIEWS: (Name, Place, Year, Interviewers)

1. **Pat Cammer**, Swift Current, Sask.,2001, Tom Hinds and Myrna Hinds Otte
2. **Judy Hinds Handestede**, Havre, Montana, 2007, Myrna Hinds Otte
3. **Alice Hinds and. Shirley Hinds Johnson**, Brooklyn Park, MN, 2001, Myrna Hinds Otte and Tom Hinds
4. **Raymond Hinds,** St. Charles MN.,St.Charles, MN, 1983-1995, Tom Hinds and Myrna Hinds Otte
5. **Cleo Hinds Litz,** Brainerd, MN, 2001, Tom Hinds and Myrna Hinds Otte
6. **Dale Pierce,** Pelican Rapids, MN, 2001, Tom Hinds and Myrna Hinds Otte
7. **Maura Newman,** County Longford, Ireland, 2006, Myrna Hinds Otte and Tom Hinds
8. **Marlys Krussow**, Aitkin, MN, 1999, Tom Hinds and Myrna Hinds Otte

9. **Ellen Poulsen**, Douglaston, NY, 2001, Tom Hinds and Myrna Hinds Otte
10. **Daphne Watt**, Molindinar, Queensland, NZ, 2014, Myrna Hinds Otte

MOVIES

The authors recommend two related movies to get a feel for the times and land. These are:

1. **GREED**, Erick von Stroheim, 1924. This film is based very closely on Frank Norris's book *Mc Teague*;

2. **DRYLANDERS**, Don Haldane, 1963, National Film Board of Canada

Many tales of mobsters and their molls have been told on film of the Dillinger days. The authors' prime choice (a little out of the box, but watch it) is one of the funniest films ever made:

3. **BORN YESTERDAY**, George Cukor based on Garson Kanin's play (1950), Columbia Pictures. We imagine that Aunt Bess had the chutzpah of Billie Dawn, BUT Aunt Bess was better read with a better vocabulary.

Many of the movies that concentrate on Dillinger can be ignored. Of the many viewed, the authors think two are OK:

4. **JOHN DILLINGER Public Enemy #1.** (1934) This J. Edgar Hoover propaganda film was created by and released through MGM as a public service.

5. **JOHN DILLINGER**, John Milius, (1973) A good cast, Warren Oates as Dillinger; it gets most of the names correct.

And one doesn't even bother:

6. **PUBLIC ENEMIES**, Michael Mann, 2009. Not a biography or accurate rendition of Dillinger.

APPENDIX

Aliases and Married Names of BESSIE HESTER HINDS and EDWARD GREEN

BESSIE HESTER HINDS

1914: Mrs. Bessie Hinds Skinner
~1926: Mrs. Bessie Walsh
1928-1930: Mrs. Bessie Moore
1932-1934: Mrs. Beth/Bessie Green; Mrs. A.J. Randall; Mrs. D.A. Stevens; Elizabeth Kline; Mrs. S.S. Maklyn Hester Hinds
1940-1983: Mrs. Bess Garrett

EUGENE (EDDIE) GREEN

1932-1934: Eddie Green; George Graham; Charles Ryan; George Green; Fred Rogge; Frederick Riley

ABOUT THE AUTHORS

THE AUTHORS WITH AUNT BESS

Thomas Hinds has been the Chief, United Nation's Publications, and Director of the Province of Koh Kong in the UN's efforts to set up a government in Cambodia. As an organizational analyst (and other things) for the UN for 25 years, he spent time in Ethiopia, Lebanon and Chile during various problems and revolutions. Tom graduated from Carleton College with distinction in English, and went on to an M.A. at the University of Minnesota in English literature and a scholarship to the Aspen Writer's Workshop. He also did graduate work in Public Administration. He has written and published in his fields. Most recently, he read and reviewed books for Doubleday Direct and mysteries for *Mystery Guild*. He was sole employee of Padfoot Press where he provided book doctoring and anything else that paid in connection with manuscripts. He also consulted in publishing and management analysis and, in his next life, he wants to come back as a landscape architect.

Tom did research on this book and most of the writing.

Myrna Hinds Otte was Co-Director of the Crossroads Adoption Services, a private non-profit agency in Minnesota that helped pioneer the field of international adoption. Over twenty years she undertook to write many home studies and counsel families, and she evaluated both adoptive families and orphanages.

She holds a degree in sociology from the University of Minnesota and is a licensed social worker. She had responsibility for establishing working relationships with governmental and private adoption agencies in the U.S. and beyond.

In her work years, she travelled to such countries the Philippines, Russia, Korea, Romania, India, Thailand and Honduras, among others. When retired Myrna was not daunted by focusing her analytical skills on her own family. She is the research arm of the team, but also edited and wrote. If possible, she has traveled to more countries than brother Tom, when she has gone to locate children in need of adoptive care.

❃ ❃ ❃

After an initial spurt of energy from 1999 to 2005, when much of Myrna's research was done, and Tom wrote an early version of this book, they took a break. Not finding a publisher after trying, they never gave up on Aunt Bess. They kept chasing her story. Who was she, and why was she what she was? Was she a victim or did she live the way she wanted to live? Why did her family (mostly) stand by her? Why did she do her utmost to protect her family. Did her life reflect anything of the times in America?

They did not answer these questions but they tried to get at answers: We have written this book as an exploration of a life and a time, places and a country. The life, the time and the country have disappeared. The places, the Dakota plains, Saskatchewan, and the wild cities of St. Paul and Minneapolis can still be seen if you look hard enough.

FAMILY FROM UPPER LEFT: GRACE PETERSON HINDS, PHAROS HINDS, BESSIE, DAVID HINDS, MINNIE PIERCE HINDS

Made in the USA
Columbia, SC
06 April 2021